_f_**P**

*Praise for*

# CUSTOMER CENTERED SELLING

"A book that is as entertaining to read as it is useful—Jolles combines an engaging writing style and impeccable credentials with a highly effective process that enables salespeople to help buyers sell themselves on the solutions offered by the seller." —Douglas E. Hughes, Ph.D., Eli Broad College of Business, Michigan State University

"In a tough economy you need to do a better job of asking the right questions, listening, and responding. *Customer Centered Selling* is your GPS to doing just that. If you can't see Rob Jolles live, this book is the next best thing!" —Alan N. Schlaifer, President & CEO, Wharton School Club of DC

"*Customer Centered Selling* is like a championship prize fight—keep jabbing with those probes until you move the client past their fear of change, and towards a proactive solution." —Dominic Martellaro, Executive VP/Managing Director, Janus Capital Group, Inc.

"When one places customers at the center of their selling activities, it's a win all the way around." —Dr. Eli Jones, Dean, E. J. Ourso College of Business, Louisiana State University

"Reading this book will show you what Rob has shown us for years. Being *Customer Centered* means moving away from being a vendor, and earning the right to becoming a partner with your customers." —Mike Wells, Group Vice President—Operations, Commercial Finance and International & General Manager, Toyota Financial Services

"Rob knows how to get to the center of the customer's issues, quickly, with insight and clarity. This book is a must-read for anyone that wants to earn a customer's business and win 100 percent of their loyalty."

—Don Neal, Chief Operating Officer/Executive Vice President, Leading Authorities, Inc.

"This book captures Rob's passion for showing sales professionals how to connect with their clients using sound, repeatable, predictable processes. Don't just make this book part of your library, make it part of your culture."

—David Larrabee, Senior Vice President, American Century Investments

"A simple yet clever strategy for building customer relationships . . . A useful read for both trainers and sales managers."

—*Sales & Marketing Management* Magazine

# CUSTOMER CENTERED SELLING

### SALES TECHNIQUES
### FOR A NEW WORLD ECONOMY

## ROBERT L. JOLLES

Free Press
New York   London   Toronto   Sydney

*f*P

FREE PRESS
A Division of Simon & Schuster, Inc.
1230 Avenue of the Americas
New York, NY 10020

This Free Press trade paperback edition August 2009

FREE PRESS and colophon are trademarks of Simon & Schuster, Inc.

For information about special discounts for bulk purchases,
please contact Simon & Schuster Special Sales at 1-866-506-1949
or business@simonandschuster.com

The Simon & Schuster Speakers Bureau can bring authors to your live event.
For more information or to book an event contact the Simon & Schuster Speakers Bureau
at 1-866-248-3049 or visit our website at www.simonspeakers.com.

Manufactured in the United States of America

10  9  8  7  6  5  4  3  2  1

Library of Congress Cataloging-in-Publication Data

ISBN 978-1-4391-4463-3

DEDICATED TO

the most influential person in my life.
He shaped my entire career as a salesman.
He taught me the most important intangibles
a salesperson can learn: integrity, honesty, and pride
within this most misunderstood profession.
His own career as a salesman inspired me,
and his actions exemplified everything
I chose to become. This book is for you, Dad.
Its lessons, like the lessons you instilled in me,
will last a lifetime.

# Acknowledgments

I would like to thank the following individuals: First, all the thousands of salespeople who allowed me to spend the last twenty-five years of my life teaching, studying, and selling with them. This book is a reflection of our journeys.

My first New York Life sales manager, Ron Thomson, whose passion for selling and desire to help me succeed instilled in me an enthusiasm for selling that remains to this day.

My first Xerox manager, Peter Toennies, who took a chance and gave me my opportunities to train and sell within Xerox, the finest trained sales force in the world. Rest in peace my friend.

My editors, Janet Coleman, who discovered my work, Robert Wallace, who nurtured my work, Dominick Anfuso, who granted me the privilege to methodically wear him down and allow me to keep this Customer Centered Selling book alive, and Leah Miller who was not only my advocate, but rolled up her sleeves and was with me every step of the way through the editing process.

My friends Glenn Cackovic, Eric Hargens, Dana Klein, and R. Scott West, who helped me to realize my own talents as a salesman, a trainer, and an entrepreneur. Your friendship, loyalty and belief in my abilities continue to inspire me to test my boundaries and soar on my own.

My children Danny, Jessie, and Sandy, who have endured my many nights on the road and gave me the greatest gifts they could provide: a hug and a smile.

And finally, my wife, Ronni, my partner and confidante. Her patience and unwavering belief in my abilities have given me more strength than she will ever know.

# Contents

## PART III   THE SUPPORT

# Preface

*"It's what you learn after you think you know it all that counts."*

*John Wooden\**

I haven't changed my mind. I know that's not the best way to start a book that represents the most important manuscript of my life. I'm also guessing this doesn't instill confidence in you, my reader. However, this book has always been an honest work that speaks from my heart, so what better place to start than there.

Those first five words that started this book have haunted me for years. I'm proud of Customer Centered Selling, as proud as a father is of one of his children. This book has lived a good and true life. It never lied, or cheated, or did anything that its father (that would be me) would be ashamed of. It told the truth, and it was honest. But here come those five words again . . . "I haven't changed my mind."

I have been blessed to give birth, I mean to have written, a handful of books. Each tells a different story, and tries to live its own truths. One of them, my seminar book, has come out in three different editions. Guess why? Yep, I changed my mind.

You see, some books need to change. That's because technology changes, people change, and cultures change. If we authors aren't careful, the messages we gave birth to become less relevant because of these changes. It was a pleasure making changes to that seminar book. A conver-

\* Author's note: All opening quotations, except the two authored by me, came from Edward F. Murphy, *2,715 One-Line Quotations for Speakers, Writers, and Raconteurs* (New York: Crown, 1981; reprinted Gramercy Books, 1996).

sation about which side of the overhead projector to stand on loses a little steam over the years!

But what about selling? What momentous changes have occurred over the past decade or two that would make *Customer Centered Selling* lose its relevance?

- Should salespeople stop asking questions and listening?
- Should salespeople stop appreciating the Decision Cycle our clients go through, and slap more sales ideas in front of you instead?
- Should salespeople stop digging deeper into a client's challenges, and replace our empathy with a dissertation on how our great product will compensate for their difficulties?
- What about trust, or urgency, or continuing to restore pride in this misunderstood, and grossly underappreciated profession of selling?

Believe me when I say that I could go on. And therein lies the problem. *I haven't changed my mind.* That leads us both to an important question you might have on your mind. "Why would I want to buy this book?" Well, I may not have changed my mind, but I sure as heck figured out an answer to that question!

When an author hasn't changed his mind, every now and then he has a publisher who stands behind him and says, "Well, if you haven't changed your mind, knucklehead, have you at least figured out how to simplify some of your thoughts?"

That I can do. It has been over a decade since I first wrote this book. I have traveled over a million miles in the air alone since then, talking with groups, consulting with clients, and gathering new insight as to how and communicate what I, well, haven't changed my mind about.

For instance, ten years ago I made an honest attempt to integrate personality into this process. I wasn't a big fan of personality models because I felt they were too self-centered. As some of the instructors I worked with would talk about personality, I would often mutter to myself, "If I wanted to learn more about me I would go to a shrink."

Well, I changed my mind. As an example of the changes you might stumble over, I want to take the role of personality a lot more seriously. I want to share with you a decade of data on personality, and show you how personality truly interacts with selling. Again, I won't be changing the selling process (I'll spare you a reminder as to why), but I do want to update and clean up some portions of this book, and personality is a classic example.

What has changed are many of the factors surrounding the selling process. How we implement what we learn is another example. In the ten years since this book first came out, I have seen firsthand examples of companies that have protected their training investment dollars and have tirelessly pursued processes to take what started as a training concept, and become a culture.

A decade ago I began this book by saying, "This is what I know to be true about the profession of selling: Selling is one of the most misunderstood careers anyone can choose. The perceptions held by many customers place salespeople in very difficult situations. Fortunately, it does not have to be this way."

As salespeople, we must stop perpetuating the stereotypes we are accused of. In this book I will tell you why these stereotypes exist and what can be done to change them. I will tell you how these misunderstandings occurred and what to do about them.

I have grown tired of the misconceptions held by many about a profession I am so proud of. I have also grown tired of the revolving door we put so many of our salespeople through unnecessarily. It is my belief that we fail to train our salespeople in skills that are vital to their survival. We fail to justify even the need for pure, simple sales training. Oh, we do a fair job inundating our sales forces with product training, but not sales training. We say, "they'll learn on the job."

Because of the lack of real sales training, we have created a culture of order-taking sales drones who do nothing but talk incessantly about their wonderful products. Quite simply, there is very little "selling" and a whole lot of "telling!" The saddest thing of all is, many who think they are selling are actually making a living boring their customers to tears and justifying the stereotypes. Unfortunately, once whatever market these salespeople are in changes and tightens up, they become the first casualties.

I have designed this book to help break this cycle. I have designed this book to teach you how to sell to those customers who need to make a change but do not necessarily want to be sold to. This is where a real salesperson—not just an order taker—steps in.

These are only some of the reasons I chose to write this book. This book is about selling and selling is about the process of persuasion. "Persuasion" is not a dirty word. My hope is that when you read how to persuade in an ethical manner, it will not only change your perception, you will open your mind to the many applications of selling. The skills that are used in selling can be applied to just about anything.

Throughout this book I am going to introduce you to some very important ideas. I call these "Rob's Rules." The first of these rules is:

▶ *There is no such thing as an occupation that does not require selling skills.*

I was lucky enough to learn to sell with two of the greatest companies in the world. It was New York Life that lit a fire within me that burns to this day. New York Life taught me to *love* to sell.

The other company that I am forever grateful to is the Xerox Corporation. Xerox took a chance with me. Xerox took me and my love for selling and taught me something New York Life did not teach me. Xerox taught me *how* to sell.

Once I arrived at the Xerox training center and became a trainer for Xerox, I began to fully appreciate the complexity of selling. When you are in a position to teach others, you are forced to become intimate with your own process.

I spent seven years becoming intimate with the Xerox sales process, spending almost half that time as the only trainer Xerox allowed to teach its customers. It was during this time I began to notice consistent areas of confusion in the training for my customers. At that point, I began to experiment with my own modifications. I did not know it at the time, but the Customer Centered Selling process was beginning to emerge.

I am proud of the Customer Centered Selling process and proud of its success with the many, many customers I have been able to share the process with. I have no doubt that you too will find this process invaluable to your selling efforts.

The name, "Customer Centered Selling," comes from my belief that nothing else really matters if you do not first center your selling process on your customer. You can focus all you want on selling, but if you do not first study the decision-making process your customers go through, your work will be futile.

There is no other book that attempts to teach the way Xerox sells. Xerox is known around the world as one of the leaders in sales training and rightfully so. Xerox offers a product that, with a few subtle exceptions, for the most part does just what its competition does. The only difference is that Xerox products cost more. How do they do it? They do not confuse their product with their selling process (more on that later), and they teach their sales force how to create urgency and sell!

I would like to ask you, my reader, for one small favor. When you have completed this book, I ask that you take a moment and either complete the reply card in the back of this book, or simply drop me a line. There is no greater joy than hearing from those of you I have worked with in one form or another. Your reaction to what you have read would be most appreciated.

So, with a nice mix of ideas from the past, and changes from the present, I hope you will find this new version of Customer Centered Selling to your liking. That means, it should perform a lot like my seminars do, and that means a combination of information, motivation, inspiration, and, of course, entertainment. Lock the door, or tell the person next to you on the plane you're busy, settle in, and let's take this journey together . . .

# Who Am I? A Poem
## by Robert L. Jolles

*I prevent financial tragedies every time I find a way to get you finally*
*to believe that your retirement and children's education are*
*more important than a seven-day cruise.*

~

*I save lives every time I persuade people to stop putting off "what if"*
*and purchase an item that protects themselves and their loved ones.*

~

*I assist companies each time I am able to get a decision maker*
*to look at the "big picture" and make decisions that reflect*
*total costs to the customer.*

~

*I looked you in the eye and asked you some disturbing questions.*
*It upset you, but your anger toward me saved your life and the lives*
*of others on a road you would have been too drunk to drive on.*

~

*I'm the person in the store. You felt put off by my questions,*
*but wound up with a solution that not only saved*
*your business that day, but saved your job a year later*
*as my product expanded along with your business.*

~

*I'm the person who changed your mind about skimping on a document that later*
*was responsible for bringing you your biggest customer.*

~

*I'm the kid standing in the rain outside your door at home. By creating*
*a commitment based on sheer pity, I took some of your money,*
*which later saved a tiny piece of land in a small natural paradise.*

~

*I put up with the stereotypical fallacies that portray me as a*
*buffoon when, in actuality, I was the only one who provided for the*
*future of your family when an early death might have meant*
*devastating and dramatic changes in your loved ones' worlds.*

~

*I could have taken no for an answer, and sometimes I wish I had.*
*I could not because I had seen the personal tragedy of procrastination.*

~

*I have empathy for your fear of change because I have similar fears.*
*The fear of the unknown sometimes outweighs the pain of the present.*
*It is my job to move you past these fears and get you to*
*take action in an ethical manner.*

~

*I may not be apparent to all, but I exist in everyone's soul.*

~

*Who am I?*
*I am a salesperson.*

# PART I

# THE NEED

# THE SELLING DILEMMA

*I didn't want a big play once in a while, I wanted a solid play every time.*

—*John Madden*

There is a dilemma that exists within selling, and it has been around for some time. On the one hand, as I will explain in this chapter, salespeople are a vital necessity in our society. Unfortunately, however, it has become fashionable to attack those who choose selling as a career. The problems within selling have been accentuated by the many advances in technology and the perceived need to transfer that knowledge to the customer. This in turn has made many salespeople fit the stereotypical mold the public has held for so long of a profession they know little about: "Salespeople talk, but they don't listen."

I had been mildly aware of this problem but did not pay much attention to it. Then one day while I was shopping in the local mall with my family, a chance meeting with an old friend made me sit up and see the dilemma for what it is.

It was a cold winter's day, and we were looking to get warm, while killing some time and keeping our kids from climbing the walls. The moment we arrived at the mall, I saw that we were not the first to come up with this idea, but we nevertheless marched onward to the toy store. While our kids were playing with the floor items, my wife and I milled around with other parents, keeping one eye on the time and the other on our kids. A friend from college whom I had not seen for many years walked up and offered a warm hello. We quickly caught up on each other's lives. Children were pointed out, wives introduced, houses and mutual friends discussed. Finally I asked my friend what he was doing professionally. The family was well dressed, and their child's stroller was top quality. He seemed to be doing well. When I asked him what he was doing now, I could not make out his response. I asked again, and he began to explain.

"I work with people finding solutions to various situations within their organizations," he replied.

I scratched my head trying to figure out what he meant, then asked, "What does that mean exactly?"

A little nervously, he responded, "I assist computer users in understanding their needs and recommend products to address these needs."

Well, some would take the hint and drop the topic right there, but I didn't. Obviously he was doing well, so why wouldn't he tell me what he did? I could not believe it would be illegal. Not this guy. So I reloaded my question one more time: "What do they call what it is you do?" I asked.

He looked down at the ground, stuttered and stammered, and finally whispered, "They call me a salesman."

Oh my! Horror of horrors. I certainly saw no need to try to pursue this point any further. The look of shame on my friend's face resembled that of a molester being led in handcuffs past the TV cameras. My mind flashed a picture of him being led out of the toy store with a coat pulled up over his head. Through the crowd, whispers would be heard, "Caught the guy selling. Can you imagine?"

Oh, don't worry. I didn't leave him in this state. Imagine his relief when I told him that I teach salespeople!

My question is, What happened? Why is there this defensiveness, even shame, about being in sales? Every profession has its stereotypes, but the public's perception seems especially tied to these sales stereotypes.

## RESPECTING THE ART OF SELLING

At times it seems almost fashionable to attack some professions. I must admit that I too have been caught up in the latest casualty of perception. When lawyer bashing began, my first feeling was that of relief. I thought, "Finally! Another profession is taking its lumps." How hypocritical! Yes, there are lawyers (unfortunately very visible ones) who discredit their profession. Does that mean all lawyers are bad people? What about the law? Is that unnecessary too?

Former ambassador and attorney Sol M. Linowitz writes in his book, *The Betrayed Profession,* "First we need to respect the law, then we can respect lawyers." I do not believe that anyone really thinks our society can exist without laws, and so we will always need professionals to help interpret the law. Linowitz's book was an inspiration to me with its reminder that the real problem in the legal profession is the respect for the law, not the degradation of lawyers.

I look at selling in a similar way. Before we can respect salespeople, we have to respect the art of selling. But selling is a profession that is shrouded in mystery. What do salespeople do all day anyway?

Many years ago, my father was in business with his brothers. They ran a heating and air-conditioning company. Every couple of months, their insurance agent would visit. As my father tells it, here was a pretty relaxed person, driving a big Cadillac, with golf clubs neatly loaded in the trunk. It did not take long before my father decided he too wanted to be pretty relaxed, drive a Cadillac, and play some golf. Good-bye heating and air-conditioning, and hello insurance company. It is a decision he has never regretted, but the reality of selling was far different from his initial perception.

The perceptions some people have of salespeople are amazing . . . of fast-talking individuals wearing fancy suits who cannot get their stories straight. Perhaps at one time the planet was infested with these creatures, but it is the twenty-first century! Times have changed. Once upon a time, doctors applied leeches to sick people, but those times are also behind us. Professions advance and become more sophisticated. So has the profession of selling.

## THE GOOD OLD DAYS

In this book, I talk of change—of new systems, new processes, and new techniques. I believe change is necessary. This is not, however, an indictment of all the old ways. On the contrary. The past was far better than we knew. With the advance of computers and technology, something very dear was lost: a generation of tremendous salespeople.

I have watched changes occur within the insurance industry. I consider myself fortunate to have sold when there were no laptop computers. In fact, no office then had its own personal computer. If you wanted an insurance policy illustration, you went to the general office, provided the ages and names, and waited. Often you did not go on a call with an illustration in hand, rather, you went to an office with a pad of paper, an application, and a rate book. Customers talked of problems and needs, while salespeople talked of concepts and solutions. In those moments, something occurred that has since become rare: *People sold—and they sold based on who they were, not how computer literate they were!*

It was tragic to me to see so many talented and tenured salespeople become casualties of the computer revolution of the late '70s. These people had ten times the product knowledge of their competition. They had experience and business savvy that was light-years away from those they were now competing with. What they did not have was pages and pages of illustrations and proposals. They could not quickly manipulate an interest rate or a payment amount. But most of them would not have done so, even if they had the knowledge. It just was not how they conducted business. They were the true heroes of the selling profession.

I am all for technology. I was one of those "young whippersnappers" who fought his battles with his computer. In retrospect, it set my selling abilities back years. It forced me to become a computing machine. Remember, machines have no feelings. I lost who I was, and I lost the empathy I once displayed with customers as well. Technology is here to stay. Used properly, it can mean better customer service and improved efficiency. Those who are careful to blend technology with character continue to display the honor within selling.

I have a rather biased view of salespeople, but hear me out. Of course, there are problems within the selling profession. There are bad salespeople in this world, just as there are bad doctors, engineers, accountants, architects, and the list goes on and on. Some of these professions have gifted people who become necessary to our very existence. We all probably know of a kind doctor who took the extra time to get to know us and reassure us that the fears we were feeling were okay and expected. He may even have saved our life.

This type of example could be drawn out for just about any professional position—any profession, that is, except sales. I do not understand why. How can we be so nearsighted? When will we wake up and realize that most people *need* a push once in a while to help make a decision? Left on our own to discover what we really need and the urgency with which we need it can have devastating consequences. Even those who preach sales every day forget this lesson from time to time.

Several years ago my wife and I purchased a car that provides a classic example of why we as a society desperately need good salespeople. When we walked in and got hit with the first "what's it going to take to get you into a car today?" I told my wife to step aside and watch her husband go to work. I informed the salesman of my profession, gave him a stern lecture on closing techniques and winked at my wife. It was time to see her man in action!

By the time we had settled on the car and the price, the salesman was nervously looking at the floor. He asked me about a number of add on options and one by one I said "no." In the middle of this list he asked me about back-up sensors. "How much is that little feature?" I asked. "About two hundred dollars" he replied. I looked over at my wife, and once again with that smug, "nice try" expression, informed the salesman the back-up sensors were unnecessary. "Yes sir" was his reply. The sales trainer won again . . . or did he?

About three months after buying this beautiful new car, while backing into a parking spot, I accidently backed into a beautiful old metal pipe that no human could have seen. That only cost me about $600. I cannot put a price on my two dogs who I dodge while backing into my garage every night. You see, just like you, the smug guy who walked into that car dealership ago needed something that was lacking. I needed a salesperson.

Look at the poem, "Who Am I?" in the front of the book. If you like it, copy it and put it up somewhere you will see it regularly. Every now and then when you need a little boost after a tough day or another thoughtless comment, take a quick glance. Remind yourself with pride who you are and what you do. We need to remind everyone who sells of the honor they carry within the profession they represent.

Unfortunately, salespeople are guilty until proved innocent. If the last contact with a salesperson was on the used car lot, the assumption is, regardless of person or product, the next encounter will be the same. Add to this the lack of understanding by *salespeople* of what it is that their real job is (I will take this up later), and you have the makings of a mess.

## WHAT CAUSED THE PROBLEM?

Let's start with what caused the problem and then I will tell you exactly what can be done about it. I believe that three major factors have created the current sales dilemma.

The first factor centers on the way salespeople are drafted into organizations. Many companies create what I refer to as a "hiring mill" approach to recruiting—that is, a mass hiring strategy. This philosophy of recruitment makes certain assumptions. Assumption 1 is that Salesperson A, regardless of experience or training, will sell a major amount of product to family and friends within a rather quick period of time. If there is talent once these simple sales have been completed, the salesperson will begin to move into real prospecting. If he lacks the kind of talent that would allow him to make it in sales, he is counseled out of selling and replaced with another person, hungry and eager to get the job.* Dozens of bodies are regularly moved into the sales bullpen, given a crash course, and told to sell. If one or two survive, wonderful. Even those who don't will probably account for a good chunk of product moved rather quickly. It almost resembles a pyramid scheme when you think about it. Countless times I witnessed this approach to hiring within the insurance industry and I have interviewed numerous others in different industries who tell similar stories. Something important is not taken into account: the long-term effect this approach has on the customer and salesperson.

Something is robbed from these people that is hard to replace: confi-

* For ease of reading, the generic *he* will be used throughout the book.

dence and self-esteem. It is discouraging to see the familiar pattern develop. It starts with an ironic, cruel sense of invulnerability. In the first few weeks of a new salesperson's career, sales are typically very good. While others struggle, the newly hired are flying high, usually because of the immediate and easy selling of family and friends. Their production can be two and three times higher than that of a veteran. Just as many of these salespeople are lulled into believing their own sales immortality, the initial business dries up and the tailspin begins. Some can pull out of it, but many cannot. Is there a more disheartening feeling than that of failure within one's profession? Unlike most other careers, this is a feeling that seasoned salespeople will tell you never really goes away.

In many instances, individuals are hired away from stable jobs they have held for many years. These jobs are sacrificed for another stereotypical portrait of sales: little work, high pay, flexibility, and reward. Haven't you wondered about the flyer on your car from time to time: "Earn thousands of dollars a month. Work flexible, part-time hours!" This is another interesting stereotype that is lacking reality. The funny thing is that when you get right down to the heart of the matter, One of the aspects of selling that the public hates is the perceived simplicity of it. "How can that !#$% make that much money and not even have to work hard!" Sadly, when someone gives in to temptation and falls prey to these hiring mills, he finds out far too late how misguided this notion is.

The hiring mill approach has negative effects on customers, too. Have you ever wondered what happens to customer accounts once a salesperson leaves the job? In many businesses, these accounts, now termed "orphaned," are handed off to (you guessed it) new salespeople. The product that was sold probably required little expertise from the salesperson and he therefore likely showed little imagination. The lack of longevity creates a direct correlation to the lack of expertise. Two months later, a new voice calls on the telephone. This voice might even sound a little desperate because this person would not be calling if there were uncles, aunts, brothers, sisters, or friends to call. The expertise is still lacking, but the pressure is not. Eventually the customer is "orphaned" again, sold more product and the process continues.

Ironically, it is training that has become another contributor to the sales dilemma. Training is often spotty, not taken seriously, and a mere formality for most organizations. This problem manifests itself in many ways. I will focus here on just one aspect: prospecting. People who have not been trained to sell properly understand little other than "get in front of bodies and sell!" You see, *the deficiency in selling has created an obsession with prospecting*. That would not bother me so much if salespeople were taught to prospect. Unfortunately, *the deficiency in prospecting has created an obsession with cold calling and telemarketing*. Although these techniques, in moderation, are necessary, they are widely overused. And as much as many customers dislike this approach to selling, often salespeople hate it even more! Careers are often snuffed out before they ever have a legitimate chance of beginning by the soul-numbing, cold-calling grind most new salespeople are forced to endure.

Another major contributor to the sales dilemma hits at the core of how salespeople are motivated: numbers. Often salespeople are given two things when they head out to the field. The first is a territory—a geographical section, that is—to sell in. The good news is that no other salesperson from the same company can come into that territory to sell. All leads are passed on to the salesperson responsible for that territory, offering exclusive rights to sell in that location. The bad news is that this same salesperson can't sell to anyone *outside* that territory, regardless of relationship to or request from the customer.

The second thing a salesperson is given, before heading out to sell, is a target number: what the company numerically expects from him. A salesperson unable to reach that number can be put on a corrective action plan and ultimately fired. Those who exceed their targets are often rewarded with rewards, like trips. If they can continue to exceed these numbers, or even achieve numbers significantly higher than projected, depending on the company, they can receive any number of lucrative incentives, including offices, secretaries, money, and status.

The challenge is intense. The lure to continue to produce at these inflated levels can be fierce. The temptation and pressure to produce numbers at the risk of breaching ethics can be overwhelming.

By the way, guess what happens to many territorial salespeople when they overachieve and hit all their bonuses? That's right: Their territories are typically cut down in size, and their expected numbers are *increased*. The climate is created for desperate actions on the part of the salesperson.

## HOW TO FIX THE PROBLEM

Clearly the current situation is not good. A selling dilemma exists, and you now have an idea of what has contributed to creating the problem. As a salesman and a sales trainer, I would not be writing this if I were not prepared to offer suggestions of what can be done about it.

The hiring mill problem can be remedied. First, study the numbers closely. The national dollar figure from various personnel departments offers some startling information. It costs roughly $15,000 to $20,000 to hire and fire an employee in this country when all the numbers (training, advertising, start-up, etc.) are factored in. Just some of these numbers represent training costs, opportunity costs, customer relations, and management time.

One thing that always impressed me about the New York Life Insurance Company was their apparent conscience when it came to hiring. Although I was hired at the age of twenty-one, I was one of only two salespeople under the age of twenty-five in the country working for this company. This was a smart move when you think about how many peers a twenty-one-year-old has who are in the market for life insurance. Let's not forget that little thing called a "need," which ethical salespeople use to sell with!

New York Life represents a great case study proving the success of organizations that avoid the hiring mill temptation. Insurance companies use a standard measurement system, the Million Dollar Roundtable, which sets a monetary standard for success. All the insurance companies have the same monetary level for their salespeople to reach, and although it does not necessarily indicate vast wealth, it does represent a minimal level of success. When I worked for New York Life the company had a sales force of approximately 7,500 agents. (Some of the larger insurance companies had 25,000 to 30,000 agents.) Throughout the history of "the Million Dollar Roundtable" (well over seventy years), not only has New York Life led the industry in placing more agents than any other company in this club, the organization's total number exceeds that all the other companies together! The lesson? Hire selectively, with a conscience, and value quality over quantity.

Most of this book is devoted to correcting to the deficiencies in training salespeople. I will say now, however, that we have to stop focusing on how to close and how to prospect and get back to teaching people *how to sell*.

The final issue dealing with the pressure of producing company-driven numbers is a difficult one. The company-driven numbers approach has been proved to gain significant results. The problem is that it satisfies everyone *except* the customer. I believe the necessary change will have to be cultural. I have mulled over this problem for many years. A buying experience I recently had inadvertently provided the answer.

I was shopping for a car, bouncing from dealership to dealership, and I met with a peculiar salesperson at an Infiniti showroom. He kept asking me odd questions: "Are you comfortable?" "Did I explain that well enough to you?" Even when we struck a deal, the questions continued: "Are you satisfied with my approach to working with you?" "Do you feel all right with the deal we struck?" Why so many questions about his approach to selling?

I probably would not have figured it out if there was not a slight problem with my car. The next day when I went to pick it up, my salesperson greeted me with a look of despair. When I asked him what was wrong, he told me the car had been scratched. With the problems that confront this world, I thought to myself, things could certainly be worse. Still, I was taken aback at his level of concern. He assured me it would be fixed immediately, and then came more questions. "Is that okay?" "Will a quality loaner be satisfactory while it is being repaired?" Yes, I thought. *Relax.*

When I went to pick up my new car with its new body work, I was once again greeted by my salesperson, who wore a much happier look. He boasted proudly, "Isn't it a perfect job? Are you satisfied with its appearance?" At this point I was starting to enjoy his immaculate approach to making sure I was 100 percent happy. As he ran (yes, ran) from the showroom to get a couple of papers yet to be signed, the manager brushed by me for a moment. "Happy with Fred?" he asked. Totally, but I was curious.

I mentioned Fred's unusual obsession with making sure I was pleased and then learned the reason. At Infiniti, the sales force makes a certain amount of money for each car sold. Nothing unusual there. However, the bonus system is directly tied to surveyed customer satisfaction numbers. Each salesperson's bonus is strongly affected by the individual's customer satisfaction rating. So long "Buyers' Remorse," hello "The Customer Is Always Right!" Could we not all learn from such a program? We need to stop rewarding successful salespeople by continually shrinking their territories and moving the finish line. It creates desperate actions on the salesperson's part and, worse, demotivates and burns out our best salespeople.

Finally, we need to tell a lot of our salespeople to *loosen up!* It's not as important to be serious as it is to be serious about the important things. There are many more important things in this world than making every sale. The monkey wears an expression of seriousness that would do credit to any great scholar. An important point to remember, however, is that the monkey is serious because he itches. Most of us in selling need to be reminded to ask ourselves from time to time, What can we take less seriously?

## THE CUSTOMER'S RESPONSIBILITY

The customer is not without fault in the selling dilemma. I have spent fifteen years training and teaching salespeople how to approach selling in a consultative manner. I attempt to inspire those around me to believe that if they learn their craft and do the things necessary to earn the customer's business, they will not have to be burdened with an unnecessary price war. I tell participants over and over again that price is only one of many factors in gaining a customer's business. It is not the most important factor, and we need to remind ourselves regularly of this.

Ironically, when salespeople become customers, they are guilty of the same offense that confronts them on a daily basis. If you do not sell cars, think about the last time you went to purchase a car. You probably played this sort of perverse game and thought, "How much can I get this car down to?" And, "If they do not meet the price of the other dealership, I'm history!" Are *we* not guilty of forcing the salesperson to participate in the exact game we so much oppose? Oh, and by the way: This is a game many of us are only fooled into believing we actually win.

When working with a salesperson, we need to add more to our buying criteria, which ultimately heavily affect price anyway. Need you be reminded that you get what you pay for? We need to add customer service to our buying criteria. We need to add integrity. We need to add dependability.

*We need to remind our customers (and remember when we are the customer) that we are purchasing a partner, not a price!*

Finally, as customers, we need to resist the temptation we put upon salespeople. We loathe salespeople who are dishonest—unless, of course, it might benefit us in some way when we are the customer. If you do not respect a lack of honesty in your workplace, why ask others to be dishonest? When a salesperson says he cannot do something you are asking him to do, accept his answer. Stop pressuring salespeople to engage in activities that are dishonest. If a salesperson gives a little wink and promises to do something that might not be "100 percent legit," you be the one to say no. Many ethics violations within selling are actually initiated by the *customer*. It needs to stop with the customer. It needs to stop with the salesperson. In my opinion, if you are honest *most of the time,* you cannot consider yourself ethical.

At this point, we have looked at the system within selling and at solutions that involve this system and customers. It is my hope that by reading this book, you will gain a deeper understanding of just what your responsibility as a salesperson is.

# YOUR BEHAVIORAL CYCLE

The time to repair the roof is when the sun is shining.

—*John F. Kennedy*

**P**eople who read about the art of persuasion and selling often already possess various skills, including opening, closing, objection handling, and prospecting. Some of you have developed these skills to a very high professional level. But regardless of experience level, selling history, or selling phobia, everyone still functions at one of four behavioral levels, the subject of this chapter.

As you read through this book, I believe you will find yourself identifying with each of the four stages within this behavioral cycle. At times you will be learning about new ideas, ones you never knew existed. At times you will be learning about ideas to help you in identified areas of weakness. At times you will find yourself mechanically plodding along, fearful that what you are learning will never become a natural part of your skill set. Still other times you might find that this book simply validates the techniques you had always believed were most effective.

## LEVEL ONE: THE UNCONSCIOUS INCOMPETENT

At this first level, the salesperson is ineffective and unaware that he is ineffective. (I also refer to this level as the "blissfully ignorant stage.") On the first day of training, a lot of salespeople are at this level. The good news is that if you are at this level right now, you do not know it! For example, all of us have known someone who got on everyone's nerves in the office, but this person had absolutely no idea those around him felt this way. He would be considered unconsciously incompetent.

One of the problems at this first level is that the people in it generally do not seek training as a solution. Why would you want to learn to do something you think you already know how to do? When I work with salespeople at this stage, I am generally pretty careful to move them slowly to the next level. It is difficult to accept suggestions about something you currently feel good about.

There are some jobs that can foster unconscious incompetency for quite some time. Selling is not one of them. When the commission checks are cut, reality often sets in. Once reality sets in, it is time to move to the next level.

## LEVEL TWO: THE CONSCIOUS INCOMPETENT

At this level, things begin to get a little more interesting. The salesperson is still ineffective but now he knows it! If you have ever attended sales training, listened to the seminar leader, and thought to yourself, "Hey, I do that! I didn't know that was wrong," you were passing from the unconscious incompetent level to the conscious incompetent level.

If there is a problem with salespeople at this level, it might be that sometimes there is some stubbornness to move on. Some even revel in conscious incompetency. Have you ever known individuals who seem to take a sense of pride when they inform you that they do not do a particular task well? They make no mention of wanting to improve. Many times they have preached about their ineffectiveness for so long and the impossibility of ever fixing it that their myth becomes a reality. They proudly remain consciously incompetent . . . forever.

Fortunately, that problem is usually the exception to the rule. Sales training programs are typically designed with the consciously incompetent in mind. Once salespeople become aware of their own deficiencies, they are much more receptive to the idea of sales training.

At the beginning of a training program, I ask the class to describe what they hope to gain from the training. Their answers speak volumes about specific areas of conscious incompetency. Generally if people don't ask about it, they believe they know how to do it.

A major reason so many salespeople I work with are in this stage is the nature of selling. Many new salespeople are forced to sell before they have been taught anything about *how* to sell. After they have taken their lumps a few times in front of an audience, they are usually much more in touch with just how much they have to learn.

For quite some time, there has been a debate over when to sales-train the newly hired. One side of the argument states the training should be conducted *before* the salesperson ever gets in front of a customer. The benefit to this theory is probably obvious: the salesperson does not make any huge mistakes in front of the customer. No sense in learning the lessons of selling on live bodies. These salespeople will often most likely be more conscious of their own incompetence.

The other side of the argument is entirely different: How can these salespeople have a realistic approach to what they are doing if they have never done it? It is difficult to teach someone what it feels like to get rejected by a customer. With no real world experiences, it is difficult to empathize with the lessons being taught.

Who is right? I believe both are right. I like a little of each theory, so I recommend combining them. If our newly hired salespeople spend a limited time in the field, even if it is just accompanying other salespeople, this experience should pay dividends. They will enter their sales training consciously aware of some of their incompetencies without costing the company too many prospective customers in the process. Some experience and a willingness to learn are major contributors in getting people to move to the next stage.

## LEVEL THREE: THE CONSCIOUS COMPETENT

At Level Three, an individual is effective *and* aware of exactly what is making him effective. Sounds about perfect, and it almost is . . . almost.

There is one issue that must be discussed when dealing with the conscious competency level: Just how conscious do you really want to be when you are performing a task? Think back to the last time you attended training and learned a new skill. When you left that training, you were probably the picture of conscious competency. You did not make a move without checking that manual or going through that checklist. You were probably able to produce methodically what you were taught, step by step. No steps missed by you, no sir! You were a machine.

And that is exactly where the weakness lies at this level. One of the frustrations of new salespeople is that while they feel good about the process they have just learned, they want to know when they will be able to implement it without using their notes or sounding like an encyclopedia. I have often felt that this level should be renamed the "mechanical competent" stage.

There is certainly nothing wrong with attempting to be effective and aware of what makes you that way. This is being consciously competent. Most new salespeople prefer to go out on a few sales calls before being observed. The reason is that by practicing and rehearsing, they are often attempting to push through the conscious competent stage and move to the next level.

## LEVEL FOUR: THE UNCONSCIOUS COMPETENT

At this fourth and final level, an individual is effective and no longer aware of the process or steps. The person is now producing the expected results without having to think about what he is doing to achieve them. The mechanical part of what he has learned to do has given way to a natural, relaxed competency.

The unconscious competent salesperson is not necessarily perfect. Some salespeople enter the selling profession at the unconscious competent level. Like natural athletes, they have an innate ability to sell. What they do not realize is the danger this scenario presents. Let's face it: No matter how talented you are as a salesperson, the selling occupation has its ups and downs. Everyone has slumps, even the most successful. Without ever being consciously aware of what it is you are doing correctly, what exactly do you fix when you hit your slump?

A natural unconscious competent who has no idea what is causing the slump is often left second-guessing everything he is doing and ends up attempting to fix the wrong problems. The Murphy's law of selling takes over. The positive attributes are eliminated and the negative attributes accelerated.

After my first year of highly successful selling, I experienced this phenomenon. Trying to repeat what I had accomplished the previous year initially seemed easy. Even management told me to "keep on doing whatever it is you are doing." As an unconscious competent, I had never bothered to analyze how I approached selling. In my second year, during a slump, I was forced to analyze what it was I did. I was clueless. It is kind of hard to fix "clueless."

To this day I have an enormous amount of empathy for the people on the top. Most have no conscious approach to selling. Most are out of business within two years. The greatest pleasure I experience in working with salespeople is watching them struggle to learn the process I teach and then watching as they realize on "very good days" they do everything I teach.

My hope is that many parts of this book will not be brand new to you. I hope that many of the things you have been doing are validated by what you are about to read. Jump back to the conscious competency: Don't do what you are doing by accident. You must spend as much time on what it is you are doing right as what you are doing wrong.

Still, this is a level most of us dream about. The frustrations associated with conscious competency give way to a more natural, relaxed approach. Everyone who learns a new process dreams of the day he can apply what he learned without having to think about it consciously.

Golfers would call what the unconscious competent stage represents "muscle memory." After careful analysis of each and every step, with practice, these steps become automatic. Anyone who enjoys the game of golf dreams of the moment of being able to hit the ball without having to go through the laundry list of techniques before choosing what seems best.

It seems like the perfect stage to operate in, and I must say that it can represent a kind of utopia. There is a problem, however. It lies in what surely will follow.

# WHAT COMES NEXT

I start every seminar with a discussion of these levels of learning to help my participants gain some perspective. I do not claim to be the author of these levels (indeed a number of different companies subscribe to this explanation of learning), but I do claim to be the author of what I have observed comes next.

I cannot guarantee how long you will remain in the unconscious competent stage: a week, a month, a year or longer. Regardless, I can assure you that eventually you will move back to Level One, the unconscious incompetent. Don't forget that when you are at this level, you do not know you are there!

See if you can remember the first customer you ever sold something to. I do. I was in the middle of a pathetic lecture about my product when the customer leaned over and said, "I'll buy it." I continued to babble for a moment more until it dawned on me that I had made the sale. After my initial panic and surprise, I filled out my first app (application for a sale). What a momentous occasion! Once our business was complete, in a somewhat emotional state, I can remember telling my customer, "You won't be sorry. I'll be here to help you no matter what. You won't [sniffle, sniffle] be sorry."

I kept my word to that customer. I was there the moment he had a question. I always returned his calls immediately. He was my first customer. If you were to ask me about my tenth customer, I would tell you that my service was good, but of course not as amateurish as my first customer. I became a lot more professional in my approach, and delivered the great service I promised.

Now ask me about my hundredth customer. Uh, my service was good— I think. No one wrote any bad letters or complained . . . that much. You see, somewhere along the line, I slipped into an unconscious incompetent state. When I received my second complaint in one month, I became a conscious incompetent. I looked at how I used to approach this issue and became a conscious competent once again. Soon after, I no longer thought about it as much and kept my vow of great service while sliding back to the unconscious competent level once again.

Does this story sound familiar? It happens every day. Do you still come to a complete stop at a stop sign? I rather think not! You are an unconscious incompetent. (That's okay. I am not judging you.)

I tend to be guilty as well. When you see the flashing red lights in your rearview mirror some day, you will become a conscious incompetent. After your ticket, you will probably be a little more careful when you come to those stop signs. You will be methodical in your stopping and looking around for other traffic and police cars. Welcome to conscious competency.

Finally, I believe you will even come to a complete stop (once or twice) without even thinking about it. You will once again be an unconscious competent. Welcome back!

I hope this discussion of your behavioral cycle will put into perspective what you will be getting out of this book. When you finish this book, do not expect to be an unconscious competent. Instead, plan on putting this book down and being in the conscious competent stage. Practice, patience, discipline, and hard work will land you in the unconscious competent stage.

# THREE

# MARRYING THE PRODUCT TO THE PROCESS

Training is everything. The peach was once a bitter almond; cauliflower is nothing but a cabbage with a college education.

—*Mark Twain*

A redundant question that is often asked about the process I will be showing you concerns the relevance of Customer Centered Selling to particular products or ideas. As you read the process that follows, open your mind and avoid the temptation to convince yourself that the "process is not right for what I sell." I am talking about *persuasion*, not product. Earlier, I made the sometimes controversial point that product knowledge is a bit overrated, and I stand by that statement. It is the *process* of selling, not the product, that I focus on in this book.

I was trained this way by Xerox, which provides a telling case study that validates this point. When I became a sales trainer for Xerox in early 1987, a process existed for training salespeople that in my opinion was ahead of its time. Xerox took a gamble and tried to separate the product and the process for selling. It was brilliant, and I believe this process helped me more than any other course I have taken to understand the true art of selling.

Xerox believed so strongly in the principles behind the separation between learning about the product and selling that it came up with an ingenious approach in its "The Fundamentals of Selling" course, which truly lived up to its name. The course had three phases: Phase One involved the process of selling. For the first two weeks of sales training, copiers were never mentioned. What was "sold" were answering machines and airplanes!

When students arrived for the course, they knew right off the bat that they were in for an interesting couple of weeks. In every student's mailbox were product profiles of two different answering machines and four different airplanes. It was no coincidence that each product was directed at a different type of customer. Many of the features were in direct competition with the other products available to sell. The students were given two days to familiarize themselves with the products. Understanding the products was crucial, and the trainers were there to help clear up any misunderstandings. It was important because these were the only products these salespeople were going to "sell" for the next two weeks!

Every example, role play, and discussion involved one of these two product lines. Each day began with another role play to be videotaped, using the selling skills being taught. The focus was on the skills, not the product knowledge (although it was challenging, to say the least, to sell without having a good working understanding of the products).

What happened in these two week was powerful. Coach Vince Lombardi would have been proud of us. He believed in practicing the basics over and over again until they could be accomplished in your sleep. In essence, this is what we were doing as well. We were teaching the fundamentals of blocking and tackling within selling, and basically saving the product or plays for later.

After two weeks, the student salespeople fully understood the selling process. They could sell the answering machines and airplanes in their sleep. I came to believe, as did many of the other sales trainers, that if I ever lost my job with Xerox, I could easily sell airplanes for a living. We could also sell anything else you pointed to or thought of and do it instantly. (A lot of the unmarried salespeople claimed they were very successful at applying the process of selling in the bars they were frequenting!) In two weeks, we wound up with salespeople who were intimate with the selling process and could sell anything.

Next came Phase Two, which lasted about four weeks. The student salespeople went back out to the field and began to study their real products carefully. They went out on sales calls with tenured sales reps. They tagged along to watch demos. They spent a lot of time sitting on benches and studying product specifications. The key here was that they did not need a sales trainer to learn product. They were not allowed back for the final phase of training until they completed observed demos and had a full range of product testing signed off on by management. Once that was completed, it was time for the third and final phase.

Phase Three involved the careful marrying of the process of selling with the product to be sold. This course, titled "Territory Management," lasted another two weeks. The first couple of days focused on a detailed review of the selling process. This time, all of the examples involved copiers and fax machines.

The rest of the two weeks was not easy. The student salespeople were thrown into a simulated territory and ate and slept selling for the remainder of their time at the Xerox Document University in Leesburg, Virginia. If they were not being videotaped selling a copier, they were being videotaped demonstrating a copier. If they were not doing either of these tasks, they were studying buyer scripts to play the role of the customer or writing proposals.

The internal name for the course found in the Xerox course catalog was L60. The trainees nicknamed it "Hell 60." One thing was for sure: After four weeks of instruction and four weeks in the field, these people could sell, and sell well! It was an innovative and successful formula. Xerox was blowing the doors off its sales projections. Profit sharing was soaring, and so was the Xerox sales force.

In the early '90s this formula was changed. In the spirit of constant quality improvement, Xerox began to attempt to "improve" this course. Many of the field managers had complained that the training was taking too long. Some complained that they did not want to have to do product training. They felt it was the responsibility of the Xerox training department to teach their employees product knowledge. The managers responsible for training made their biggest mistakes: They listened.

Before long, a new course was created, crafted to please the field managers. No longer would these managers be responsible for teaching their direct reports product information. No longer would they have to worry about having their employees out of the field for four weeks of sales training. The old adage comes to mind: "Be careful what you wish for. You just might get it."

The course was shaved down from four weeks to one week. To accommodate the requests from the field, almost all of the raw selling skills portion of the course was removed. In its place was product, product, and more product. Due to the enormous amount of product and the time required to train our own sales trainers to the degree that was being requested, another innovative idea was hatched: The trainees would move from classroom to classroom during the week, spending roughly a day with each trainer learning product. It was the trainer's responsibility to give out tips on how to sell some of the products that were being taught. The actual selling process was lost!

Historically, training departments have to beg and plead for patience to decision makers they are trying to sell on training. It takes time to see results from the training efforts. Often it takes time to see the repercussions of poor training as well. Not in this case. Within six months, sales figures began plummeting. The managers were once again screaming about the training being conducted at the training center. This time their cries were of a different nature. They wanted the art of selling once again localized and taught. In a frighteningly fast period of time, Xerox had changed a significant percentage of its field force from savvy sales professionals to product-obsessed robots. Amazingly, some at the training center were strongly reprimanded, and the course was eliminated. Mercifully, it was the shortest-running course I had the displeasure to witness in my seven years at the training center.

Here are the lessons from this case study: First, isolating the selling process and becoming familiar with the tactics involved in persuasion are critical to salespeople's success. Their training should be designed to support those goals.

Second, learning the art of selling must never be compromised or rushed. As with most other things in life, you get what you pay for. Invest little, and you'll receive little.

Finally, the actual art of selling has little to do with specific features or products and much more to do with the art of persuasion. The original formula that Xerox had created was brilliant and effective. I believe the process of selling and the study of product can go hand in hand. To this day, when I am asked to step in as a consultant to sales-train a company, I try to implement the original Xerox formula and intentionally time my course around key product launches.

Although Xerox no longer has its new employees selling answering machines, I do! I mail out product profiles before the course begins. I spend a day or two teaching the selling process, sit through the next day or two of product information, and take the final day to *marry the product to the process*. When companies are willing to take a risk and get past the discomfort of not talking about their products for a couple of days, they are rewarded with sales training that takes on that much-anticipated, much-desired cultural change everyone dreams about.

As you read through the process in this book, apply what you learn not only to the products or concepts that you sell but to other situations as well. Look at the people you manage, the children you raise. Look at the ideas you have dreamed of pitching. If you apply what it is I am about to explain to you only to the particular product you are selling, you are missing out on a greater opportunity. Ultimately the ability of the Customer Centered Selling process to relate to these other endeavors or situations will become the true test of its effectiveness.

PART II

# THE PROCESS

# FOUR

# THE CUSTOMER CENTERED SELLING PROCESS

Many receive advice. Only the wise profit from it.

*—Chinese proverb*

**W**hen you actually look at how innovative processes and imaginative techniques were created, often their births take on almost mythlike qualities. The Customer Centered Selling model follows in that tradition, built and assembled by trial and error.

The process itself has an interesting history, beginning with my work with Xerox. Since the '70s, Xerox had been using a process of selling called SPIN, created by a company called Huthwaite. It was a dynamic process that Xerox purchased and used for almost twenty years. Ironically, Canon, a major competitor of Xerox, purchased the same process from the same vendor and has been using the process as well. It was the process of selling that I was originally taught to sell with and later became a certified instructor to teach.

All was well until the late '80s, when Xerox stumbled on an ingenious idea to increase market share within authorized office dealerships across the country. These are the dealerships you see in your town that typically sell low-end products from a host of vendors like Panasonic, IBM, Canon, Sharp, and Xerox, to mention a few. Xerox was experimenting with allowing dealerships the opportunity to sell Memorywriters (Xerox typewriters) and fax machines to increase their distribution. Additionally, this would free up the internal field force to sell larger equipment. The trouble was, with all these vendors for a salesperson in the dealership to pick from, how could Xerox get the salesperson to recommend Xerox?

One technique was a quota system that the dealership was given to fulfill. Xerox, for its part, made a commitment to the dealership not to flood the market with too many other authorized dealerships, essentially giving it exclusive rights to sell Xerox products. The dealerships felt a sense of loyalty from Xerox and did all they could to meet their quota (and retain their rights). Most of the other vendors did not take this approach, and instead gave the rights to sell their equipment to just about anyone who would hang out a sign for them.

The Xerox strategy worked well. Unfortunately, however, this loyalty to keep Xerox dealerships from competing with one another did limit sales somewhat. The question continued to gnaw at Xerox: How do we keep this loyalty, not flood the market with vendors, and increase sales? The answer was in training.

An idea was hatched to offer sales training to the dealerships. The course would spend a majority of time teaching sales skills, role playing, and putting on demonstrations, using (coincidentally enough) Xerox equipment. The course would be five days in length and held at the Xerox training center in Leesburg, Virginia, the crown jewel of Xerox Corporation's collection of buildings. Nestled on almost 2,300 acres next to the Potomac River, the facility was perfect to train customers from across the country. With well over a million square feet of office and training space, it can handle over 1,300 trainees on any given day.

There was only one problem: What curriculum were these trainees going to be taught? The program Xerox had been using was licensed for Xerox to use internally only. Any attempts to take this training to customers would violate the contract Xerox had signed and would result in an ugly lawsuit.

A natural option would have been to teach "Professional Selling Skills" (PSS), a "Xerox" program that had been taught to Xerox customers for over a decade. But Xerox had sold all rights to this course for a hefty sum a couple years before, to another vendor with a five-year noncompete clause, which meant Xerox could not compete in the sales training marketplace. It was tricky getting around the noncompete clause. These were Xerox dealerships and therefore excluded from the noncompete. And PSS no longer belonged to Xerox. So what would Xerox teach these dealerships?

There was certainly going to be no difficulty in attracting trainees. Xerox was offering every dealership in the country free room, board, and tuition for any two salespeople they chose. A task force was developed to design and deliver what would be called "Buyer Focused Selling." I was one of the five trainers who would make up this team. It was late in 1987.

By 1989 a few things had happened. The course was a smashing success. The dealerships were thrilled with their sales increases of around 25 percent. Xerox was thrilled with its strategy to increase market share. Among those who had attended the school, Xerox sales within the dealerships had increased by a staggering 68 percent. When you convert a salesperson to want to sell your product, that is called "mind share," and those who had attended were demonstrating exactly what Xerox had hoped for.

Things got even better by 1990. The success of the Buyer Focused Selling model had spread throughout the sales industry. Xerox still had two years remaining on its noncompete clause, but the course continued to grow. It was the Xerox authorized agents' turn to try their luck with the model.

Xerox authorized agents are not employees of Xerox, but they are authorized to sell Xerox equipment. The Buyer Focused Selling program was created to try to salvage the Xerox reputation in rural areas. For years, Xerox internal salespeople from larger towns had been given territories that had included pockets of rural sections of the country. For some Xerox sales reps, these little pockets could represent traveling distances of a couple of hundred miles. The sales reps would literally blow into town, sell equipment, and leave. Their next trip back could be months away, and the customers in these small towns would get frustrated by the sales reps' lack of support and attention.

It became a strategy of Xerox to find individuals who lived in these small towns and make them authorized agents for Xerox. What they sold would be shipped directly to the customers, so inventory was unnecessary.

Eliminating the necessity to plan and pay for inventory made the program appealing to many, including some of the company's finest salespeople.

The agent program to this day represents a tremendous success within Xerox. Customers were thrilled to have one of their own selling and monitoring their accounts. The agents were content because many were making a lot of money in places where a lot of money could buy a lot! Xerox was happy because it was able not only to salvage its reputation in these small towns but to increase market share in areas that had been all but moribund.

As these agents grew more and more successful and interacted with more and more customers, it became clear that sales training was going to be necessary. This time, putting together a training program was a little bit easier because the course was ready. It was my task to launch Buyer Focused Selling for the agent program. The results were once again astonishing.

These courses were not free to the agents, but into Xerox Document University they came. Quickly it became my job to cross-train and monitor other trainers to teach these courses. The agents' sales numbers were skyrocketing, and so was the number of attendees. What started as a program designed to stem the tide of lost market share in rural America became one of the most successful marketing programs for low- to mid-range products in the history of Xerox. Today the Xerox Agent Program has expanded into larger cities with salespeople called metro agents. With the continued success of this program, there is the strong potential that someday this may be a channel that Xerox will use to move most, if not all, of its low- to mid-range products.

With one year to go on the noncompete, word of the Buyer Focused Selling success had spread far. Departments within Xerox began to pass up the internal SPIN training and sign up for the Buyer Focused Selling training. The rush was on! News of this Xerox selling process began to appear in various magazines and newspapers, and customers started inquiring about what Xerox was up to in the sales training arena.

The noncompete finally ended. You might think Xerox would have gone flying back into the customer training arena, but the move was slow, mainly because the entire internal sales field was now converting to Buyer

Focused Selling. In a few years, Xerox had not only converted its customers to this way of selling, but had converted itself as well.

The first true customer sales training course rolled off the shelf in early 1993. Titled "Advanced Marketing Techniques," it was aimed at a select market. The printing industry would be the first to receive the training, and for good reason: It is where some of the largest Xerox customers are found.

With the Buyer Focused Selling model as the program backbone, the rest of the course was designed in an unusual and unique manner. Typically Xerox would turn a project of this nature over to its own curriculum developers and designers, but in a stunning turn of events, this course was designed and written by a group of individuals Xerox rarely even solicited an opinion from, let alone asked to write a course: a team of eleven Xerox sales trainers.

As a Buyer Focused Selling subject matter expert and a senior sales trainer for Xerox, I became a member of the team. The team itself actually represented what Xerox calls a "quality family," whose task it was to create the course using the principles of quality Xerox has become so famous for. It was exciting seeing two of the corporation's most famous processes come together: quality and selling.

The original intent of the course was to mirror another highly successful program, called Advanced Customer Training (ACT), designed for Xerox customers from the technical operational side—the folks who run the larger copiers in major corporations and print shops. ACT courses are one week long and are located at the Xerox training center. For one week, these customers go through a shorter version of the technical course that their own Xerox technicians take: they trouble-shoot the machines, debug the machines, and basically learn how to fix problems far more significant than paper jams.

The program is brilliant for many reasons. First, after completing the course, these customers have the knowledge to fix about 80 percent of the problems that occur with their machines. This translates into more uptime for the customer and fewer service calls for Xerox. This program is ingenious for one other reason that I don't believe Xerox even anticipated: These trainees went home with a deep appreciation and attachment to

Xerox. As anyone who works for Xerox likes to say, they "bleed little blue Xs."

Not only had Xerox made a friend in the customer, it made a friend in the local sales rep as well. Guess what happened when Xerox competition came visiting these most prized accounts to sell their wares? It was like trying to sell a Kodak copier to a Xerox employee! The sales force was in heaven, and every time Xerox launched a new high-volume copier, the customer waiting list soared into the six- to nine-month range.

It was in the spirit of this massive success that the sales trainers decided to benchmark the program. Once again, Buyer Focused Selling became the core of a huge success.

The success and reputation of this course for print shop salespeople finally lifted the floodgates for Xerox external sales training and Buyer Focused Selling. Customers began calling from far and near inquiring about the course and wanting to send their salespeople to it. Our original strategy was to let the course mature for a while and just teach print shop salespeople. Before we knew what hit us, we had a six-month waiting list with salespeople from companies like Microsoft, Motorola, Aetna, and TDS Telecom. At this time, I was the only trainer in Xerox working with customers and teaching this course.

In 1993 I became a member of a team of three responsible for launching the Xerox Institute of Customer Education (ICE). Our task was a simple one: launch the external training efforts for Xerox Corporation.

The three of us got a quick education in the marketing of training. The Buyer Focused Selling model was our calling card and our lifeline. The existing Dealer, Agent, and Advanced Marketing Techniques courses all followed a similar formula: five days in length, class size limited to eight to allow for direct trainer-trainee observation and feedback, and multiple videotaped role plays.

In came a customer named Van Kampen Merritt (now Van Kampen Investments). Out went the comfortable formula for delivery I had spent years developing. Times were changing. Van Kampen Merritt, a mutual fund company formerly owned by Xerox, wanted to form an alliance and take Buyer Focused Selling out to the banking community. They would market the course, assist in coordinating all the necessary activities, and host the programs. A few things, however, would have to change. First, they felt there was no way they could get the salespeople in the banking community out of the field for five days. The courses would have to be cut down to two days in length. This was not as difficult as it might have sounded. Eliminating the videotaped role plays and allowing for all role plays to be conducted in simultaneous triads took care of most of that. Once the role plays were no longer going to be conducted one at a time, the classes were increased in size to twenty salespeople. If I was no longer going to be listening to each role play, I could allow the trainees to take turns evaluating in their groups of three.

Finally, because it would not be cost-effective to fly twenty salespeople to Xerox for two days, the course hit the road and was taken to the customer. To this day, the launching of the Xerox two-day Buyer Focused Selling course remains one of the corporation's smartest, most lucrative moves in the training area. I owe Van Kampen American Capital for that one.

All was well except for one small problem. Cutting a course from five to two days creates what in training is referred to as gray areas. There are subtleties that can be worked through in a five-day format but not in a two-day format. With seven or eight role plays going on at the same time, it became challenging observe and work out the tough areas. Realistically the trainees would not be leaving with unconscious competent skills—understanding the process without notes or hesitation. The challenge was to get the trainees at least consciously competent, understanding every move but not necessarily having the process committed to memory.

I began to notice easier and faster ways to teach the training program and was encouraged by many customers to put the process in writing. Customer Centered Selling was created and launched in April 1994, and the reception was mind boggling. Within the first six months, the process exploded into a dozen banks, insurance companies, and various other businesses. I had learned a tremendous amount from PSS, SPIN, and Buyer Focused Selling and melded them together into the Customer Centered Selling model.

Customer Centered Selling has been taught to thousands of customers around the world with many different applications toward mastering the art of persuasion from hostage negotiators to medical supply companies and from management to parenting. It is the most powerful, innovative selling process in corporate America. This book will show you how the Customer Centered Selling process works.

# THE CUSTOMER CENTERED DECISION CYCLE

I have found the best way to give advice to your children is to find out what they want and then advise them to do it.

*—Harry S. Truman*

Through the years I have attended many sales training courses, covering any number of topics. There may even be a few that you recognize within this book. I will show you a repeatable, predictable process that will assist you in your day-to-day persuasive en-counters. Before I do, ask yourself this one question: Do you believe customers go through a repeatable, predictable process when they make a decision to commit to change or buy?

I hope you said yes. If you are on the fence regarding a *decision cycle,* I intend to prove the process exists. I will teach you to identify the steps your customers go through each time

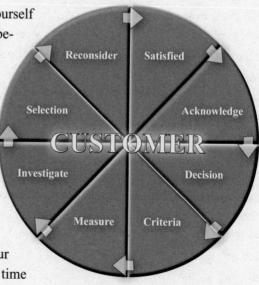

they make a decision, and you will benefit in a couple of different ways. First, you will become a better buyer. Often after I teach this process in my seminars, participants tell me that their ability to persuade has improved a lot, and so has their ability to make decisions. Another benefit to studying the decision cycle is the effects it will have on your ability to make strategic selling decisions. You can learn persuasion tactics until you are blue in the face, but if you are not aware of the decisions your customer has to make, or for that matter, where the person is in his own decision cycle, your chances of making a successful sale are diminished.

The key concept of Customer Centered Selling is to learn to analyze where your customers are in their decision cycle and assist in moving them through to a decision. In doing this you must learn what tactics are appropriate for which part of the decision cycle.

I have learned much of what I am about to teach you from observations, surveys, and studies of customer behavior. I must credit Xerox for pointing me toward the topic of buying and away from selling. It was Xerox that taught me that a decision cycle even exists. Xerox referred to this phenomenon as a "buying cycle." Once I began to work with outside customers, I realized this process related not only to how we buy, but also to how we make decisions. As you read this chapter, let your mind wander to the many purchases you have made and picture yourself going through the cycle over and over again.

One quick word of warning: The cycle that I am about to describe seems to fall apart when applied to minor decisions—that is, any commitment under $100. Plain and simple, these commitments or purchases are acted upon on impulse. Little validation exists as to why these decisions are made or what influences them. This also explains why, in a mall, for instance, many of us make quick and irrational purchase decisions. Once that commitment goes over $100, however, you become *extremely* predictable.

The most effective technique to learn the process is to track the process yourself in a decision you have made. I strongly urge you to go through the exercise that follows. It will put what I am about to convey to you in perspective and make the message a lot more powerful. Remember, there are no right or wrong decisions. What I will be describing is a process, not a straitjacket.

# TRACKING YOUR DECISION MAKING PROCESS...

Think back and try to recall the answers to the following questions relating to the last time you purchased an automobile:

1. What car were you driving?
2. What car did you buy or lease?
3. What were some of the things you did not like about the car you were driving? Try to list at least three or four.
4. What were you looking for in a new car? Please do not necessarily list what you actually got. Within reason, this list should resemble more of a wish list. It should not necessarily be a list of everything you actually ended up getting.
   - When this list is complete, please prioritize the list by placing a number one by the most important item, a two by the second most item, and so on.
   - When you have finished, highlight this list.
   - Finally, if you quantified any of the items on the list, i.e., price range, gas mileage, cubic feet, please go back and try to quantify this.
5. When did you first realize (rough estimate on date) that the old car was less than perfect?
6. When did you start seriously looking for a new car?
7. When did you actually buy the car?
8. What other cars did you look at?
9. Where did you get the information on these cars, (i.e., friends, dealerships, etc.)?
10. If you could go back, and at no penalty to you, make that decision all over again, would you make the same decision?

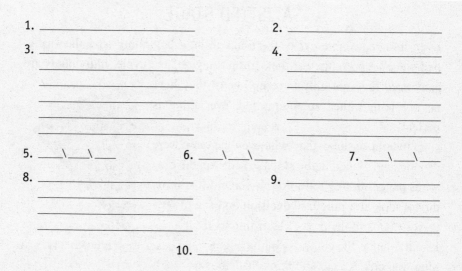

1. _____     2. _____
3. _____     4. _____
   _____        _____
   _____        _____
   _____        _____
   _____        _____
   _____        _____

5. _____     6. _____     7. _____
8. _____     9. _____
   _____        _____
   _____        _____

                    10. _____

I like to use the example of a car purchase because it is a major commitment, and most of us have made this purchase at least a few times in our lives, but you can apply most of the questions I am about to ask you to any number of tangible or intangible decisions you have made. Simply replace the word *car* with *home, job, investment,* or some other large purchase. Answer the questions that follow, and place your answers in the fields that correspond to the question numbers. To get the maximum benefit from this activity, have on hand a highlighter and a pencil or a pen.

Now I will break down the eight steps a customer goes through when making a decision that creates change. From time to time, I will be asking you to go back and look at some of the decisions you made and track them, using the sheet you filled out for the questionnaire. Remember that what I will be showing you is a process, not a straitjacket. People make decisions, not processes, and there are exceptions to every rule. Still, brace yourself, because you will be amazed to find how predictable so many of the decisions of the past have been.

One last point before we move on. After this chapter, I will show you, step by step, how to move someone through the cycle from a persuasion perspective. But do not look for it here. What follows is a synopsis of what is happening in the cycle from the *customer's* perspective.

## SATISFIED STAGE

Even in a repeatable cycle, there has to be a beginning, and the "satisfied stage" represents just that. In this stage of the cycle, individuals are convinced they not only have no needs, they have no problems either. In their mind, everything is perfect.

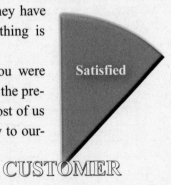

I would assume that whatever car you were driving, and placed in the slot marked 1 on the previous page, initially fell into this stage. Most of us do not look at a purchase decision and say to ourselves, "This looks pretty bad, I think I'll take it!" Quite the contrary. In the beginning, we look at a car and think that car is perfect. For a period of time, sadly far too short, we are 100 percent happy.

Amazingly, it was not until 1988 that Xerox acknowledged that this step even existed! The thinking was that everyone has problems and needs. That is simply not so. There is a percentage of the population that is totally happy with what they have and therefore see no benefit in looking at the particular ideas that you intend to persuade them to adopt.

The bad news is (and it should appear fairly obvious to you) that customers who are in the satisfied stage are extremely difficult to persuade. The good news is that there are far fewer people in this stage than most people believe. When I ask salespeople what percentage of their customers they believe are in the satisfied stage, they will often guess at a range between 50 and 60 percent. Not even close.

At the end of this section, you will see a graph that outlines the research I have done, illustrating just what percentage of people fall where. It will act as a visual summary, because in each step I will show you separately where the numbers will fall. These surveys, conducted over a three-year period, covered a wide range of issues. The first question I asked dealt with the satisfaction level of the individual. The participants were not feeling any threat of being sold a product by me, and therefore they gave candid, honest answers. I rotated the products among the following items:

- Homes
- Cars
- Printing
- Insurance
- Financial planning
- Jobs

I selected those products based on what my audience was not currently selling. Of the six products, three represented tangible solutions and three did not.

There are many myths associated with persuasion, and before we move on, now is as good a time as any to dispel one of my favorites.

## MYTH: THERE IS A BIG DIFFERENCE BETWEEN SELLING TANGIBLE PRODUCTS AND INTANGIBLE PRODUCTS.

That happens to be categorically false. Remarkably, with over 3,000 surveys analyzed, regardless of the product in question, the numbers did not deviate by over two percentage points! I will prove to you within the Customer Centered Selling process that there is no difference. Yes, near the end of the process, a Xeroid (a term many Xerox people call themselves) can place a copier on a desk and an investment counselor cannot. Understand that the sale was won or lost well before the tangible copier appeared.

Now, let's get back to the good news. When not feeling the pressure to make a commitment, only about five percent of the customers I have surveyed have said that the product they have is "perfect." How could the numbers be so far from the 50 to 60 percent many salespeople associate with this stage? Simple. When a salesperson circumvents the customer's decision cycle with his own selling process, customers lie. Here is your first, and sad truth, one of my Rob's Rules:

► *Buyers can be liars.*

And there is even better news for those who are concerned about the satisfaction stage. I believe that at least half of that 5 percent of the customers in this stage *do* have problems. They are not lying; they just don't know they have problems.

Think back to the late '60s when Chevrolet came out with the now-famous Vega. A brilliant idea was hatched to equip these cars with aluminum engine blocks: lighter engine block, better mileage. In a way, Chevrolet was ahead of its time, addressing the American car gas-guzzling issue a couple of years before the rest of us realized the problem existed when we began lining up at the pumps for gas. Chevrolet had actually taken a step to avoid the upcoming crisis, but in the process created a crisis within its own cars. When the engines heated up, as engines have a tendency to do, the extreme heat began to warp the aluminum engine blocks. This created a host of mechanical problems, and a lemon was born.

The moral of the story as it relates to the satisfied stage? Many customers may truly believe what they have is perfect, but often it is not. Customers are simply unaware. Just because they have not come face to face with a problem does not mean that a problem does not exist.

This is sometimes referred to as the honeymoon stage because a customer can stay in this stage for only so long. Eventually the honeymoon ends, and we must deal with reality. We make do with what we have, but when we become aware that what we have is no longer perfect, we make the first move within the cycle . . .

## ACKNOWLEDGE STAGE

. . . and a prospect emerges. When I deliver a seminar, I usually tell my audiences there will be "nice to knows" and "need to knows."

Basically, I do this to reserve the right to focus listeners on the more important aspects of what I am telling them. At this point, I would like to direct you, the reader, as well. This stage represents the most critical element of the *decision cycle*. It also symbolizes the most misunderstood component.

The acknowledge stage represents a basic dichotomy within the customer's mind. In this stage, the customer will readily admit that, yes, he does have particular problems that could be addressed with your solutions. Unfortunately, he will just as readily state that, no, he does not want to do anything about these problems at this time.

What you are looking for here is the most critical Decision Point a person will reach. The Decision Point can be referred to as the "fix or don't fix" point. I call it that because, regardless of the amount of talk from the person, he must cross this line before anything can really happen. Look at it as a sort of line in the sand. People will approach it, moan about what's bothering them, peer over the line, and then run the other way.

Are you frustrated by reading this? Many people tell me that this is where most of their customers are in the cycle. According to my numbers, they happen to be absolutely right. Brace yourself: 79 percent of the people I survey admit to me this is exactly where they are in the *decision cycle.* "It hurts," they say, "but it doesn't hurt that badly." There is no sense of urgency. The person simply does not want to do anything about his problems.

Look at what you listed in question number 3. Your car was certainly not perfect. If it was, why in the world would you get rid it?

I sometimes refer to this stage as the whining stage. Many of us whine but do nothing about it. For a classic example, think back to your first day on a new job. There you were, excited, nervous, and taking things out of one of the boxes you packed for your new desk. Wow! Your first day! It didn't take long for your first visitors to show up. They appeared at your desk with a scowl, buttons neatly pinned to their left chest pocket with the words, "The We Hate It Here Club." The recruitment drive was on, and you were on the welcome route. As you popped up out of your chair to shake a visitor's hand, the scowl turned into a weak handshake. The dialogue can vary a little bit, but it usually goes something like this:

"Hi! Pleasure to meet you."

"Ya, whatever. Say, you're not working for Mr. West are you?"

"Well . . . uh . . . yes, I am."

"Figures."

"Why . . . uh . . . is there a problem?"

"Look, I'm not saying anything . . . but this guy is an animal! He'll chew you up and spit out the pieces, just like he does everybody else."

"Oh my."

"Ya, whatever. Me? I'm a ghost. Better get a good look at me now because I can assure you, I'm a memory. I'm outta here!"

Dazed and depressed, you continued your unpacking. Well, it was good while it lasted.

I present this example to illustrate something else. How long do you think your whining friend had been wearing that pin? You will get a good idea by looking at what you filled in for question 5. Look at the date you first entered the acknowledge stage and admitted the car you owned was less than perfect. Now look at your answer to question number 7, showing when you actually purchased your car. My bet is that you are probably looking at something between two and three years. Pretty scary.

Not only are 79 percent of our customers locked into the acknowledgment stage; they stay there for a long time. Think back on that person you pictured in your mind who told you he was a "ghost." That could have been three jobs and five years ago. Go back to that office, and guess who is still most likely going to be there?

Some people get stuck in the acknowledgment stage and literally can't get out. We all know of people we might consider to be complainers. I see them as *people who need to be sold!* I say that because of what I have learned of human nature. Two things keep customers paralyzed in the acknowledgment stage. The first is the perceived size of the problem. Here's another Rob's Rule to remember:

▶ *People don't fix small problems. They fix big problems.*

Regardless of the problem, if customers do not perceive the problem as a big one, they will feel no urgency to do anything about it. Customers procrastinate and put off acting on difficulties that face them. That's human nature, and that's what keeps us all pinned down in the acknowledge stage for long lengths of time. As the problem grows in size, we gravitate closer and closer to the next stage. When the problem becomes too enormous, we move on. If a salesperson comes along to "take an order," there will be no sale. We need to be sold first.

The second reason customers remain in the acknowledge stage for so long is an issue that will come up a few more times in this book: fear of change. All of us fear change. It often becomes the one stumbling block that even good salespeople can't overcome.

In the next chapter, as I show you how to move a customer through the decision cycle, I will be paying special attention to this step. There is a solution, and it requires honest-to-goodness persuasion. The "load the customer down with product information, order-taking mentality" will not work here.

Want to know the exciting part of this dilemma? The strategy I will be showing you to move a customer out of the acknowledge stage will teach you how to persuade the 79 percent of the customers who have no needs and are not shopping around looking at your competition. This 79 percent of the customers represent greatness from a persuasion perspective, and we're going to sell them! Unfortunately, as we track the decision-making process of people in their decision cycle, there is no salesperson "to assist them" and the customer is left paralyzed in this stage, waiting and waiting . . .

## DECISION STAGE

. . . with nothing happening. So there the customers are. Not totally happy with what they have, but not willing to do anything about it. Their problems are growing in size or severity, but nothing is happening . . . often for years. If asked, they will honestly tell you that they have no needs and no interest in hearing about your products or ideas.

Then something *does* happen.

It is hard to say exactly what, but something happens. Often it comes down to one of two scenarios. Sometimes it is simply a wearing down of the individual from a lot of small problems. These problems mount up until the person finally becomes fed up and begins to look at alternatives.

The second, and more common, scenario involves a more traumatic situation—a scare, a tragedy, a bad dream, or something else that wakes the customer up. The problem that the customer has been living with has somehow become unmanageable. I sometimes refer to this stage as the "straw that broke the camel's back stage" because often that is what the traumatic event really symbolizes.

It could be a bad transmission resulting in a stalled car and missed appointment. It could be a lost investment opportunity. It could even be someone else's misfortune that scares a person enough to cross that fix—

don't fix decision line. Once the problem grows, the customer wants to look for alternatives. Sadly, often this newfound realization comes too late.

When I sold insurance for New York Life, one thing the managers hated to see was agents sitting by the telephone, waiting for it to ring. Customers do not just sit down and call their agents unless something is very wrong. On the rare occasions when I did receive a call from a customer looking for insurance, our conversation would go like this:

"Hi, I'm looking for insurance."

"That's wonderful. What did the doctor tell you?"

"Pardon?"

"Well, when you went to the doctor, what did he tell you today?"

"Uh . . . well . . . he said my blood pressure was going up."

I call it the decision stage because it represents a crucial, and perhaps the most important, decision a customer goes through within the decision cycle. What's amazing is how often as customers we can come across the line and back again in a matter of seconds.

I remember struggling through some of my accounting classes at the University of Maryland. Each time a test approached, I toyed with the idea of seeking a tutor. After every test I would check the posted sheet of grades, see that I had done fairly well, and promptly dismiss the thought of a tutor.

One time, though, as I approached the "wall of truth," I had an extra-bad feeling about my test score. Searching for my social security number (which acted as my identification), I was very nervous. "This one definitely got by me," I thought. "I should have studied harder." When I saw my grade my heart sank. It was a D.

I needed a tutor, and I needed one now! Why had I been so foolish and waited as long as I did? What was I thinking? I began to map out my plan. I would call a tutor that afternoon. I would meet once a week until this misery was over. I would get some names from my roommate. On and on my mind raced.

Then, just for the heck of it, I decided to check my grade one more time. My mood changed from depression to elation in a split second: I had read the wrong person's grade. I hadn't gotten a D. I'd gotten a B! "Let that guy get a tutor," I thought to myself. "I'm hanging in there!"

What had happened in a matter of seconds illustrates the shaky ground at the first decision point people hover around. In those few seconds, I had crossed the line and come back again. Like many people, I chose to roll the dice once again.

Now look back at the answer you wrote down for question 6: "When did you start seriously looking for a new car?" Think back and ask yourself, Why? What made you start seriously looking? My bet is you will be able to recall something fairly traumatic that affected your decision.

Now look at something else that is also rather startling: the gap in time between question 5, which places a date as to when you *acknowledged* you had a problem, and question 6. Chances are there is a healthy gap in time. Then look at the gap in time between questions 6 and 7, which look at when you bought the new car. My guess is that the gap is probably six months or less. This second gap represents the infamous window of opportunity that every salesperson longs to find customers coming through.

One last point needs to be made: When tracking customers in the decision cycle, I have found that as crucial as this stage is, it represents more of a flash point for the customer. It is rare to find a customer actually in this stage, but, interestingly enough, it is almost impossible to find a customer who has *not* gone through this stage. It can take years of slow and frustrating difficulties to reach this stage, but once met, the fix—don't fix decision point is crossed in a flash, and the decision has been made. Now the process of making a decision, which has been dragging along for quite some time, begins to move . . .

## CRITERIA STAGE

. . . and move quickly! Once customers cross that first decision point, they immediately move into the criteria stage. With no seller in the picture, the individual has often gone through an emotional crisis of some sort and is looking to fix whatever is bothering him. What many people do not understand is that customers do not move immediately to making decisions once they make a commitment to change. It is natural, and expected, to begin to figure out what it is we are looking for *before* we go out looking for it!

The single most critical lesson you must learn within the process lies right here. It centers around the eerie connection between the customer's concerns (question 3), and the customer's decision-making criteria (question 4), which you highlighted. I asked you to highlight this so you could clearly see the difference between these two lists.

► *Customers' problems dominate the shape of their needs.*

Want to know where a piece of decision-making criteria came from? Take a long look at the customer's problems! I'll illustrate this point individually with a classic example.

When my wife and I purchased our last home, we came face to face with the problem shaping our need. The house we were looking to buy was seventeen years old and in fairly good shape. Every appliance in the kitchen was brand new . . . except the dishwasher. "That's okay," the agent told us. "That rumbling, tumbling sound you hear is the sound of quality." Well, I bit, but not before clever Rob had an addendum put in the contract: The dishwasher was given its own thirty-day guarantee. If anything happened within the first thirty days after settlement, the seller would have to replace the dishwasher. I wasn't born yesterday!

Literally thirty-one days later, a small puddle appeared on the floor next to the dishwasher. At that moment, the Jolles family officially entered the acknowledge stage. Unfortunately, like many other customers in the decision cycle, I did not perceive the problem as a big one, so I reacted like most other customers: I put off the thought of purchasing a new dishwasher.

One of the problems that I faced was cost. The house we purchased was in good shape but the kitchen was a fixer-upper. We had already put in a new subfloor and new tile, to the tune of almost $2,000. We were not in the mood to spend another $325 for a new dishwasher.

The plan I sold to my wife was a simple one: We would go back to basics for a while, washing dishes by hand during the week, and once a week we would run the dishwasher for sanitary purposes. On the days the dishwasher was to be run, we'd place a washcloth on the floor to collect the small amount of water that would trickle out. (To this day, I look back on this brilliant idea as one of my tougher sales.)

This pearl of an idea worked—for about a month. One day while giving my obligatory "first six months in your new house" tour, I saw the ramifications of my lack of action. The tour was a simple one: "Here's the kids' room, there's the living room, there's my office, and over there you will see . . . the flood in the kitchen!"

The gushing sound confirmed my worst nightmare: water was shooting out from under the dishwasher, and already about two inches of water covered our new kitchen floor. As if to present me, symbolically, with a visual exclamation point, my infamous washcloth floated by as if to say, "Welcome to the decision stage."

Do our problems shape our needs? Absolutely. It is proved over and over again, day after day. Look at the last home you purchased. If you were looking for a low-maintenance yard, I would wager you put in a few too many hours around the house you lived in. If your most important criterion was the neighbors in your community, I am willing to bet you lived in a neighborhood with knuckleheads. If a customer tells you his most important criterion is the service you offer, I am willing to bet that this customer had a bad experience with the previous service on his account. Our problems clearly shape our needs.

The Jolles' biggest problem clearly happened to be a lack of dependability. Our most important criterion centered on the need for a reliable dishwasher. Perhaps that represents a bit of an understatement. I was obsessed by reliability. I never wanted even to say the word *dishwasher* again. A new moral can be added to our first lesson:

▶ *Customers do not make decisions based on needs. They*
*make decisions based on problems. The bigger the problem,*
*the bigger the need.*

I bet, if you think about it for a moment, you can even guess which dishwasher we purchased. You guessed it. A Maytag. It wasn't the most feature-rich, or quiet, or fancy machine. It represented to us the most reliable machine on the market.

I respect Maytag for that very reason. Maytag is a brilliant company that has figured out what many other companies have yet to decipher: It is impossible to be everything to everyone, so segment the market toward people with dependability issues. Its advertising has been dedicated to this issue since I was a child.

Once I mentioned a need for reliability, didn't the name *Maytag* pop into your mind? Score one for the folks who make those Maytag products!

Another crucial lesson comes from this harmless story of dishwashers: The Maytag we purchased did not cost us $325; it cost $425. And I wrote that check in a heartbeat. Let's add to our previous two morals with a new one:

▶ *People do not make decisions based on needs; they make*
*decisions based on problems. The bigger the problem,*
*the bigger the need. The bigger the need, the more*
*customers are willing to pay.*

I guess if I were to sum up this story, I would do it this way: Needs appear for predictable reasons! I was not struck on the head by a coconut and woke up wanting a dishwasher. My wife and I, just like people you are attempting to change, went through a repeatable, and predictable, process. I did not just waltz into Sears one day, stop, and say to my wife, "You know what? I can't exactly tell you why, but I've got this irresistible urge to buy a dishwasher! Call me crazy, but let's live life to its fullest and do wacky things. I FEEL LIKE BUYING A DISHWASHER!"

I can't stress enough how crucial the lessons are that illustrate the relationship between the acknowledgment stage, decision stage, and criteria stage. If necessary, reread these sections until you are clear as to how they mesh. As a salesperson, you must be interested in all customers who are in these two stages. They represent over 90 percent of the customers out there. All the customer must do now is . . .

# MEASUREMENT STAGE

. . . tighten that list a bit. This next stage that customers go through in the *decision cycle* is a step that not all of them consciously experience. From a salesperson's perspective, I wish they would. The measurement stage provides the customer with the opportunity to move from the vague to the specific. This would eliminate many potential disputes that haunt seller and customer.

In the car exercise, you were asked to go back and put in measurements where appropriate. You may have wanted better gas mileage, but my guess is, when pushed, you came up with a specific numerical range. The last time you bought a house, you may very well have been looking for a larger home. If you were asked, my bet is there was an actual square footage desired.

This stage for the customer is nothing more than an adjustment of what is already desired. When customers consciously go through the measurement stage, they tend to be rewarded with smart buying decisions and peace of mind. When they do not, they run the risk of making poor buying decisions. Additionally, they face the possibility of being manipulated by less than ethical salespeople.

Want a classic example? In one of the funniest movies I have ever seen, National Lampoon's *Vacation*, there is a classic car buying scene that takes place with Chevy Chase, his son, and the seller from hell. It's a wonderful example of what happens when a customer does not measure his criteria. Chevy comes to the car dealership looking for "something sporty." He gets an A for showing us an example of the criteria stage. He gets an F for his attention to the measurement stage.

What happens next is a priceless piece of cinematography. Without a clear sense of definition or measurement, he becomes vulnerable to a salesperson whose goal is to provide *his* measurement of the criteria. The result? The infamous family roadster, pale green with mismatched wood side paneling and at least six headlights, in a stale, hideous wagon form.

Sadly, what blemishes the sales profession so deeply is clearly exemplified in this movie: unethical salespeople who attempt to manipulate customer criteria to benefit themselves, not the customer. Hopefully, with a better understanding of this natural and necessary step within the decision cycle, you will not fall prey yourself to this poor approach to persuasion.

One last critical point: At this stage in the decision cycle, the individual must make the second of four crucial decisions. As you will remember, that first decision was, "Do I want to fix the existing situation?" The decision the customer must now make is, "What is it going to take to fix the situation?"

At the end of the measurement stage, although some customers do this better than others, the decision has been made to move on through the cycle. The highly celebrated window of opportunity is wide open . . .

By the end of the measurement stage, although some individuals do this better than others, this decision has been made. It's time to move on through the cycle. The highly celebrated "window of opportunity" is wide open . . .

## INVESTIGATION STAGE

. . . and our customer is now ready to go looking for bargains! Now that the he has come up with a list of criteria and, hopefully, developed a sense of measurement, it's time to go shopping. Armed with a basic idea of what he is looking for, the customer is closing in on a selection decision.

In this stage, the customer, ironically enough, often comes looking for the salesperson. If the telephone does ring when you are alone in the bullpen and staring at the phone, it will probably be someone calling you from this stage of the *decision cycle.*

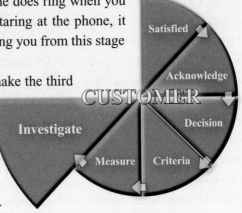

The customer must now make the third of four crucial decisions. Once he passes through the decision to fix, and feels comfortable with what it is going to take to fix it, the salesperson becomes involved. The third decision point a cus-tomer must now make is, "Who am I going to trust to make this decision?"

In the exercise you completed, if you look at your answer to questions 8 and 9, asking you about the cars you looked at and where you got the information to assist you in your decision, you will get a better idea of your own proficiency (or lack thereof) in the investigation stage. In this stage, the customer is really trying to accomplish two things. First, when making a sound decision, he will methodically apply the list of criteria to each and every product under consideration. That can be illustrated by looking at how you answered question 8, "What other cars did you look at?"

It is more the norm than the exception that not everything on the list of criteria is necessarily addressed when the ultimate selection is made. More often than not, the selection is made based on the solution that ultimately does the best job at addressing the top two or three items on the list.

The second task customers accomplish in this phase of the decision cycle involves the degree to which they will shopout their selection. Your answer to question 9, "Where did you get the information . . ." should show an example of this. At this point in the cycle, various solutions are eliminated based on their ability to meet the prescribed criteria. The cus-tomer then begins to do his homework. Advertising magazines like *Consumer Reports,* dealerships, friends, and previous experiences are all examples of how the investigation stage can be influenced.

Some customers may very well have already decided on the final selection. This last portion of the investigation stage may involve the customer's actually shopping out the same product at different distributors. For instance, in selecting a car, you may decide on a Ford Taurus. The second half of your decision would be where to buy it. Chances are you might visit a couple of dealerships, looking at the same car.

While tracking the decisions customers make, some have proudly told me, "I went with the first car or house I saw." This would *not* be something I would brag about, even if the first selection was the best one. Often, the better job a customer does in the investigation stage, the less buyer's remorse he is likely to experience. Now, with the comparing and shopping out of the way, our customer has finished his homework. At last, he is about ready to buy . . .

## SELECTION STAGE

. . . and all that is left to do now is pull the trigger. The customer has wandered down a long and frustrating path, but finally is ready to commit. Despite the slow process to get here, the customer often feels a sense of euphoria, finally being able to say yes and act on the urge to buy. There is a lot of emotion here, but unlike what you might have learned before, this is one of the few areas that allows for such emotion. The decision cycle is not as emotional as some would have you believe. The selection stage, however, is emotional.

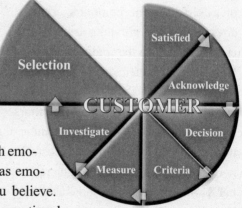

At this point in the decision cycle, there is just one final decision left for the individual to make. To do this, the customer must be convinced that the selection he has made in fact addresses all his needs.

Strangely enough, the final decision is often the easiest one. I am also willing to bet that when it finally came time to make *your* last decision, you felt a sort of release of tension when you ultimately made your choice.

There really is not much more that can be said about the selection stage. It might just represent the most basic and quick step within the cycle. Unfortunately, you'd better not blink, because the customer will not stay here for long. Almost instantaneously the customer moves on . . .

## RECONSIDERATION STAGE

. . . and heads to the reconsideration stage. Sometimes referred to as "buyer's remorse," this is an inevitable stage. It is really not a matter of if a customer goes through this stage, it is more a question of when.

The severity of this stage is often in direct proportion to the size of the commitment; that is, the purchase of a $400,000 home carries with it a lot more remorse than the purchase of a $2,500 home computer. That's obvious. What is not quite as obvious is the perspective that individual customers have of their decisions. It appears clear that the $400,000 home would have a large amount of remorse attached to it. We need to remember that this number is relative to each customer. A new home buyer would have as much remorse in the reconsideration stage paying $150,000 for a new home as the $400,000 buyer who is parlaying the last two purchases to make the next dream possible. Many salespeople lose sight of this valuable lesson.

The reconsideration stage can also be misunderstood when relating to the size of the solution. There is a clear distinction between a $400,000 home and a $2,500 computer, but what about a $2,500 computer and a $1,500 computer? The decision can be almost as slow, carry a lot of remorse, and once again be relative to each customer.

When tracking your buying decision, look at how you answered question 10, asking you, in essence, if you could go back and make this decision again, would you do it differently? Twenty-five percent of the time, when I ask someone that question, the answer I hear is "I would not make the same decision again."

If I were the seller in these situations, I would not be happy. I would be a little nervous. There has been an enormous amount of research tracking the satisfaction level of customers during the "quality craze." I found the research done by Technical Assistance Research Programs (TARP) of Washington, D.C., to be fascinating.

Most of us have heard that an unhappy customer will tell other customers of his displeasure. TARP tells us that they actually speak to anywhere between eleven to twenty other customers about their unhappy experience. But wait. It gets worse.

When it comes to what a customer will actually put in writing, the numbers become a lot more disturbing. A business often has no idea how bad the situation is because most customers do not speak to them about their problems. What a typical company does see and hear, if it is observant, is what is often referred to as the tip of the iceberg. It has been statistically proved that a typical business hears from only 4 percent of its unhappy customers. But wait. It gets even worse.

Of the 96 percent of the customers who do not bother to complain, 25 percent have serious complaints. Sadly, many misguided companies pass off an occasional complaint as unimportant. The numbers say otherwise.

After a brief touch of remorse, the customer moves on through the cycle, landing in the satisfaction stage, and the process begins to repeat itself. A benefit of Customer Centered Selling that will appear obvious to you is the increase in selling, and therefore income, that will result if you are a professional salesperson. Again, what many people are surprised to realize, as a benefit to this approach to persuasion, is the positive results you will see in how *you* perform as a customer making decisions.

Within the decision cycle customers encounter three critical "Decision Points." The three decisions made are as follows:

## THE FIRST DECISION POINT—"AM I GOING TO FIX THIS OR NOT?"

The first and most critical decision point is also the most difficult. It is human nature to fear change, and many of us simply sit, and wait for small problems to become big problems. However, this decision point represents a psychological "line in the sand" for many who take a long time to move through this. Once they do cross this line, they move briskly through the rest of the decision cycle.

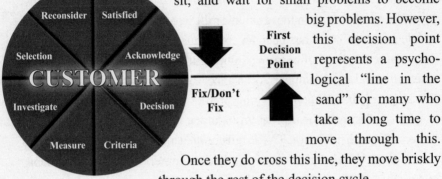

## THE SECOND DECISION POINT— "WHAT AM I GOING TO FIX THIS WITH?"

Buoyed by a sense of relief that his problems at last are going to be resolved, the client moves to the next decision point and now must figure out what it will take to fix their problems. Some will prioritize, and some will measure, but the infamous "window of opportunity" is open clients try to decide they will fix their problems. The most important thing to remember is that these needs did not develop by accident, but are linked to specific problems the client is looking to address.

## THE THIRD DECISION POINT—
## "WHERE AM I GOING TO GET THIS FROM?"

With a commitment to change, and a list of needs to address this change, it's time to simply take these needs, and apply them to various solutions. This leaves the client working towards the third and final decision point: "Where am I going to get this solution from?" Once this last decision has been made, the only thing left to do is make the *final* decision, and that is to actually make a purchase.

So there it is. A repeatable, predictable process that tracks the decision-making process individuals go through, along with the decision points they pass through. One quick reminder and word of caution before we move on. What you have just looked at is a *process*, and nothing more. It is not a straitjacket, just a process.

Now it's time to clear up a few misconceptions that hamper many in their approach to persuading. Then we'll turn our attention to the art of influencing and creating change by learning how to work within that decision cycle.

# SIX

# TEACHING SALESPEOPLE ...TO FAIL!

The definition of insanity: Doing things the same way you always have and expecting the results to be different.

*—Anonymous*

So now you have a better idea of how people make decisions. It's a shame salespeople are not taught this the first day they begin selling, but at least they are receiving some sales training. The question is, what exactly *are* we teaching? I believe the only thing we are really teaching our salespeople is how to fail, and I intend to prove it to you.

When I discuss selling in my seminars, I typically start by asking three questions about the participants' sales training background. Jot down your own answers here.

1. Have you ever taken a sales training course or seminar? _____

2. What were the names of the sales training courses you attended?

3. What are you implementing now, in your approach to selling, that you learned in the sales training you attended? _____

I have consistently noticed the same responses to these three questions. The answers to the first question, are rather consistent: roughly 95 percent of the participants claim to have been sales-trained before. On numerous occasions! From time to time, I have asked participants in my seminars how many have attended more than ten selling seminars. About half the hands remain raised. Imagine that! All that training.

The trouble begins when you look at the answers to question 2, about the names of the courses. Of the salespeople who claim to have attended all these sales training courses, 75 percent can't remember the names of these courses. It is rare if they can even remember the *year* they attended. This does not represent what I would call memorable training. (Were *you* able to answer the second question?)

Question 3, "What are you implementing now?" is the response I am actually most interested in. Typically those who can't answer question 2 have a real problem with the last question. Many times as participants are answering the last question, I can see them staring blankly into the distance as they attempt to recall information they have not used in years.

What went wrong? Why are we spending so much time and money to train salespeople, only to find they are not implementing any of the ideas they are taught? The problems that come from our failure to train salespeople are extensive. To begin, salespeople approach their training with a bad attitude, and I don't blame them. A salesperson makes money in front of the customer. If he is not in the field, he is not making money. To tell salespeople they will be spending two or three days out of the field makes them very uncomfortable. When anyone attends training without a feeling of benefit to themselves, they do not learn effectively. However, there does seem to be one consistent group of salespeople who do look forward to training: the top tier of the most successful salespeople. Never was this more apparent to me than when I was transitioning from sales to training at New York Life.

This was some years ago, and the office had just invested in a new-fangled contraption called a videocamera. It was decided that we would try filming the agents' selling and give them an opportunity to evaluate their tapes. In addition, they would be provided with feedback from the trainers.

The Washington general office, where I worked, was made up of seventy-eight agents:

- Twenty-one apprentice field underwriters (AFUs), agents who had worked with the company for fewer than twenty-four months.
- Fifty-two tenured agents with varying degrees of success.
- Five Chairman's Council agents, members of a select club of extremely successful agents. This club consisted of roughly the top five percent of the agents in the country, and the Washington general office was always among the leaders in the placement of Chairman's Council agents.

A flyer was placed in everyone's mailbox about this new, and rare, opportunity to view our approach to selling and get some feedback. It was a mandatory exercise for all AFUs, but optional for the other fifty-seven agents. All agents were requested to respond either yes or no.

As expected (and ordered), all twenty-one AFUs sent their forms back requesting various filming dates and times. Only five other agents asked to be filmed. You guessed it. The only other people who felt it was worthwhile to be filmed were the five Chairman's Council agents! Wait, it gets better.

Many of the AFUs were a little put off by the experience. They went through the motions and casually nodded at the feedback they received. When the Chairman's Council agents were evaluated, each one brought a pad of paper and never stopped asking questions and taking notes. I estimate the *least* successful of the five was probably making close to $500,000 a year (this was almost fifteen years ago). The Chairman's Council agents came to the filming obsessed with getting better.

The moral of this story was an easy one for me. What those five agents taught me that day was that successful salespeople share many common traits. One that seemed of paramount importance was a desire to improve, no matter what their level of success might be. The successful wannabes were too good for this training.

It would be unfair to say that everyone but the most successful salespeople approaches sales training without a feeling of benefit. On the contrary. Some others come to training eager and energized about the opportunity to learn more about their craft.

These courses typically fail. We herd hundreds, sometimes thousands, of salespeople into a room for a day of training, typically in a large university-style lecture. The drawbacks to this approach are obvious: There is no trainer-trainee direct contact; there is much theory but little activity; and trainees who come to the course eager leave disappointed and confused.

The failure to train salespeople effectively can create a ripple effect within organizations. Management, often shelling out the dollars to train staff, can become disillusioned as well. The only person more upset than the salesperson who spends a day out of the field not being productive is the manager, whose bonus depends on the success of the sales team. To hear from the salespeople that the training was "the same old stuff" creates an air of distrust from management. A cloud appears over the concept of sales training.

# WHY SALES TRAINING OFTEN FAILS

The failure to sales-train our sales force properly can be attributed to a few different factors. The first and most crucial reason it fails is that the initial sales training that just about all salespeople receive is *not* sales training. What most companies call sales training is actually *product* training masquerading as sales training! This is probably the most significant contributor to why salespeople will not stop talking and thus fail.

## CONFUSING PRODUCT WITH PROCESS

What does a customer hate more than anything else? What stereotype do you have when you think of a bad salesperson? What is the biggest sin a salesperson can commit? The answer is the same for all three questions: talking too much. When all you have been taught in "sales training" is product, your first reaction, when talking to a customer, is to do just that: talk. We want to tell the customer all about what we have learned. Factor into that "need to educate the customer" the fears a new salesperson has about his product knowledge. Frightened he will appear inexperienced, he is even more likely to want to show the customer all that he knows.

I will never forget my first week as a New York Life agent. The four of us starting with the company were led to a tiny room with poor ventilation. We sat in this room for four and a half days. The first three days started at 7:00 A.M. and ended around 10:00 P.M. It was our "core sales training." We were taught all there is to know about insurance. We learned about whole life and various dividend options. We learned about term insurance with convertible opportunities. We learned about health insurance and preexisting conditions with first-dollar accident options. Finally we learned about disability and cost-of-living opportunities. I was becoming a virtual genius in the field of insurance information. I was learning to sell!

Finally, on the fourth day, I saw the light, literally. We began at our usual 7:00 A.M. start and by lunchtime our "core sales training" was complete. Each of us was given about a dozen applications to put in our briefcase as we were marched to the front door. Squinting from the sunlight, which we had not seen in four days, we milled around waiting for our final instructions from our sales manager. I will never forget those last few words . . .

"Remember boys," he bellowed with a sly grin. "Two a week, ten a month. Now get out there and bring me back some apps!"

He was referring to insurance applications. He was also giving us our only real sales training. Looking back on my first day as a salesman, I now realize I was trained to fail. To this day, I wonder how I survived. When I was lucky enough to have a live prospect in front of me, I did exactly what I had been taught: explained various dividend options and carefully spelled out convertible opportunities within term policies. If customers were kind enough to tell me they did want to talk to me about their health insurance, I would shift gears and immediately oblige them with a perfect rendition of preexisting condition clauses and first-dollar accident options. I was guilty of committing the same sin that I loathed in salespeople whom I did not respect: I was talking way too much and not listening.

If you want another example, think about the last time you walked into a sporting goods store to buy athletic shoes. You most likely would not be walking up to the shoe display if you were not interested. If this is so, why is it we so often leave without new shoes? The reason is simple: We fall prey to the salespeople's inability to sell. Instead they tell us: "This running shoe here has shock rods on the bottom, a reinforced heel, and Velcro straps instead of laces. Now the other shoe over here costs a little more, but it has reinforced grommets, higher arch construction, and a breathable front. Finally, this last shoe [you're lucky if it is only three shoes] in the corner has the addition of a pump for better fitting, a waffle bottom to avoid pronation, and a leather upper."

I'm sold. How about you? Before we blame the salesperson in this case, let's look at where this salesperson probably was a few days earlier. Most likely, he had met with the regional wholesaler whose sales training consisted of banging a stick on a prepared flip chart and asking those in the room to join him in their sales chant. I can just hear that sales training now:

"AGAIN! Shock rod bottoms, reinforced heel!"

"AGAIN! Reinforced grommets, higher arch construction!"

"AGAIN! Better-fitting, leather upper!"

The real problem was that when the sales training was over, you were one of the first people the salesperson saw. That is how we teach people to insult customers' intelligence. That is how we teach salespeople to fail.

We do a great job of teaching *product* in this country, but most sales organizations do a poor job of teaching salespeople how to sell. Many industries make continuing-education credit mandatory to remain licensed in their chosen fields. Unfortunately, these courses are simply more product classes. This means that, *still*, no one is teaching our salespeople how to work consultatively with their customers.

Teaching someone to sell this way is like teaching others to bake a cake by showing them the finished product, letting them taste it, and then telling them to go bake it. This approach benefits no one.

For years now I have been attempting to add ethical, consultative sales training as a continuing-education credit alternative. Actually I believe this should be mandatory. I would not suggest the removal of all product training. I am merely endorsing a compromise on the mix of this training. Ultimately customers will benefit.

In short, we have to stop dumping enormous amounts of product information on salespeople and start teaching them to sell. By locking these salespeople away in rooms across the country and jamming product information down their throats, we are doing a disservice to them and to customers as well. I can't help you with your product knowledge. But I can assure you that by the time you finish reading this book, you will know exactly how to sell any product or idea you represent.

As a matter of fact, I've had people finish three-day training programs that I have delivered and then comment, "The most important thing I learned was to ask questions and listen." Part of me is disappointed that these participants did not get more from the training I conducted. My goodness, three days allows me to teach decision cycles, urgency, trust, trial closes, probing sequences, objection handling, opening tactics, and I'm just scratching the surface! To hear a participant tell me he is leaving with a new commitment to ask questions is initially a crushing statement.

But then again, if a participant leaves a training program truly committed to asking questions and listening for the rest of his life I want to go on record as saying this might represent the greatest class he's ever attended. Yes, I sure would like my participant to learn more, but without this lesson, a training program and this book are useless.

## CONFUSING STYLE WITH PROCESS

Sales training often fails because of the confusion between style and process. The definition of the word *process*, according to *Webster's Dictionary*, is "a series of actions or operations conducing to an end." The definition of the word *style* in this same dictionary is, "a distinctive manner or custom of behaving or conducting oneself." In other words, the process refers to *what* we do, and the style refers to *how* we do it.

Too often these two words are confused. Salespeople are evaluated and critiqued on their style, not process. When I work with salespeople, I show them what to do based on a sound, logical process that is repeatable and predictable. That process is not debatable. It is based on how people make decisions. There are times when salespeople ask me about how they personally verbalize these skills, and that's when I back off. Everyone's style is unique to that person. No one should ever criticize or try to change that.

The best example I can provide is from a person I believe to have been the greatest salesperson who ever lived.

In 1979, while I was with New York Life, Ben Feldman led the industry in sales—for all insurance companies, not just mine. And he didn't just lead the industry. He dominated it. The top nine agents were all fairly close to each other. Ben Feldman tripled his next closest competitor! He sold $1.6 billion of life insurance in his lifetime. This is a record I don't think will ever fall. What's more, Ben sold in the sprawling metropolis of East Liverpool, Ohio.

I had never seen a picture of Ben, but I imagined what he looked like: tall, aggressive, good looking. One day we received a videotape of Ben Feldman in the office. When I watched his tape, my life changed. Ben Feldman stood about 5 feet 4 inches. He was somewhat overweight and had hair a little like Larry's (of the Three Stooges). He spoke with a heavy lisp. Not what I had expected, but I watched on. Within seconds, I was drawn to the process that Ben Feldman was using. It was then and there I learned the most valuable lesson I would ever receive in my life regarding style: I could not be Ben Feldman, but I could focus on his technique or process and continue to ask myself, "How can I do that so it sounds like Rob Jolles?" Rob Jolles can't do Ben Feldman, but then again, Ben Feldman can't do Rob Jolles.

In summer 1994, Ben Feldman passed away but not without leaving us a few final gifts. He showed us many process behaviors that are repeatable and effective when working with clients. He also taught us that if you commit to your own personal style, and don't try to copy anyone else's style, you can become as great as you want.

## CONFUSING MOTIVATION WITH PROCESS

Sales training often fails because of the way it is structured. A lot of sales training is really more motivational than instructional. I have nothing against motivational training. I do quite a bit of it myself. When I conduct a motivational seminar, my intent is to do just that: motivate. I want participants to feel good about what they are doing and the way they do it. I am not speaking to educate as much as to entertain.

One of my favorite motivational sales trainers is Zig Zigler. I could listen to his tape, *Prime the Pump*, every day. It makes me feel good. It inspires me. He creates a tremendous visualization about the act of pumping water from a well and the energy necessary to start the flow of water. Once the water flows, the person pumping must continue to pump, or the water stops. He does a masterful job of relating this to selling and the activities associated with selling. It is brilliant. Nevertheless, it should not be confused with sales training. It is motivational training.

Many salespeople listen to tapes like this and think they are learning to sell. The first time I heard this tape, I thought the same thing. I remember playing the tape right before I went to see a customer. As embarrassing as this might sound, I vividly recall standing in front of the customer, attempting to sell a concept, when the customer broke in to ask me what I was doing with my arm. It was then that I became aware that I was moving my left arm up and down, simulating a pump on a well.

I remain a big fan of Zig's and some of the others, but I recommend keeping the lessons learned in perspective. Before seeing a client, I look over the process I intend to use to sell. I play the motivational tapes to fire up my attitude and inspire me to be enthusiastic while using my process.

## LACK OF PROCESS PRACTICE

A third reason for the failure I so often see in the training of salespeople is the lack of a clear-cut process to sell by. I have read brochures that actually boast that what is offered is not a process but rather simple, sound ideas. To me, this is mind boggling. Why in the world would anyone boast of *not* offering a process?

Often while I am asking for expectations of the participants in my seminars, someone raises a hand and offers the following immortal comment: "If I could learn one or two good ideas, I will be happy." One or two ideas? Boy, is this a symptom of some bad sales training! My response is almost always the same: "I am not here to give you a couple of good ideas. I am here to teach you an entire, complete approach to selling. If you are counting, however, and I do not give you at least fifty new ideas, see me when the session is over so I can give you your money back."

The whole idea behind learning a process is to give a structured series of techniques that are repeatable and predictable. The most powerful benefit of a process is that when you are performing predictable, repeatable techniques in a sequence, you are able to measure your performance.

When I think about the art of being able to measure what it is you do, I can't help but think about a story I recently heard. Two men went moose hunting in Alaska. This was an annual event that both men looked forward to. The men had a favorite location and a system they had developed over the years. On a Monday they would be flown in to their favorite spot. They'd hunt for a couple of days, and meet back at the drop site to be flown out. They were hunters who believed that you take what you can eat, so each year they limited their take to one moose each.

On the third day they returned to their drop site, each proudly displaying the animal he had hunted. When the pilot looked at the size of the two moose, the men, and their gear, he quickly realized they represented too much weight. Nervously he told the two men. Frustrated, the two men searched for a solution. Finally, one of them moaned, "It just isn't fair. Last year we each bagged a moose, had about the same amount of gear, and with a similar airplane, the pilot agreed to take us out!" Upon hearing this the pilot agreed to fly them out (against his better judgment).

The takeoff was rough. There wasn't a lot of length to the crude runway, so the plane had little room for error. As the plane picked up speed, it ever so slowly began to rise from the ground. A stand of trees loomed at the end of the runway, and each man began to swallow hard. More speed, and the plane continued to inch its way upward. If the trees were going to be cleared, it was going to be close! The plane reached the tree line, and the limbs of the first row of trees could be heard scratching at the underbelly of the small plane. For a moment, it looked as though the plane had made it to safety, but the second row of trees was higher than the first and seemed to reach out and grab the tiny plane. The plane bounced a few times and fell to the ground with moose, camping gear, and men strewn all over the ground.

Although bruised and badly shaken, miraculously the three men were not seriously injured. As one of them was shaking his head, trying to recover from the initial shock, he heard a call to him from above. The second man had landed in a tree. Bewildered, he asked, "Hey, Larry, can you tell where we are?" After looking around for a moment, Larry replied, "Yep. We're about forty feet farther than last year!"

It might be an old story, but look at the moral: At least they were able to measure what they were trying to do! *You have to be able to measure what it is you do.* Athletes can measure what they do by time. As a runner without a watch, I am fooling myself as to the effectiveness of my workout. As a salesperson, I can be fooling myself as well without a measurement system. This leads me to another one of Rob's Rules:

▶ *What gets measured, gets fixed.*

One of the most important lessons I learned in my long association with Xerox was the value of a process. I saw it work for me not only in the way I sold but in the way I approached quality. Xerox won the Malcom Baldrige Quality Award in 1989, and the Xerox Leadership Through Quality program has been benchmarked by many other companies. As a former trainer for Xerox, I can tell you why the Xerox quality program was so successful: Quality is taught as a *process*, not a slogan.

Xerox does not preach that problem solving is a nice thing to do; rather, it provides a process by which to problem solve. The employees are either using it or not. The process allows for measurement. Many companies that attempted to join the total quality management (TQM) movement in the 1980s became disillusioned and gave up. They gave up because they were given a handful of ideas but never a process that allowed them to use and measure these ideas. Without a process, sales training, like quality, can fall into the dreaded "flavor of the month" category and be perceived as a waste of time.

## THE TRUTH ABOUT SALES SCRIPTS

People initially may be turned off to learning a process to sell with because they inadvertently confuse a process with a script. After a few months of floundering around selling insurance, I was given a script (called "The Live, Die, Quit Story") and told to memorize it. With my theatrical background, I memorized that bad boy with ease and performed it for my colleagues (who, I might add, were a bit envious). I performed this script for management. They loved it. The office had a competition between all the apprentice field underwriters to see who could perform this script the best. Need I finish this story? Of course, I won. One of the secretaries came up afterward and told me I had actually brought a tear to her eye. Everyone loved the way I performed this script—except the customer. I never performed the script for a customer. I found it artificial, unforgiving, and personally insulting.

I am not totally against scripts when presented properly. In fact one of the first things I was given at Xerox was a ten-page demo script, with orders to memorize it. I felt as if I was reliving a bad dream. I once again called on my theatrical training techniques and memorized the sucker. After performing it for my manager, I was asked what I thought of the script. I gave the expected new-hire "Xeroid" response: "I love it, sir!" With a kind smile, my manager then asked me if I had any idea why I had been asked to learn the script. I had been told by a grizzled veteran that it was a rite of passage, but I didn't make that my response. I also didn't totally believe it. I could not believe that a company with sales training as sophisticated as Xerox would want reps to perform a demo from a script. At one point, I even thought it was more of a hazing than a help. But I didn't know the answer to the manager's question and stood blankly in front of him.

Finally he spoke: "We don't expect you to ever recite that mess in front of a real customer! We just hope that when you need it, when you are at a loss for words, when you are asked difficult questions, you will have an articulate bank of information to draw on."

Are scripts always bad? Of course not. They serve a purpose, though they will never take the place of a well-tuned process. They can teach us how to articulate difficult concepts. Sadly, many who are given a script to learn are never taught how to use it.

## THE DANGERS OF MONOPOLY MENTALITY

The final failure that can be a by-product of sales training is no training at all. Sales are good, and as long as they remain that way, why bother? This dangerous attitude can often be traced to company attitude, or what I refer to as "monopoly mentality." Xerox's history gives a classic example of monopoly mentality. Back in the '60s and early '70s Xerox was a prime example of a dominant company. Want a photocopier? You're buying a Xerox machine.

I still have a videotape that is a collection of all the commercials Xerox ever made. In the mid '60s, Xerox ran a series of commercials with a copier set up in a storefront window in downtown Manhattan. Hidden cameras in two different locations filmed customer reactions. I mention this not to point out any fascinating dialogue between the customer and the Xerox employee in the storefront, but because of what was subtly going on outside the window. In certain sequences, the crowd outside is standing four and five people deep. In one commercial shot, it is obviously raining outside, and, umbrellas in hand, people are lined up outside the window with their noses literally pressed to the glass. Well, that sounds like a pretty difficult sale, doesn't it? The most difficult aspect of selling a copier was finding the time to fill out all of the applications. Sales training? Why? Business was wonderful!

That was all well and good while the Xerox patents held and its copiers were the only show in town. After the patents expired in the early '70s, Xerox was warned of serious Japanese competition on the way. It ignored these warnings. Even after the Japanese began flooding the market with copiers that were less expensive, did more, and were every bit as dependable, the attitude did not change: "People will buy Xerox because . . . we're Xerox!" If there was a category in the *Guinness Book of World Records* for "Fastest Lost Market Share in the Shortest Period of Time," Xerox would head the list. The losses were devastating; the company was almost lost. Fortunately, a man named David Kearns came along, knocked the chip off the Xerox shoulder, and implemented two ideas: a commitment to total quality management (which Xerox referred to as Leadership Through Quality) and plans to utilize fully the Xerox training facility (Xerox Document University) and get back to serious sales training.

This is not a new story to many in business, yet major corporations continue to make the exact same mistake. Look at IBM. In the late 1980s, I sales-trained many office product dealerships that had been previously trained by Xerox. I was told the same thing over and over again: with an IBM product, they were taught to sell three things: name, name, and name! This strategy worked well when the personal computer industry was in its infancy. Unfortunately the competition grew faster, stronger, and hungrier. By the time IBM realized it was in a fight, the competition was putting out product that was less expensive, did more, and was every bit as dependable. Sounds familiar, doesn't it? The fall has been quick and well publicized. (I am a fan of IBM and a firm believer that IBM has learned from its mistakes and will recover as a better, more customer-focused corporation. But it has been an awfully expensive education.)

These are two well-known lessons that Xerox and IBM learned in different decades. Sadly, there are many, many more examples every day that do not make the front page. The time to divorce from the monopoly mentality is not when problems begin to be noticed. Then it's too late. No organization, regardless of its success, is above sales training. The first barrier is to convince them that it is necessary.

## AVOIDING THE "BOOK OF THE MONTH CLUB" SYNDROME

Another barrier to sales training can, ironically enough, be attributed to an overzealous approach to sales training. On numerous occasions, high-level managers and senior staff members will approach me during a break or at the end of a seminar and tell me how much they believe in training. It's always good to hear that. They then tell me that they believe in sales training so much that they have their salespeople read a different sales book each month! Oops. Here come the makings of another problem.

Salespeople should be receiving training that teaches an approach centered around a repeatable process. Some processes are more up to date and more effective than others, but if it is measurable, I can live with it. There are some tremendous processes out there: SPIN, Buyer Focused, Consultative Selling, and (my personal favorite) Customer Centered Selling, to mention a few. Each process offers a little nuance here or there, but the core is similar. They are not dramatically different from one another. Trying to learn them all scares me. A golf analogy will explain why.

Imagine going to a golf pro and taking a series of lessons for a month. We will assume the golf pro is competent and provides a fairly simple process for hitting the ball. Next month you decide to take lessons from a different pro. His credentials are similar, and he is competent as well. There are many similarities to the first process learned, but a few minor exceptions too. Next month, a different pro, a different couple of exceptions. After twelve months, what would your swing look like? Probably a mass of contradictory processes and no swing at all.

## EXPECTATION PERSPECTIVE

Finally, sales training often fails because many salespeople lack a sense of perspective on what they should expect to gain from the training itself. Many feel that their moderate amount of success excuses them from learning new ideas and considering change. I want to clear this point up right now.

Take just a moment and consider the difference between a .200 hitter in baseball and a .300 hitter. For those who do not follow the sport, a .200 hitting average means the player gets a hit two times for every ten times at bat; a .300 average means that the player gets a hit three times for every ten times at bat. Logic measures the difference this way, but in no way does this represent the true difference between these two baseball players. The difference is far greater.

One hit out of ten separates these two players; however, that one extra hit out of ten is consistent. In fact, that one hit out of ten often comes down to one pitch, usually a curve ball. Not every pitcher can throw a curve ball, but most can. Just about any baseball player can hit a fast ball, but those curve balls are murder. Learning to hit one takes a lot of time and dedication. All that extra work often comes down to one extra hit for every ten times at the plate. You can play the game without hitting a curve ball, or you can play the game well when you can hit a curve ball. It's that simple.

Now look at the difference between the two players. The .200 hitter spends his career in minor league baseball. He rides a bus from city to city, gets about $35 a day for meal money, and tries to make ends meet with various side jobs. The .300 hitter is in the major leagues. The average salary is over $1 million a year, and a .300 hitter is well above average, probably making close to $3 million a year. There are no more buses. These players travel first class, often on private jets, and meal money is irrelevant.

Within the profession of selling, this scenario plays itself out on a daily basis. The .200 hitter is represented by a salesperson who has achieved some good sales figures. This person sells enough to remain employed, and if a customer literally seeks him out, he is equipped to sell what the customer needs.

The .300 hitter is one of the stars in the office. This person in no way sells every customer but he consistently sells more. On a regular basis this salesperson is able to "hit the curve ball" and sell a percentage of the customers the other salesperson cannot.

I will not preach to you that the Customer Centered Selling process I will teach you is rocket science or the reinvention of the wheel. I will tell you it is a sound process that incorporates fifteen years of selling and can certainly teach you how to get that one more hit on a consistent basis. It has been successful for tens of thousands of sales professionals selling hundreds of different products or ideas. I hope you use it and prosper. The most important lesson that can be learned here, however, is that whatever method you commit to, stick with it. Perfect it and watch out for the book-of-the-month club approach to learning.

# SEVEN

# EXPOSING THE BIGGEST MYTHS IN SELLING

I respect faith, but doubt is what gets you an education.

—*W. Mizner*

The title of this chapter may sound a bit strong, but there are misconceptions within the sales profession that trouble me. These misconceptions perpetuate various lies and are fed meticulously to salespeople. You have seen the way salespeople are taught to fail. Now let me show some of the more damaging myths that add to their failure.

I must tell you that I swallowed these lies hook, line, and sinker. I would still be floundering if it were not for this thing called a decision cycle. Once you understand how people make decisions, you begin to realize that the selling tactics often taught are, figuratively speaking, in a bubble. Plain and simply put: Our customers make decisions in a certain way, and our salespeople are taught to sell in a completely different way.

In this chapter I present an argument that will shake the very foundations of just about everything you have learned or heard about selling. I start by looking at what it is a salesperson does, or should be doing. From there, I systematically expose myths in the profession of selling and explain why these fallacies hamper a salesperson in doing what he should be doing. Ultimately, most of what I will show you will be based on one person whom the sales profession lost sight of years ago: the customer!

Let's start with the basic core of what a salesperson does. This issue deals with the most basic principle of selling. For years, I have started many of my seminars with a survey question. I ask the participants to define what a salesperson does. I invite you to take a shot at the correct answer yourself.

## HOW DO YOU DEFINE WHAT A SALESPERSON DOES?

Here are five of the most common definitions I hear from salespeople. Put a check mark by the definition that best represents your own.

Selling Is:

1. Doing what you say you will do.
2. Taking customer needs and providing solutions.
3. Doing it right the first time.
4. Persuading customers to fix existing problems.
5. Linking customer needs to the benefits of your product.

Which did you select? The chart shows where you fall within a survey of over 3,000 salespeople who have answered the same question. The results are fairly obvious and hardly surprising: the most common definitions chosen were "Taking customer needs and providing solutions" and "Linking customer needs to the benefits of your product." This chart thus represents and supports the first and most fundamental principle behind selling, one that is taught in the universities and taught to every new salesperson. It is the basic battle cry representing the heart of selling: "Customers buy [or make decisions] based on needs."

*Webster's* provides the following definition of selling: "To develop a belief in the truth, value, or desirability . . . to persuade or induce to make a purchase." This is actually not a bad definition; the problem is that most salespeople do not know *how* to do this. They assume that to sell, they must adhere to the definitions I have provided. As you can see, most people believe the way to do this is by "taking customer needs and providing solutions" or "linking customer needs to the benefits of your product." This is strongly supported from the graph displaying how salespeople define what they do.

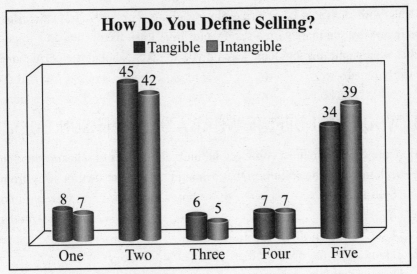

## How Do You Define Selling?
■ Tangible  ■ Intangible

*Source: Jolles Associates, Inc., Great Falls, VA.*

Interesting couple of definitions. Sounds good, and Lord knows I have heard this response for many years now. As you can see from the chart, you are in strong company. These definitions dominate the responses I hear. There is only one small problem with these two statements that everyone seems to believe so strongly in: *they are categorically wrong!*

This is no longer just my opinion. Research proves it is a fact. If you study the decision cycle customers go through, you begin to see how mistaken this entire assumption is. If customers make decisions based on needs, then why is there such a strange relationship between problems and needs? Take a look again at the exercise you completed in Chapter 2, tracking your decision to buy a car. Look at the problems you listed under question 3. Now look at the needs you listed under question 4. Your needs happen to represent alternatives to the problems you listed. Here's a Rob's Rule that will probably shake you up a little:

▶ *Customers do not make decisions based on needs. They make decisions based on problems.*

This is the first premise that is important for you to grasp. Here is a personal example that proves this point perfectly. When we bought our last house, the most important criterion to us was peace and quiet. Now, where do you think that need came from?

We bought our previous house in 1986 in the Washington, D.C., area where houses were being sold in less than twenty-four hours. We had already lost one house by waiting two days to make an offer and were bound and determined not to lose another.

The house we looked at seemed perfect: Cape Cod style, brick construction, meticulously taken care of, and a location that was too good to be true—ten minutes from the D.C. line and only two blocks away from the Capital Beltway. We looked at the home the night before it went into the multiple listings, sat in the peaceful, wooded backyard, and bought the house one hour later. It was the Jolles family's turn to win one. The house was ours.

Everything seemed perfect, and we counted the days until the closing. About a week before we were to move in, my wife and I drove to our new neighborhood to take a quiet walk and celebrate our upcoming move. Well, we took our walk, but it was by no means a quiet one. It sounded more like a walk along the Beltway. We were told by neighbors not to worry; it was just a shift in the wind.

As if to add insult to injury, our section of the Beltway was elevated above the neighborhood. If you are not familiar with the Washington Beltway, a portion of it—my portion of it—acts as a bypass for route 95, the highway that stretches from the bottom of Florida to the top of Maine. Every eighteen-wheel truck on that highway passed by my house. Have you ever heard air brakes being applied by one of these trucks? Not pretty.

So there we were, moving into our dream house that was already flawed. We did not spend even one week in the house in the satisfaction stage. To mask the noise we purchased outdoor speakers. We put up storm windows . . . in the *summer*. We even bought a big air cleaner for the bedroom we affectionately called the "soundalizer." I would like to tell you that we purchased this machine to clean air, but we did not. It put off loud, white noise, and was perfect at muffling our little air brake heaven.

We spent four years in this house. We loved our neighbors and friends, but when it came time to leave, what do you think our most important criterion was? Now you are catching on! We were interested in quiet.

*Interested* is probably not the right word. *Obsessed* would be a lot more accurate. For months, I would look at houses either on the way to work or on the way home. Equipped with stacks of multiple listings, the first thing I would do when I pulled up to see a house was put it through what I called the sound test. This test consisted of turning the car engine off, opening the car window, and hanging my head out of the car. If I heard anything that sounded like traffic, ANYTHING, I would not go in the house. I did not care if there were twenty bedrooms, with a bathroom for each. I was not going in.

Do you think our problems shape our decision-making criteria? I'll stake my reputation on it. So far, I do not expect any big bells or sirens to be going off in your head, but they will.

Now that we have looked at how you sell and what affects the customers you are selling, let's shift focus to how you are at making decisions. Let's stay with this house example a little further.

## WHERE ARE YOU WITHIN YOUR DECISION CYCLE?

The purchase of a house represents one of the largest decisions a customer ever makes. Let's see how *you* feel about your home. Answer these as honestly as possible.

1. With regard to your home, you feel:
   a. It is perfect, flawless. You could be offered top dollar today for the house, and even given the money necessary to buy your "perfect home," you would stay put.
   b. It is not perfect, but it is good enough. You are not looking for a new home. The one you are in will do fine. For now.
   c. Fed up! Funny I should ask. Something rather traumatic happened recently that was really the last straw. You have not contacted a realtor, but that call is imminent.
   d. Actively looking for solutions. You have a realtor. You are going out and looking at open houses every couple of weeks. On Sundays, you find yourself mapping out various houses of interest. You are in the market.

e. Honeymooning. You bought a house within the past six months and would prefer not being made to feel bad about it, so back off!

2. Circle the numbers that best represent how long you have felt that way:

| 0–6 | 7–12 | 12–24 | 24 |
|------|-------|-------|-----|
| months | months | months | months or longer |

Now let's interpret those selections. Each of the five choices represents a stage (or stages) in the decision cycle:

| a. It is perfect. | Satisfaction stage |
|---|---|
| b. It is not perfect . . . but good enough. | Acknowledgment stage |
| c. Fed up! | Decision stage |
| d. Actively looking for solutions. | Criteria, measurement, and investigation stages |
| e. Honeymooning | Selection and reconsideration stages |

Perhaps the biggest misconception in selling revolves around the assumption that most customers have needs that require a selling solution. Nothing could be further from the truth. After polling over 25,000 seminar participants (and still polling), asking purchase-related questions (similar to the questions you have been asked), the numbers strongly indicate a complete *lack* of needs but a convincing acknowledgment of *problems*. (See the chart on page 83.)

My guess is that you chose the second statement when asked how you feel about your home. "It's not perfect, but it's good enough." Once again, you're not alone. Almost 80 percent of the population agrees with you. And there's the problem right there.

And that's not all. Not only are most customers lodged in the *acknowledgment stage* numbers indicate they stay there for a long time. Sadly, most customers still have to absorb what amounts to a traumatic event before they move to the *decision stage* and begin once again to move through the cycle.

*You see, if this is how you look at selling and this is how you look at making decisions, then you are missing out on almost 80 percent of your prospects!!*

How can I make that claim? you ask. Simple.

- Research tells us salespeople are taught to seek out and sell customers who have needs and link those needs to the benefits of their products.
- Research tells us that almost 80 percent of the time customers have no needs or the need for a salesperson.

So here is the bottom line: Go out and sell all customers who are in the criteria, measurement, or research stages. These are your precious customers with needs. A few quick words of warning, however. There are not many of these prospects—about 8 percent of the customers out there—so take your time, and treat them like gold.

Reconsider 4%

Selection 2%

Criteria 8%

Satisfied 5%

Acknowledge 79%

Decision 2%

Source: Jolles Associates, Inc., Great Falls, VA.

Remember that you will not be alone. Nearly every salesperson is essentially fighting over the same type of customer. Bide your time, take your best shot, and don't let a little competition get you nervous.

Oh, and cross your fingers regarding those cherished needs. You must remember that you have entered the customers' decision cycle so late that they have already had their criteria heavily influenced and molded by existing problems and other salespeople. For example, if you are selling older homes with small closets and your customer wants large closets, you will figure something out. With any luck you might match up okay.

Finally, if all you are doing is taking a customer's needs and providing a solution, be prepared for a price war. Let's face it. If you take only the information the customer gives you and you and don't ask any questions, why should the customer pay you more? Why shouldn't price be the customer's most important criterion? By definition, you are an order taker. I will be happy to make you a deal: You go out and sell all 8 percent of those customers who have needs, and I will not interfere. It would be nice from time to time to sit by the phone and wait for one of these customers to call, and Lord knows occasionally they do, but a deal is a deal. The good news is that when customers have needs, they call you! Unfortunately, the bad news is that they probably will call everybody else in town too. In return, I want exclusive rights to the 79 percent of the customers you do not seem interested in.

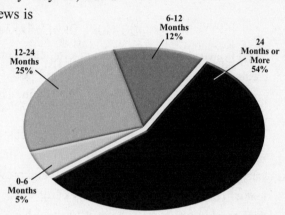

I want these customers because they have no needs or criteria they are aware of. A conversation involving a solution I have in mind will fall on deaf ears.

*Source: Jolles Associates, Inc., Great Falls, VA.*

I want these customers because I can influence their criteria to look more like *my* solution or product. It's called selling and I expect to accomplish this in a consultative, ethical manner.

I want these customers because they have called no one else. We all want the customer who has a list of needs and wants us to provide them with a solution. (A royal flush wouldn't be bad either!)

I want these customers because if I do a good job selling, the development of their criteria, measurement, and research will be done with me by their side. That's how salespeople earn their commission, and I intend to earn mine.

I want these customers because if I sell them, I can create a sense of urgency to combat the expected fear of change these customers have. This happens to be one of the biggest objections most salespeople face, and I wouldn't mind eliminating it early on.

I want these customers because if I can find one thing, just one problem they were not aware of, and get them to look at it carefully, my customer will be grateful and look to me, not my competition, for help. What a nice way to eliminate price as an objection.

I want these customers because my success as a salesperson depends on my ability to sell this customer. Enough said.

## NO MORE ORDER TAKING!

What I have attempted to show in a logical manner is simply this: We have created a society of salespeople who are fairly knowledgeable about their products but lacking the skills to sell them. The results are dangerous to the salesperson as well as to the customer.

The order-taking mentality is dangerous to salespeople because of what it does to their ability to recognize viable customers. Teaching a salesperson to identify customer needs and provide solutions is the equivalent of teaching a gambler to play cards by dealing him a full house and then teaching him how to bet it. As you have already learned, most customers have no idea what they need and will lead you down a path of price objections and stalls. When someone has not committed mentally to fix an existing situation, why would he or she offer needs upon request?

Salespeople constantly tell me they want to learn how to sell customers who appear unmotivated, slow to react to their recommendations, or unwilling to sit down and even have a conversation. What they are really saying to me is, "Teach us how to stop order taking and start selling."

Another danger to accepting an order-taking mentality lies in the danger to the customer and the exposure to the salesperson. "Exposure?" you might ask. Let me provide you with a scenario using investing as an example.

A customer comes to your investment firm. You ask what she needs, and with a smile she tells you what you want to hear. You provide her with the best product on the market to address those needs, and a sale is born. What a perfect layup for a salesperson . . . or is it?

Two months down the road, interest rates shift, and the customer you sold to is burned in the market. You had no idea, but she had planned this investment to supplement her children's education and had little else to fall back on. You placed this customer in a short-term, high-risk investment, as she requested. The customer is now furious. Of course, it was her idea, but here comes the $64,000 question: Who do you think the customer is going to blame: you or herself?

In many sales professions, salespeople purchase insurance called "errors and omissions" for protection in the event of lawsuits for situations like this one. The premiums are not cheap, as you might guess. The order-taking mentality that we teach our salespeople sees to that.

Another downside to adhering to an order-taking mentality is the lack of control salespeople have over the customer needs they are asked to match up to. I am referring to the helplessness of attempting to react to needs you cannot match. I am an ethical person, but I would certainly like to know how my customer arrived at his decisions. Just about every customer I have ever attempted to sell originally listed price as a key decision criterion or need. The training I conduct is not inexpensive. If I don't question the list of needs my customer arrives with, and sell, I am wasting my time. Aren't I being paid to ask these questions *before* the customer realizes his needs should be reexamined?

Waiting for customers with needs is a layup. I do not discount these customers. I simply say there is no need for a salesperson. A clerk will do since almost anybody can make a layup. I want to start a revolution. It is time to stop order taking and start persuading. It opens you up to another 79 percent of your customers, and it invites success.

# EIGHT

# QUESTIONING TECHNIQUES

The difference between the almost right word and the right word is really a large matter—'tis the difference between the lightning bug and the lightning.

*—Mark Twain*

I kicked around a couple of ideas for this chapter. One of my favorites was, "The Oldest Lesson in the Book . . . That Nobody Uses." In this chapter, what I will be teaching will not be new to many of you. Most who read this will discard the message of this chapter as something they already know. Be careful. Some of the key elements of the process I explain rely heavily on your ability to understand the two questioning techniques that are available to you. As a reward to you for reading this chapter, I will commit to you to get right to the message that these two techniques contain (as I always do!).

Rest assured, there are many types of questions that you can choose from, but at this point, I focus on the *way* you use these questions. I refer to this as the *technique* salespeople use in questioning, and this is where open and closed questions fit into the process.

## OPEN QUESTIONS

The first technique used in asking questions involves the use of open questions: those that cannot be answered with yes or no. As easy as this might sound, it is surprising how many people have a great deal of difficulty trying to employ this technique when questioning a client.

I believe salespeople have difficulty trying to use the open question technique because the definition often taught is vague. You see, some people take exception to the definition that I have given you for open questions. Instead, they define an open question as any question that does not allow the customer to give a limited response. From a practical viewpoint, they are absolutely correct. From an implementation viewpoint, they run into some trouble.

The discussion of open versus closed probes represents an old, basic lesson that just about every salesperson has heard. Never have I heard that the difference between the two is of no value. Quite the opposite. These techniques are fundamental and critical. I began to ask myself, "If so many salespeople think understanding the value of learning open and closed questions is necessary, why are so few of these salespeople actually using the technique properly?" After some experimentation, I realized the problem lay in the way these techniques were defined and taught. You now know the definition. Now let me show you how to remember and use the technique properly.

The secret to using an open question lies in the first word out of your mouth. You do not need to obsess on limited responses or lengthy responses. You need to focus on whether the customer can answer the question you ask with a yes or no, or if he will be forced to expand on his answer. Here are some words that encourage a longer response:

| | |
|---|---|
| what | tell |
| where | describe |
| when | how |
| why | share (for you West Coasters) |

When you start questions using these words, you will not receive yes or no responses. Someone who is asked, "What type of work do you perform?" is unlikely to answer "Yes."

## THE BENEFITS OF USING OPEN QUESTIONS

Among the many benefits to using the open question technique, an immediate one lies in the economy of questions you have to use. I can't tell you how many times I would be out with Xerox salespeople (who had once been taught this technique) and heard the following barrage of questions:

"**Do** you use the equipment?"*

"**Do** the secretaries use the equipment?"

"**Do** the temporaries use the equipment?"

"**Do** the partners use the equipment?"

"**Do** you have personnel who come in on the weekend and use the equipment?"

I often felt tempted to put my hand over the salesperson's mouth and break in with, "What my friend here wants to know is, Who uses the equipment?!"

Another benefit to using open questions is that this technique can often open up a reserved customer. As we all know, there are certain personality styles that do not lend themselves to the gift of gab. If you want these customers to talk, you are going to have to use open questions—for example:

### "**What** are you trying to accomplish with your business?"

Even the most reserved customer won't answer that question yes.

A third benefit to using open questions is their ability to get customers to expand on information. It is amazing what questions like, "Tell me more," can do to a conversation. I do not care for the game, "What's My Line?" and I certainly do not want to play it with my customer. When a customer is asked to expand on certain information using open questions, you will not have to worry about being a panelist on that show anymore—for example:

* Throughout this text I have boldfaced key words in all examples.

## "**How** does that work?"

The bottom line, and perhaps the biggest benefit, to using open questions is that it gets the customer talking. People love to talk, and they love to talk to others who make it easy for them to talk.

Think back to the last party you attended. At most parties, there are some people you want to talk with and some you avoid. Think about why. My guess is, if you really study it, that a lot has to do with this topic, that the first person we often want to avoid is the person who will not stop talking about himself. Almost as frustrating as the person who will not shut up is the person who has long-winded questions that typically end up requiring no real reply. My favorite example of this can be found on the new genre of television talk shows that dominate daytime television—shows with stirring topics like "Wives Who Cooked Dinner and Then Left Their Husbands for Their Husband's Cousins." The castigating mobs called audiences are famous for these long-winded, waste-of-time questions that are launched something like this:

> I have a question for the wife.
> Please, go ahead.
> Ya. If you knew you were going to leave him, why would you bake him a muffin, 'cause I wouldn't bake anyone a muffin. I just wouldn't do it.
> Uh . . . thank you for that question.

We are often guilty of almost the same ridiculous nonquestions. When we do ask questions, they are so loaded and take so long to ask that by the time it is the customer's turn to answer, all that is left is a pathetic yep or nope.

Now think back to the last time you saw an individual across the room and eagerly approached him. I want you to remember how easy it was to have a conversation. Try to play back that conversation, and I believe you will be surprised to find out why you liked talking to this person so much. The answer is simple: *You* did all the talking! What's more, he made it easy for you to do all the talking because he asked you wide-open questions:

"**What** are your kids up to?"

"**How** is your job going?"

"**What** are your summer plans?"

"**How** is your golf game going?"

The use of open questions as a technique for questioning is critical. Those who are uncomfortable with such a simple definition typically are not exposed to the thousands of salespeople who struggle with such an easy concept. People have asked me, "How can a question like, 'What is your name?' be an open question? Certainly you do not expect a detailed response?"

Well, they are right. I do not expect someone to answer that question, "My name is Steve because on a cloudy day back on August 10, 1958, I came bouncing into this world." I will lose that battle . . . but I will win the war.

When you focus on the key words I have provided, you are training yourself to open conversations up. I visit salespeople I have trained a decade ago who tell me they still use the key words, and they no longer have a problem with open questions!

## CLOSED QUESTIONS

Thus far, I have sung the praises of open questions. There is a time and place for everything, and I can assure you that I would not mention closed questions if this technique also did not present value to you.

First, I'll spell out a simple definition for this technique: A closed question is one that *does* provide the customer with the opportunity to give a yes or no response. The key to using or identifying a closed question also centers around the first word you use. Once you start a sentence with one of these words, chances are you will be receiving a yes or no answer.

| | |
|---|---|
| do | if |
| so | can |
| is | will |
| are | would (and the whole "ould" family) |

It is always the customer's prerogative to expand on a closed question, but when using this technique of questioning, you are not encouraging an opportunity for a good conversation with the customer.

## THE BENEFITS OF USING CLOSED QUESTIONS

So why use closed questions? Well, properly placed within the selling process, they can provide many benefits. In the chapters that follow, breaking down the selling process for you, I will show you exactly where closed questions should and should not be used. For now, however, let me tell you of their strategic benefits.

Using closed questions can assist you in the event your open questions function too well. Occasionally you might be faced with a customer who is a little too talkative. A harmless open question like, "How was your day?" might begin to take you through conversations about what was for breakfast and the day's traffic patterns. Closed questions can actually act strategically to limit the responses of a customer who monopolizes the conversation with meaningless information. For instance, in this example, watch as the closed question sets up another, more focused open question:

**"So** [breaking in on a rambling customer] it sounds as if your day was a busy one, wasn't it? Is your day as busy when you're at work?"

Closed questions can also help to qualify customer information. Sometimes, as hard as this may be to believe, customers can be unclear as to what their problems or needs are. Their statements can be vague and their intentions unclear. It is up to the salesperson to help clarify this conversation, and closed questions can be just what the doctor ordered—for example:

**"Are** you saying that you purchased the first product and then became unhappy with the results?"

Probably the biggest benefit to using closed questions is their ability to test and confirm information. For instance, most trial closes that are used (and all within the process I will be showing you) are administered using the closed question technique. Once again, these questions do not guarantee a direct response, but they certainly improve your chances of a shortened response—for example:

**"Is** this what you will be basing your purchase decision on?"

Positioned properly, closed questions can be extremely effective. Remember that the key to using these questions or open questions lies on the first word out of your mouth. Be careful not to overuse closed questions, and this technique for asking questions can be of great benefit to you.

## TIPS FOR IMPLEMENTING THIS LESSON

Oh, I know, you are probably saying to yourself, "I am glad he kept his word and kept this section brief. Now tell me something I don't know!" First, *never* talk to me that way again, and second, I suggest you watch yourself. Let me provide you with a case in point: Try taping yourself conducting a persuasive conversation. My guess would be (and I have listened to well over a thousand of these tapes), that for every open question you ask, there will be ten closed questions clustered around it. In other words, typically I hear ratios of 10:1 closed versus open.

Let me tell you why these numbers should concern you. To tell a salesperson to ask a lot of questions and listen to the customer is only half the story. The real goal is to get the customer talking. Remember, it is supposed to be a conversation, not an interrogation!

Think back to a time when you were stopped by a police officer for speeding. Did you enjoy that conversation? If police officers in the state of Maryland are representative of their profession, you will not hear, "Share with me your feelings about the speed limits in the state of Maryland." No sir! Their questions probably sound a little more like these:

"Do you know how fast you were driving?"
"Do you understand the laws in this state?"
"Do you have your license and registration?"

I do not question their tactic! They have a job to do, which I respect a great deal. However, you are not being sold this ticket; you are being issued this ticket. Although firing closed question after closed question might be the expected strategy for the police officer, it can be intimidating to customers and must be avoided by salespeople. (As a side note: I have worked with a half-dozen different state police departments around the country, teaching them the selling techniques that you are now reading about. How is that for progressive thinking by our police?)

The moral of the story is a simple one: Watch out for the temptation to overuse closed questions, particularly early in the sales cycle. I recommend that you simply listen for the first words out of your mouth to control your questioning technique. Do not panic if you hear yourself leading with a bunch of questions that start with classic closed question words like *do* or *are*. The biggest obstacle is to simply hear yourself using these incorrect words and be conscious of their use. There is no need to fumble around and restart your question in front of the customer. Simply make a mental note, and work on decreasing the percentage of their use. In no time, you will be rolling out the open questions.

Another practice you should work to avoid is closing down your open questions. Some salespeople cannot seem to leave a good question alone. For example, you might make this mistake and ask a question like this:

**"What** type of work do you perform? . . . I mean **do** you prepare client briefs?"

As you can see, the question is started open and then closed down. The result is to limit the response of the customer, it can also potentially keep you from hearing about other work the customer is performing. The customer could perceive this "other work" as not very important and disregard it. The problem is, this "other work," when found and analyzed, could represent an important need to the customer. That is precisely what we pay good salespeople to find out.

A similar problem to closing down your open questions is becoming impatient and answering your own questions. Often, we want to hear particular responses from the customer, and unintentionally offer these in *our* questions to the customer. A question like that would sound this way:

**"How** do your customers react to that? I'll bet they get pretty angry, right?"

That is not the kind of question you want to ask your customer. You should bite your lip and try as hard as you can to leave your questions alone once you have asked them. If a customer asks me to restate a question, I am more than happy to oblige. Otherwise I let that question stand on its own. Besides, something tells me it will not be the only question I end up asking this customer. There is more than enough time to rework the question and ask it again later.

A third, very typical problem salespeople experience when trying to use open or closed questions concerns the length of the question being asked. There is often so much salespeople want to know and need to know that they inadvertently cram all their thoughts into one question. This limits the customer's response and once again forces the salesperson to talk way too much. Here is an example:

**"When** you get to your office, and find there are messages waiting for you, **what** typically goes through your mind in terms of your performance with your clients or even other personnel? **Do** you think they know about what's going on, or would they rather be left alone, given the fact that some are unaware of the situation?"

How does that question grab you? As silly as it might sound, this is quite common to hear from salespeople who initially attempt to introduce more questioning in their sales approach.

Obviously, my suggestion here would be to shorten this question. A visualization might be helpful. When I was a boy, I used to go camping a lot. We would go backpacking up into the Appalachian Mountains for days, and sometimes weeks, at a time. I was an Eagle Scout and learned a great deal from my scouting experience: how to tie knots, lash, use signal flags, even march. But one aspect of camping that I was never very good at was cooking. I later found out the reason for this: I was not a good cook. I had a little trouble getting near the "blazing inferno" I called a fire. Finally, once while camping in the Shenandoah Valley, I met a seasoned hiker who was backpacking the entire 1,800-mile trail. I watched as he tended his fire. Small and manageable. He was practically crouched on top of the fire. Not much smoke, just enough flame. He did not appear to be working hard at all. Occasionally he would place another small twig directly on the fire. He was relaxed, in control, and deep in thought.

*My* fire was another story. The fires I built could be seen from miles away, and this one was no exception. I had collected just about every piece of dead wood around and was bound and determined to show off my fire prowess to Mr. Camping Guru. As usual, I hacked and coughed, trying desperately to get near the food I was burning—I mean, cooking. If I was not scorching my hands trying to stir my food, I was obsessively stoking my fire. We shared our food that night. His was tasty, and he was relaxed. My food was charred; I was exhausted. I looked as if I had come out of a burning building, with black circles under my eyes and smoke seeping out of my clothes. It wasn't difficult to see who was the better cook and camper.

I was envious and curious. How was he able to do so little and accomplish so much? He was kind as he explained it to me. "Let the fire do the work," he told me. "Keep it manageable, and work it a little at a time." He added, "You will get a great deal of power from one twig."

Words to live by. I see the conversation I have with my customer as that fire. I can ask long, difficult questions that are hard to answer and even harder to compose. Symbolically this represents the camper's trying to stoke a bonfire over which he has little control and which is exhausting to tend. Keep your questions short. A rule of thumb I try to use as often as possible is, Keep the majority of your questions under ten words. Now you are crouching over the manageable flame—easy to tend and easy to sustain.

It is my *customer* who does most of the talking. Strategically used, open questions and closed questions help me to accomplish this task. Particularly early on in the selling process, the ultimate goal is to stop talking. I envision my job as more of a caretaker of the conversation.

I'll conclude this chapter with one simple Rob's Rule that is a fact of life when it comes to selling:

► *The more the customer talks, the more the customer likes the person he or she is talking to.*

# THE CUSTOMER CENTERED SELLING CYCLE

Everything must be made as simple as possible but not one bit simpler.

—*Albert Einstein*

**A**t last it's time to take a look at the selling cycle contained within Customer Centered Selling. I don't want to obsess on the selling process, but rather to analyze the need for such a process to exist. This process, or any other process, is of little value without first studying the process a customer goes through when making a decision. This is the logic I have learned from Xerox, and this is what I will pass on to you in the chapters that follow.

As you read and study the selling cycle, remember a few things. First, at all times, attempt to keep the customer's *decision cycle* in mind. Do this so that you will see the logic of attempting to sell the way customers make decisions. Also remember that my intentions in using this process to persuade are ethical and honest, as yours should be. The process of persuasion is an extremely powerful tool. The process can, at times, challenge your morals relating to whom you choose to persuade and how you intend to use this process. I know you might be thinking to yourself, "This guy takes himself a little too seriously," but I do not believe you will think this at the end of my explanation of this process.

The process of making decisions and selling is cyclical in nature, which is why it is best illustrated with the use of a wheel. A customer will enter the cycle at the satisfaction stage, although he or she usually will not stay in that stage for long. With this in mind, I start the explanation of the selling process in the selling stage that aligns itself with the customer's being unaware. Salespeople who do the persuading may see this customer in any of the stages of decision making and will strategically align themselves to match up with the customer.

The best way to explain the process is to illustrate every move, step by step. Once again, remember that the process is not a straitjacket. I can't teach the process to you by teaching short-cuts or "what ifs." The only way to describe the process is by explaining and demonstrating each step in its entirety. After you have mastered the process, you can decide if there are particular steps that are more appropriate or less appropriate, depending on your situation. After you become more familiar with the process, I discuss strategic decision making, to provide you with strategies of how to utilize the steps of the process that best fit your situation. In addition, strategic decision making allows you to take an intelligent approach to matching up with your customers regardless of what stage you meet them within their decision cycle.

A second reminder is really more of a warning. One strategy of the *selling cycle* that intimidates people when they are first exposed to the process is the enormous number of steps. Be prepared now: When all the substeps are added together, there are twenty-two steps to this process. I can give you an explanation as to why the process is so involved.

When I first came on board with Xerox and learned the SPIN process that used to be taught there, I was spared the pain of so many steps. The SPIN process is four simple steps. That was the good news. The bad news was that it took two weeks to work on and role-play before it began to make sense. There were many subtleties and ride-on tactics that came together, but it took a long time and a lot of coaching to get through the gray areas.

Customer Centered Selling was designed to accommodate trainees who were to be taught in a shorter period of time. It seemed like an unrealistic demand, but it was a customer requirement just the same. As with many other inventions, this may have been a blessing in disguise. These requirements, in my mind, account for one of the most significant advantages to Customer Centered Selling. The process was designed to spell out every move. That's *every move,* no matter how small or trivial.

The selling cycle within the Customer Centered Selling process will not contain areas that ask you, for instance, to "make the customer feel comfortable." You will be told to follow three steps in sequence, and the customer *will* "feel comfortable." You will not be given the impossible assignment to "get the customer to feel a sense of urgency." You will be told to follow another pattern of steps and the customer *will* "feel a sense of urgency." The selling cycle systematically attempts to eliminate the gray areas.

This should be particularly helpful to you. I am unable to listen to you and give you feedback. I can, however, construct your selling process, step by step, which is what you will discover in the pages that follow.

Finally, I will tell you now that I like to start every sale and process from a cold-call, new-customer perspective. If you can become comfortable in these situations, you can certainly become comfortable in warmer situations. I have no intention of applying this process to your brother or sister. This process of persuasion is for those who do not necessarily want to be sold. Make no mistake about it: The process was designed to persuade.

*Webster's Dictionary* defines the term *persuade* as "to move by argument, entreaty, or expostulation to a belief, position, or course of action . . . to get with difficulty." Now *that's* a definition I can live with. The process I will now be showing you allows you to persuade in a systematic, repeatable, predictable manner. I have already preached to you about the ethics involved in persuading a customer. This is an issue that will require you to look deep into your soul to make sure you are persuading a customer to do what is right. With this in mind, allow me to provide you with my definition of selling, along with a catchy little Rob's Rule:

► *Selling is taking an idea, planting that idea in your customers' minds, and making them feel that they thought of it.*

Now reread that rule, and keep reading it until it makes sense to you. If you can understand that statement, you have just been given a window into the theme of what I believe selling is all about. Customer Centered Selling is simply the vehicle that initiates this process.

This is not by any means a new concept. It is, however, a forgotten concept. Recently I was at a garage sale and spent $1 on an old book, *Salesmanship and Sales Management,* written in 1917 by John G. Jones from the Alexander Hamilton Institute. His definition of selling went this way: "Salesmanship, in its broadest sense, is essentially the selling of one's point of view—the ability to start with the other fellow's point of view and to lead his mind to the viewpoint of the seller." This is not new information. It has been around, but it has been forgotten.

## CASE STUDY APPLICATIONS

When I teach people the selling cycle within the Customer Centered Selling process, or any other process, for that matter, I believe that the only way to learn is for the learning to be interactive. I hope that you enjoy these lessons, and profit from them. In this spirit, I have provided exercises that allow you to interact with the instruction that I present.

So far in this book I have asked you to audiotape your sales presentation and twice check its content. Now, as I move you into the process, I strongly recommend you participate in the outlined activities. They will not take long to accomplish, but they are crucial toward your comprehension of the process.

Throughout the study of the selling cycle, I will ask you to complete activities labeled "Test Your Comprehension." At the end of each chapter are my answers. My answers are by no means perfect, taking into consideration such factors as style and geographical location (I live on the East Coast), but they will provide you with acceptable, documented examples of the steps you are learning.

In each stage of the selling cycle, I provide examples tracking a couple of different customers in selling situations. I track tangible and intangible purchase decisions and how to persuade within these situations through four case studies that overview four fictitious companies.

You may want to place a mark at this section so you can quickly flip back and forth throughout the book. This will allow you to analyze and apply what you are learning to these case studies. It will also allow you to begin to implement strategically the lessons of the entire Customer Centered Selling process on your own clients.

To sell any product, you must first know its strengths. Here are the four companies in question and their particular strengths. You can make notes below each case study.

# PJ INVESTING CORPORATION
## (an intangible selling scenario)

If someone is looking into making investments, PJ Investing Corporation might be the company for them. There are many options to making investments, but your company feels it can offer certain benefits others cannot. To begin with, PJ Investing has assembled a research team that other companies can only drool over. The research department alone has nearly twice the staff of a typical investment company. The company has also recently upgraded its ability to turn around customer investment checks from eight days to one day. This means customer money begins working for the customer that much faster. It wasn't cheap, but now your company can claim the title of the quickest transfer in the industry.

You read all about the best approach to setting an appointment for a cold-call situation from this book, used it on this customer, and miraculously were able to set up a meeting. Your timing finally paid off. The Bracken family's faith in the Internet and *Money* magazine has finally been shaken by another unlucky no-load (no commission) investment. For the amount of money "The Bracken family has" in the market, you were surprised their investment "hobby" lasted as long as it did. Now that the family is "paralyzed by fear," it's time to challenge the Brackens with a little persuasion.

Notes _____

_____

_____

_____

# TO CLEAN A ROOM
## (a parental scenario)

Your oldest child has always been near the top of his class in schoolwork. With minimal effort, he has gotten by and his grades have been good. If anything, you wish he were challenged a little more often.

Unfortunately, this ability to get by with little effort has now leaked into other areas as well. He seems to approach many things in a lackadaisical and sometimes lazy manner. His bedroom has become a battleground. At least one of his good friends keeps a tidy room. This along with an occasional lost item or two may very well be your only source of support. Punishment hasn't worked up to now; perhaps persuasion will.

Notes _____

_____

_____

_____

# A TON OF TALENT, A LACK OF TRUST
## (a management scenario)

John has been with the company you work for longer than most, including you. He is a hard worker, dedicated and talented. He is also quite outspoken. If an internal company issue rubs him the wrong way, you can count on John to bring it to the forefront. He tends to voice these opinions at the most inopportune moments, with an air of innocence that his fellow employees have come to expect and, at times, even enjoy.

John would have been promoted long ago if it were not for his outbursts, which have been interpreted by senior management as disloyalty. Being passed up for a managerial position has made John increasingly bitter and cynical through the years. Most of his previous supervisors have not fared well with him. Now you are to be his manager. The few times you gave John responsibility, he responded well—as long as he didn't have to "compromise his ethics." You not only would like to reverse his behavioral tendencies, you would like him to attend interpersonal training to better understand some of his shortcomings. It's time to persuade John.

Notes _____

_____

_____

_____

# EVERY MOTORS, LTD.
## (a tangible selling scenario)

With an upscale clientele, Every Motors was prospering a few years ago, until everyone began to produce and sell cars to this clientele. Now the war is on, and the cars you specialize in are not so special anymore. Fortunately, the newest cars that you received came with a few interesting bells and whistles. One has an adjustable seat that memorizes two other predetermined settings. Also, the service department has come up with a new arrangement that assigns each customer a service representative. Now customers have a consistent person with whom they can develop a relationship as well as hold responsible.

Across the lot, you saw a typical customer looking at stickers on the cars. Once you approached, the customer told you he had just started shopping for cars and was doing a little "homework." You suggested he allow you to help him with his "homework," and he agreed. The conversation is about to start and so is the persuasion that is in order.

Notes _____

_____

_____

_____

# THE RESEARCH STAGE

## THE VALUE OF A GOOD CONVERSATION

You ain't learnin' nothin' when you're talkin'.

—*President Lyndon Baines Johnson*

I worked with a customer once who wanted to shoot a video demonstrating the Customer Centered Selling process as it applies to banks. We decided to start the video with some unsolicited comments from customers who were coming into the bank. I will never forget a comment made by one of the first customers. He was an older man who had a chiseled, distinguished look. When asked about what he looks for from the salespeople he works with at the bank, he grabbed his chin, squinted his eyes, and said, "Son, I value a good conversation. That's what I look for from the salespeople I work with."

There is an art to sitting down and having a conversation with a customer. It requires skills that seem to be lacking in many salespeople today. In this first stage of the Customer Centered Selling process, I will outline these skills and spell out exactly what to do to get a customer to value your conversation.

When the research stage is performed properly, it provides a rare opportunity to learn about and study the customer's world. Taking the time to learn about the customer's world is not just good business. It is essential in order to do business today.

The research stage is the Rodney Dangerfield of the selling process. For some reason, it seems to get no respect. But if this stage is not performed properly, the rest of the selling process becomes extremely anemic. It is a stage that is often underestimated, and that is dangerous.

Certainly you have heard the phrase, "People buy from people," indicating that people often end up buying from people they like. If you believe this is true, this stage represents your first, and probably most significant, opportunity to get someone to like you.

## DETERMINING DECISION MAKERS

If you are about to have a good conversation, one of the first things you must know is if you are speaking with the right person or persons. It is another one of those easy questions that so many people get wrong! I often ask salespeople I work with how they go about finding out if they are talking to the right person. With a smile and a roll of the eyes, I typically hear something like this:

**"Are you the one who will be making the decision on this purchase?"**

It is a simple question that some might even categorize as a no-brainer. The problem is that this question is worded improperly. Picture yourself as a potential customer who needs approval of a purchase decision by your spouse, boss, or any of a dozen others. You have been asked, "Are you the one who will be making the decision on this purchase?" Your ego is on the line. You don't want to appear to be not in complete control, so you do what many, many customers do: You lie! Before you can catch your breath, you respond, "Yes I am!"

Now what if you were to change that question ever so slightly to accommodate these fragile egos? Try this question instead:

**"Who, besides yourself, will be responsible for this purchase decision?"**

Phrasing your question this way allows your customer to maintain his dignity *and* provide with a truthful response.

# THE THREE RULES OF RESEARCH

The research stage is the only one within the selling process that has no other subsets. Once again, this may have been a case of underestimating the difficulty of getting a customer to open up and talk. It may seem easy, but when asked to make this skill repeatable and predictable, it's a whole different story.

## STEP 1. BACKGROUND PROBES

The first type of question that is used within the research stage is a *background probe*. It is used to obtain basic information about a customer's current situation.

Asking background probes can appear quite easy, but when asked to make this skill repeatable and predictable, it's a whole different story. With this in mind, consider these three rules when asking your background probes.

### RULE 1. KEEP YOUR QUESTIONS OPEN

As you may have guessed from my earlier chapter that dealt with techniques for questioning, open questions are critical in this stage of the selling cycle. It seems easy, but I can assure you that the temptation to use closed questions is hard to resist.

It is especially difficult for salespeople who work in vertical markets, that is, specialty markets. Some salespeople specialize in the legal "industry," some in working with hospitals, others in working with accountants. Specializing in a vertical market can often put salespeople in a catch-22 situation: They know a lot about the organization they are attempting to sell, but often have difficulty avoiding telling the customer everything they know about their organization.

It is the *customer* who should be telling you about his situation, not the other way around. Customers love to brag about their companies or their current situations. They are turned off by salespeople who talk too much. They don't trust know-it-alls. You can sit down and literally tell customers more about their company than they can, and you will be right. The bad news is that the customer will not like or trust you, or want to do business with you.

Regardless of your knowledge level within a customer's situation, let this customer tell you. Open questions are tailor-made for this first stage, where trust and perception are so critical. Remember once again, "The more the customer talks, the more the customer likes you."

This is not to say your expertise and knowledge within a particular vertical market are of no value. On the contrary. If you are dealing with a customer in a vertical market you feel comfortable in, your questions will reflect your expertise. It would certainly put off a lawyer, for instance, to hear you ask, "So tell me, how does a law office typically work?"

The strength of keeping your questions open and letting the customer do the talking is the first step in earning a customer's confidence in your abilities as a salesperson. Watch out for the temptations to use closed questions, and you will be taking your first step in achieving the type of conversation you are looking for.

## RULE 2. AVOID PROBLEMS

When I give a seminar and mention to participants the relatively small number of people who are totally happy with their particular situations, someone usually takes me to task. A voice will usually cry out from somewhere in the room: "You don't know my customers! Almost all of them tell me they are satisfied." Yep, and almost all of them are lying to you. It is an earlier Rob's Rule I want to remind you of:

► *Buyers can be liars.*

Rule 2 provides an explanation as to why they are not telling the truth. Too often salespeople jump into customer problems prematurely. This can often force a customer's hand and also often force a customer to become untruthful.

Let's say I was trying to sell you on my accounting services. You were kind enough to meet with me and have a conversation about the services you are using now. I even went so far as to assure you I want to get to know you and your business and was prepared to ask you questions and listen to all about you.

Sounds good so far, right? As a matter of fact, although I will touch on opening tactics later, what I have said so far might begin to warm you up for a friendly conversation. Then I go and spoil it all with one of my first questions:

## "**Do** you have problems with your current accountant?"

To begin, I don't think this person would be sitting here if there were not some problems with the current accountant. However, talk about a wolf in sheep's clothing. With this question, you are leaving the sanctity of the research stage and crossing into an area that requires a great deal of trust. In a split instant, I believe the customer's mind is racing, and it's sounding something like this:

"Do I have a problem with my accountant? Let's see. If I answer that question yes, I am probably committing something to this salesperson. If I answer that question yes, I will probably have to buy something. Heck, I'm not sure if I really want to change accountants or not. Do I have a problem with my accountant?"

The answer you hear is far simpler: "No." Now, that no will probably be followed up with an excuse or a lie as to why he is there talking to you, but chances are that the customer's nose is about to grow. What's worse, you pushed this customer into telling you that lie.

You have probably told quite a number of these little lies yourself. When you are approached by a salesperson who sells real estate or insurance and early in the conversation you are asked whether you have problems with your home or insurance, how do you react? No doubt you lie or shade the truth. When push comes to shove, you would not mind talking about your home or insurance, but you will not admit to problems for fear you are committing to something you will later regret.

Often when I tell people about disciplining themselves regarding this issue, as with the open questions, they will say, "Thanks for the tip . . . but I already do this." I believe this is a classic case of unconscious incompetency. Taping a sales call, as I suggested in an earlier chapter, takes care of identifying open and closed questions. Looking at the customer questionnaire often takes care of identifying this second issue.

A customer questionnaire can be called many things, but it's typically a document that most sales organizations keep around. This document acts as a research sheet to be followed by the salesperson. It is a brilliant idea. The only problem is that I have never seen one that does not mix problem-related questions throughout the entire document. When I work with companies, one of the first things I ask to examine is this document. I do not eliminate these problem-related questions; I merely move these questions to the bottom half of the document.

I am not the only one who feels this way. A classic example exists within a profession that I have come to know well: polygraph examiners. In a typical three-hour session with a polygraph examiner, the first hour (referred to as the "pretest") involves nothing but very simple questions, designed to put the person being tested at ease and to get a true reading from the person being tested as well as earn trust with the person doing the testing. The ultimate goal is to get a confession, and that will not occur unless there is trust. You will not hear a question like, "You stole the money, didn't you?"

The art of working within the research stage is to get a customer to trust you. Staying away from customer problems goes a long way in beginning to earn this trust from the customer you intend to persuade.

## RULE 3. PLAY YOUR STRENGTHS

The third rule is probably the most important but also the most difficult one. One reason it may be difficult for salespeople is that we are not taught to think the way a customer thinks. In the past, we were taught to tell customers a whole series of solutions and hope one or two might interest them. By "playing your strengths" I am referring to asking questions to make a case for solutions you want to show your customer later.

Most companies attempt to specialize or have particular strengths. A law firm might specialize in contracts, taxes, or estate planning, for instance. A manufacturer might specialize in service, price, quality, or selection. Most companies realize that you cannot be everything to everybody, so they begin to carve out a niche. Some companies want to be known as the least expensive place to buy, while others want to be known for their quality.

In the copier wars, Xerox prided itself on its quality, service, and ease of use, while Canon moved toward being feature rich (e.g., magnetized paper clip holders) and low cost. If you sold for Xerox, it would be no coincidence for you to ask harmless questions like:

**"What** types of companies do you typically interface with?"
[*quality*]
**"How** often is the machine currently being serviced?" [*service*]
**"Who** uses the machine?" [*ease of use*]

If you sold for Canon, the nature of your questions would change but not their intent—for example:

**"What** do you usually do with the paper clips you use on the documents you copy?"
**"How** much are you paying for the equipment you have?"

Examples like these can be found in industry after industry, company after company. At this stage in my career, I am more than happy to demonstrate how to sell anything anyone wants me to sell them within my seminars. The only thing I ask is, "What do you want the customer to want?" In other words, what are the solution's greatest strengths?

Here comes the scary part. Usually I am meeting with senior managers, vice presidents, and heavily tenured salespeople. When I ask them to give me the three or four biggest strengths of their own organizations, they look at me with a blank stare. It often becomes a homework assignment, but it is not uncommon for senior members of the organization I am working with to come up later and tell me how shocked they were with their own inability to answer the question.

Let me provide you with a few examples of "playing your strengths." Doctors, for example, often back you up and do this when you come into their offices. You tell the doctor that your shoulder is hurting, and most of them will essentially force you to back up and not talk about the problem. Rarely will they ask you to talk more about the shoulder pain you are feeling. Instead, they will ask questions like these:

**"What** types of sports do you play?"
**"What** kinds of exercises do you perform at your health club?"
**"How** old are your children?"

All of these questions, in the doctor's mind, have right and wrong answers. The answers either eliminate or potentially create further questions that give insight to a problem. If you play tennis, or if you lift a lot of heavy weights at a health spa, this would provide clues to your shoulder pain for the doctor. If you have young children you pick up often, again, the doctor would be given key clues with which to perform her diagnosis.

Another example of playing your strengths was exhibited by a television character, Lieutenant Columbo. I think this series *(Columbo)* presents a prime example of the research stage at its sometimes bizarre best.

As Columbo enters a case, he typically encounters a shrewd, rather closed-lip suspect. I have watched many episodes and have yet to see one that has our beloved lieutenant walking into the room and greeting the suspect with, "You killed her, didn't you?" You know what the answer to that question would be. Watch a good rerun of a *Columbo* episode, and you will see a far different tactic—one that is actually a combination of all three rules that I have outlined. First, you will hear a number of open questions being asked. Columbo's goal is to get the suspect to start talking.

Second, you will not hear any problem-related questions early on in the conversations. His goal, like mine, is to loosen up the person he is talking to. It doesn't take long for the suspect to start relaxing, and the conversation takes some more helpful turns.

Finally, mixed into many of these harmless open questions, which intentionally avoid problems, are some questions that do have right or wrong answers: "Pardon me, ma'am, but **what** type of cigarettes do you smoke?" Columbo does not say he found the butt of a Camel cigarette on the sidewalk next to the crime scene. He simply asks if this person smokes and what brand. There is a right or wrong answer to the question.

Something else occurs in these *Columbo* episodes that I find interesting. If you watch these shows, you will often see the defenses of these suspects come down. When these defenses are lowered, it does not take long for the suspect to start saying a little *too* much.

You will notice this phenomenon often occurs with a good manager. We have all had managers who mastered techniques within the research stage. You will remember these individuals as the ones who got you to say a lot more than you intended to say. We have all approached this type of person's door saying the same thing: "I know what this guy wants, and he isn't getting it from me today. I'm not talking. I'm going to be the human sphinx. He may think he's going to crack me, but he's wrong this time. I'm not talking!"

One hour later you emerged, smiling and laughing. You shook hands and wandered back to your desk. It was only then that your smile began to fade. The questions in your mind began to take over from there. "What did I tell him? I didn't have to tell him *all* of that. Why did I tell him *all* of that? Son of a gun, he did it to me again!" You were up against a master researcher, a Lieutenant Columbo type. Don't blame yourself. You never stood a chance!

The bottom line is that most companies' products typically do almost exactly what other companies' products do, with a few minor exceptions. The mark of a successful salesperson is not only to get you to want some of his minor exceptions badly, but to make you feel as if you came up with the idea.

Now let met give you an example. Recently I was conducting a seminar in Kansas City and rented a car. I was minding my own business, looking over my city map while leaving the airport, when I heard a strange sound—a short, quick sucking sound. I was not sure exactly what it was, but it certainly got my attention. I came to a red light and found myself looking the car over, attempting to figure out what the bizarre sound I had heard was.

The only thing that caught my attention was the door locks. I could have sworn that I had not locked the car, but all the locks were down. It had sounded a little bit like a door lock, but I could not figure out how I had accidentally hit the lock button. Anyway, I shrugged it off and just for the heck of it unlocked my door. I thought to myself, "If I want my doors locked, *I'll* be the one to lock them!"

Up went the lock, and the light turned green. I found myself looking out the corner of my eye at the possible "lock with a mind of its own." No change. Yet the moment I took my eye off the lock, I heard the short sucking sound again. I quickly shot a look over to my door lock, and sure enough, the door was once again locked!

By the time I arrived at my hotel, my study was complete. There was no short in the electrical system. This was no accident. At ten miles an hour, the car automatically locked itself. Believe it or not, this was a feature.

I laughed to myself. What a silly feature, right? Wrong. It was time to start thinking like a salesperson. I thought to myself, "How would I try to sell this feature if I sold this car?" This "silly" feature represents exactly what I am attempting to illustrate to you now.

Stop and think for a minute. Compare two cars that fairly face off against each other:

Both have radios.
Both have engines.
Both have four tires.
Both have cruise control.
Both have decent service plans.

Are you getting the point? For the most part, minus a few bells and whistles, they are pretty much carbon copies of each other. So what actually drives your decision? Your fascination with a particular bell or whistle. If there is no unique bell and whistle, then the obsession turns into a fascination with a common feature. This common feature on monumental proportions and is satisfied by premium solutions.

I would love every customer I sell to walk in craving the few things I happen to do well, but that's unrealistic. My job is to create that desire for what I do well, and of course, get the customer to feel as if he came up with these needs. I would prefer not to play the "What's My Feature" game, so I ask background probes. I also begin to play my strengths to see if a further conversation is even necessary.

Now, back to Kansas City and the car example. Questions began to pour into my mind. Two questions would be of particular importance:

**"Who** rides in the car?"
**"Where** do you typically drive the car?"

These questions help me play my strengths. They are open questions, and they avoid problems. If I were to hear that children ride in the car, my ears would perk up. If I were to hear that occasionally the car is driven to less-than-safe areas, I would take note.

I never went on a sales call for Xerox without my asking (or the person I was with asking), "Who uses the equipment?" Xerox prides itself on building equipment that is easy to operate. When you hear that question, there is a right and a wrong answer. The answer I would love to hear is, "Everyone uses the equipment." I have just received my first hint at what I will be talking about in a few minutes. I am thrilled. I have the potential for an ease-of-use issue.

Sometimes that answer was not to my liking; "My cousin Louie. He has been with the company for ten years now and no one else gets near the equipment. By the way, Louie used to be a technical representative for Xerox. He knows this machine as well as your service reps do!"

Well, now I am not thrilled, but I still benefit from that question. That answer just saved me from spending ten minutes getting this customer to want something that was a waste of both of our time. I have some other features and some other questions to fish with. I can use my time wisely and move on. You see, I win either way.

## STEP 2. ANYTHING ELSE?

The next issue becomes, How long do you take to ask all of these questions? One of the most commonly asked questions with regard to the research stage relates to timing. So how much research is enough research?

Your guess is as good as mine. But I will tell you the signs I look for that help me. The most common indicator of time relates to the size of the account. A good rule of thumb is that usually the size of the account will be proportionate to the length of the sales cycle. All stages are affected. If I were dealing with a "mom and pop" (small account) customer, ten to fifteen minutes in the research stage is enough. If I were dealing with a larger customer, this stage would take a lot longer.

Some people suggest watching the customer's body language, but that has always made me nervous. Some people fidget, cross their arms, or look at their watches because, basically, that is what they like to do! I personally have never put a lot of stock in the subtleties of body language. You might want to look at the customer's body language, but you are on your own here. I know I often fold my arms and supposedly "close down" because I am cold, not because I am put off.

The best suggestion I can offer might be the most obvious: Ask. My favorite approach to finishing off the research stage is to ask the customer this question:

**"I feel as if I have a pretty good handle on the background of your business. Is there *anything else* that you think might be pertinent to this conversation?"**

I can't read minds, so I have always trusted this question. If there is more, the customer will tell me. If not, I feel the customer is saying to me, *"You understand my business and have the right to move on."*

## SOME FINAL THOUGHTS

With the two steps involved in the research stage and three rules to support these steps, it would seem that the first stage of the Customer Centered

Selling process is in place. I must warn you, however, there are always some subtleties and gray areas that must be watched for. Here are a couple of ideas that might help you.

## REMAIN CALM AND STAY PUT!

Now, here is something that can shock people, but here goes. You will never guess what I recommend you do if these questions begin to shed some light on particular problems. After you write the question down, so you will not forget it, I recommend you do nothing . . . for now.

The mistake so many salespeople make is to jump all over the first problem they hear. Even if this is an important problem, chances are it will not be enough to move on through the process. This is no longer just an opinion of mine; it's a fact. Look at the purchases you have made and frustrations with products you are dissatisfied with. Was it one problem that moved you? Even if it was a severe problem, chances are you would not do anything about it.

I began to notice this in my buying habits as well as my selling. I could identify a problem and transfer this problem to a strong need. Still, I noticed customers stalling and resisting change. I decided to create a survey to attempt to settle this issue. How many problems are enough to create change? With a sample pool of 2,500 participants, the question was asked, "On an average, how many problems will you live with before deciding to fix the problem?" This question was followed up with a scale of perceived severity showing little change.

Of every poll or survey I conducted, this was probably the most difficult. The question was difficult to word, the results a challenge to measure. However, the message appeared clear. The chart shows that for most customers, it takes three significant, separate problems before they actually do something. If you are in the research stage and discover a problem the customer is experiencing (whether this customer is aware of the problem or not), initiating change will not be easy. Discipline yourself. Stay put, and continue to learn about your customer. The odds are that no matter how severe the issue, the customer will probably not want to do anything about it.

The research stage disciplines the seller to avoid talking about prob-

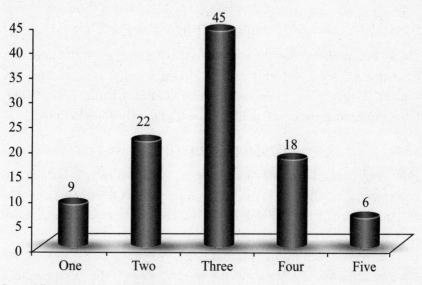

Source: Jolles Associates, Inc., Great Falls, VA.

lems with the customers. But if the customer does bring up a potential problem during the conversation, write it down. Leave it alone! I believe that unskilled salespeople take the bait and immediately assume the first hint of a customer problem is a cue to move onto a solution. This is a flawed perception. This is not what the customer pays a commission or premium for. It is our responsibility to keep learning about the customer and looking for problems the customer may not have fully identified before he came to see you.

There is a commercial (one of my favorites) that illustrates the importance of this point. Two men are talking to each other. One man, in a rather dejected mood, confides to the other about his problems: "I don't know what I'm going to do. I have to scrape up money for the kids' college, the house needs an addition, and my parents are going to require more and more of my income as they continue to get older. What a mess."

The other man tells him, "I had a broker years ago who set up a number of different accounts and plans to take care of all of that."

Bewildered, the first man looks at his friend and asks, "How did your broker know to do all of that?"

The answer: "He asked."

## BE FLEXIBLE

Even when implementing the concept of playing your strengths, not every customer will have problems or needs in the areas you are probing. Be flexible. Have as many options as possible. As Emile Chartier put it, "Nothing is more dangerous than an idea when it's the only one you have."

## CONSIDER YOUR TIMING

How many background probes are enough? When Xerox sells its high end equipment, the selling cycle can last an average of six to eight months. The research stage can last a month or two. Of course, the equipment cost can start at a quarter of a million dollars.

The second step of the research stage, "Anything else?" was not put there by accident. The beauty of the research stage is that it represents a no-risk opportunity. "The value of a good conversation" can pay huge dividends later in the sales call. I want my customer to trust me and to open up to me. I desperately want to find one thing, just one thing my competition could not find that is of importance. The rest of the process will teach you what to do when this occurs.

Worst-case scenario? There really isn't one. I spend twenty minutes with a customer, and in that time we never even leave the research stage. I refuse to believe this was wasted time. This chapter has come full circle. In twenty minutes, I learned more about my customer than any other salesperson will learn about him. My customer spent most of his time talking to me. I avoided problems, which ultimately allowed me to listen at a deeper level to this customer. I positioned a couple of potential features that I will not even mention until the process is complete. Most important, however, it took me only twenty minutes to get this customer to like me. That is the value of a good conversation. I call that success.

# TEST YOUR COMPREHENSION: RESEARCH STAGE

Go back to the four case studies in Chapter 9. Here is your chance to test what you have learned. Write two background probes for each scenario that incorporate the three rules outlined thus far. Then write two questions that apply to the product or idea you are trying to sell. On the following page, I give you my two background probes that address the strengths of each of the companies outlined in the case studies.

## PJ INVESTING CORPORATION

1. _____

_____

2. _____

_____

## TO CLEAN A ROOM

1. _____

_____

2. _____

_____

## EVERY MOTORS, LTD.

1. _____

_____

2. _____

_____

## A TON OF TALENT, A LACK OF TRUST

1. _____

_____

2. _____

_____

YOUR OWN SCENARIO

1. _____

_____

2. _____

_____

# SUGGESTED ANSWERS TO TEST YOUR COMPREHENSION: RESEARCH STAGE

Here are my answers. See how closely they resemble the answers you gave. Do not worry about the difference as it relates to style. Watch closely for technique instead.

## PJ INVESTING CORPORATION

1. **Walk me through** the typical process you use when making an investment decision. [*I am looking toward research here and the decision-making process.*]
2. **What** is the size of an average investment? [*The size of the investment will strengthen my argument for transfer speed down the road.*]

## TO CLEAN A ROOM

1. **Who** else comes into this room? [*This begins to position the child's friend and his feelings about a clean room.*]
2. **When** was the last time you couldn't find what you were looking for? [*With any cooperation, we might be able to set up a conversation about lost items.*]

## A TON OF TALENT, A LACK OF TRUST

1. **Tell** me about the last project you were given a leadership role on. [*I am looking to see how receptive the person is to this topic. I don't want to irritate or agitate this person in this stage of the process.*]
2. **What** type of formalized training have you received to date? [*I am looking to do my homework and find out what type of resistance I might expect to encounter.*]

EVERY MOTORS, LTD.

1. **How** many people do you anticipate will be driving this car? [*Let's see if we can begin to position the adjustable seats here.*]
2. When you have had your car serviced in the past, **what** were the typical procedures? [*It would be nice to hear the customer spout off about a lack of procedures, but I'll take whatever he can give me here.*]

Look over these question as well as your own, and put them through the test:

- Is the question an open question?
- Does the question avoid your bringing up a problem?
- Does the question begin to play a strength of the company in question?

# ELEVEN

# THE ANALYSIS STAGE

## THE BEST-KEPT SECRET IN SELLING

FOR WANT OF A NAIL

For want of a nail, a shoe was lost

For want of a shoe, a horse was lost

For want of a horse, a rider was lost

For want of a rider, a message was lost

For want of a message, a battle was lost

For want of a battle, a war was lost

And all for want of a nail . . .

*—Ben Franklin*

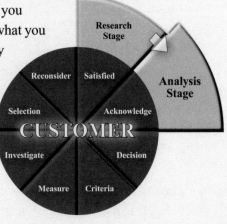

So far, the process I have shown you has probably reaffirmed much of what you have already learned. There are many different approaches to researching with a customer. I hope that I was able to present a logical argument as to why you should be more careful and deliberate in that stage. I trust that my arguments were sound and that you saw the wisdom of what I was explaining to you.

Now I worry that, with this newfound knowledge, you will fall prey to the trap that most salespeople fall into. The questions have been open and the customer has been talking . . . and talking. The customer felt truly comfortable with you and began telling you of difficulties he did not predict he would be discussing. Listening carefully, you were even able to sense a couple of problems he did not mention. At this point, you not only know what the customer's problems are, you already know how to fix them. Now, buoyed by a false sense of security, you will make the most damaging decision you can arrive at: You are ready to fix the customer's problems.

Think about it. How many times have you heard a customer describe a particular problem and you found yourself literally squirming in your chair to offer a solution:

| Customer: | We have been handed over from one sales rep to another sales rep to . . . |
|---|---|
| Salesperson: | . . . to another. I know. You see, at our company . . . |
| Customer: | Then when we bother to complain . . . |
| Salesperson: | . . . you are probably given the runaround. We promise . . . |
| Customer: | Yeah. You promise. We have heard promises before. The last time we . . . |
| Salesperson: | . . . we have a customer assurance guarantee! It's in writing! How does that sound? |
| Customer: | It sounds expensive. I don't have to pay extra for that, do I? |

Does this exchange sound familiar to you? It should. It has been going on for decades. You see, doing a little research and then offering a solution would be perfect if it weren't for one little thing: the *decision cycle*.

I have already established that decision cycle. I have tracked hundreds, if not thousands, of decisions customers make, and I think you will agree that this is how you make decisions as well. Remember this Rob's Rule:

► *People do not fix small problems, they fix big ones.*

The example I just gave indicates a customer who is aware of a small problem but is not really ready to do anything about it. This is a classic case for most of us and a typical representation of the awareness stage for the customer.

Well, you have come to a crossroads. Here is where success—or failure—lies. Those who can move customers out of this stage and across the first decision point yet to come are the fortunate ones. Those who can't are often the ones who feel life has somehow dealt them an unfair blow. It is *not* an unfair blow. It is often just a lack of selling skills in this area.

If you can master what I discuss in this chapter, it will serve you the rest of your life. That is the good news. Let me prepare you for the bad news: It is no coincidence that this part of the selling cycle is the most challenging, most difficult, most misunderstood, and grayest of all the steps. It is also the most important.

The reason for the difficulty here is understandable. Typically, just about everyone I work with has had what they feel is extensive sales training. Strangely, it has never been in the area I am about to develop. Like anything else that is new, the tendency is often to avoid it. I ask you, don't reach for the easy excuses . . .

## "I don't need to learn this part."

You do. Almost 80 percent of your customers are lined up in their decision cycle directly across from this stage in the selling cycle.

## "I pretty much do this step with my customers."

I role-play and observe salespeople for a living and I have never seen a salesperson naturally use the skills I will be showing you before they are taught. If people use this step, they are keeping it a well-guarded secret.

## "I don't know what the fuss is all about. I have read it, and this step does not seem that hard to me."

Oh, make no mistake about it. This is a difficult step. I will explain it to you carefully and slowly. I will provide you with numerous examples and case studies. Do not be fooled. You need to use the skills either in a role play or with the customer to learn them.

Now the good news. If you study this chapter carefully and immediately try to practice what you have learned, you will succeed. Most people I work with see marked improvement the second time they implement this step. The second time!

Enough of the fanfare. Let's get at it. It is now time for you to learn the best-kept secret in selling. It is time for the analysis stage.

# LETTING THE CUSTOMER PAINT THE PICTURE

Once a salesperson enters the analysis stage, a subtle change begins to occur. In the previous stage, you were taught to avoid problem areas at all cost. Now quite the opposite is true. The analysis stage is the one and only step where problems are the *main* focus. The customer would not be talking to us (and vice versa) if there were no problems. Hopefully, our patience has paid off, and the customer is ready for an in-depth conversation dealing with these problems.

This is a challenging step for salespeople and must be approached carefully. With caution in mind, let me break down the analysis stage into three repeatable steps. These steps focus on three different types of probes that should be used in a sequence that I refer to as the *probing sequence*.

Remember that I am not referring to customers who are asking us to take their business. Rather, I am referring to that mass of people who have problems they consider minor and are not willing to look at alternatives. Refer back to the decision cycle, and you will be once again reminded of these customers. If we tell them they have problems, they may very well lie and say it is not so. This first probe begins to get the ball rolling.

## STEP 1. IDENTIFYING PROBES

*Identifying probes* is step 1 because that is what needs to happen first. Until the customer identifies a particular problem, there is no logic in working to solve it. When you are using this first probe, you must get the customer to identify or agree there is a problem. This can be difficult. Most customers, early on, resist admitting to a problem. If they do, they often will not admit to the size of the problem. This can be due to a fear of being "sold" something. More often than not, surprisingly, many customers will not admit to the size of a problem because they truly have never sat down and analyzed it carefully.

The good news here is that you will not be deviating too much from the pattern you established in the research stage while working with background probes. It is once again critical to use open questions. You are beginning to tread on sacred ground here, and you definitely do not want to be perceived as pushy. Just listen to the difference in these next couple of questions. Let's start with closed questions:

**"Do** you have problems with your finances?"
**"Aren't** you unhappy when you can't get an answer to your questions?

Now consider the open questions:

**"What** sort of challenges do you currently experience with your finances?"
**"What** kinds of difficulties are created when you can't get an answer to your questions?

Which set of questions would you rather be asked? When you take care to avoid the temptation of using closed questions, you decrease the perceived aggressiveness of the question. This is important, especially for the first couple of questions asked in this stage. These are quite often disturbing to the customer.

I have one other concern about the use of closed questions in the identifying portion of this stage. Closed questions force customers to decide too early whether or not they actually have a concern. The customers might really enjoy talking with you and trust you as a salesperson, and be wanting to help you. However, when faced with a yes or no choice as to whether they have a problem in a particular area, their answer may very well be no. The door is closed. You sense a problem does exist, but now you have to move on. You have backed yourself into your own corner.

In keeping with this theory of treading carefully, let me give you another hint about how to soften these questions. Notice something else about the example open questions. In this case, do not look for what is there; look for what is missing.

If you notice, the word *problem* is not used in either of the open questions. This is by no means an accident. Back in the early 1980s, Xerox did one of its many studies with customers and quickly learned that customers hate it when salespeople use the word *problem*. It sounds aggressive and pushy. "Do you have a problem with that?!"

There is no way to perfume that pig; the word *problem* must go. Fortunately, the study did not stop there. To this day, I have always pictured people in lab coats working in a laboratory on new words that would work. Well, it was not a laboratory, but here are a number of words that can be substituted for the word *problem:*

| | |
|---|---|
| concern | barrier |
| difficulty | limitation |
| dissatisfaction | obstacle |
| challenge | trouble |

These words will swap nicely for the word *problem* and allow you to arrive at the same conclusion with the customer. The major difference at this point in the conversation is the intentional turning of the conversation toward customer concerns.

Hopefully, if you are patient and use nonthreatening background probes in the research stage, continuing to use open questions, and avoiding the word *problem*, the customer will more readily admit to having a particular difficulty. Sometimes they need just a little push.

This "little push" involves spelling out more of the customer's problem than I would like, but sometimes it is necessary. Some customers truly would rather not deal with a particular issue or problem until it actually occurs. You and I know it is probably too late at that point, but let's continue to look at real-world situations. It is not a reflection of customer stubbornness to procrastinate and avoid the thought of serious problems; it is human nature. In a worst-case scenario, this might be a reaction to an early identifying question.

Salesperson:  **What** kind of **concerns** do you have with your inventory?
Customer:       None. We run it kind of tight, but so far we have been hanging in there.

Well, that did not seem to identify a thing. What is necessary at this point is to help this problem along a bit:

Salesperson:  I see. Well, **what happens if** you do run short on your inventory?
Customer:       Uh, well, I would probably be a little late on some of my deliveries.

Bingo! Now, we have ourselves a problem to work with. Watch the temptation to overuse the phrase, "What happens if/when." I hesitate even to make this suggestion for fear that all your questions will begin this way. Keep it in your hip pocket, just in case.

So now we have identified a concern in the customer's mind. Where do we go from here? Well, I can certainly tell you where 99 percent of people in a selling position would go from here: right to a solution . . .

Customer:       Uh, well, I would probably be a little late on some of my deliveries.
Salesperson:  Well, with ABC Enterprises, you won't have that problem anymore! We have developed a new technology that . . .

And so on, and so on, and so on. Wrong! That is *not* the way it should be done. For all those who can't understand why I am so adamant about not recommending a product, I have one small, haunting Rob's Rule:

► *If customers are so intelligent and know fully about their problems, how come they take so long to do anything about them?*

Chew on that one for a minute. The answer is, the problem does not hurt enough. As you have read in the decision cycle, people do not fix small problems; they fix big problems. In the customer's mind, this is not a big enough problem. The enticement to launch into a solution tempts the salesperson the way a mouse is tempted by baited cheese. Both offer damaging consequences.

A solution here often results in a lack of urgency by the customer, along with an obsession with cost. Obviously the consequences for the mouse are a little more severe.

# TEST YOUR COMPREHENSION: IDENTIFYING PROBES

Go back to the four case studies at the end of Chapter 9. Here is your chance to test what you have learned. Write an identifying probe for each of the four scenarios. Then write an identifying probe that applies to the product or idea you are trying to sell. See if you can link these probes to the questions you used at the end of Chapter 10. At the end of this chapter, I give you my suggestions for probes that apply to each of the companies outlined in the case studies.

PJ INVESTING CORPORATION (an intangible selling scenario)

1. _____

_____

TO CLEAN A ROOM (a parental scenario)

1. _____

_____

A TON OF TALENT, A LACK OF TRUST (a management scenario)

1. _____

_____

EVERY MOTORS, LTD. (a tangible selling scenario)

1. _____

_____

YOUR OWN SCENARIO

1. _____

_____

# STEP 2. DEVELOPING PROBES

Within the analysis stage, perhaps the most important step lies right here. It is not easy, and for many people it is not instinctive. Your temptation is to move on. But to persuade or sell, you must stay put and develop the problem more.

The way you develop a problem is to continue to ask questions about it. Often customers do not want to talk much about their concern. I do. Customers will avoid thinking about the long-term effects a particular problem might have. I won't. Customers evade contemplating "what if." I will. (That is precisely what I am paid to do.) Once the customer has experienced a major problem, there is no longer a need for a salesperson. It's too late. A Rob's Rule is in order here:

▶ *The intent of selling is to protect the customer from "what if," not "what is."*

We once owned a car (the name will be left out to avoid embarrassing a rather large American manufacturer) that will provide a good illustration of this point. It was the classic family truckster. It was my wife's car, and it was used for all the family dirty work. It was the car that we took on long trips. It was the car in which we hauled lumber and other odds and ends. Most damaging of all to the vehicle, it was the car we hauled the kids around in. At that time, I drove a little red convertible that really was of little help in these matters. (Don't be so surprised. I *am* the salesman in the family.)

In a nutshell, the car had some small problems—little things like a broken plastic door lock, a jammed window, a radio stuck on FM, and a tire that rattled, to mention a few. Nothing too severe, but annoying just the same.

One day, my wife came home and informed me that the car had developed a new problem. For no apparent reason, at random times, the car would "hitch"—that is, lose five to ten miles per hour in an instant. Seconds later, it would regain its full power. It was as if someone was pinching the fuel line and then releasing it. Sometimes it would happen twice a day, sometimes twice in a month. It took almost three weeks before the car hitched with me in the car.

I know a few things about working on cars, and when I exhausted both of them, I took it in for repairs. The problem seemed serious enough to take it back to a dealership specializing in this particular car. That's where things got interesting.

Three days later, I went back to pick up the car. I was not happy with the $700 bill, but I was assured the problem had been fixed. Almost on cue, as I was pulling out of the dealership, the car hitched. Somewhat mortified, the repairman nervously called out, "Don't worry Mr. Jolly. The car just needs a few miles on it!"

Two days and three hitches later, I brought the car back in. Once again, I was told they had repaired the problem, and once again the car began hitching almost immediately. To make a dangerously long story short, over the next month we brought the family truckster back five times. In fairness to the dealership, we were never charged a penny after the first bill was paid and were given a loaner car while ours was being repaired.

Meanwhile, the family truckster was getting some astounding work done to it. Computer chips were methodically replaced one by one until the car was finally given a new computer. All sorts of repairs were being made in hopes the hitch would go away. A computer was strapped to the engine as the car was driven hundreds of miles to research the hitch better.

To this day, I cannot tell you why, but the plastic door locks were fixed, the rattle on the tire was repaired, the window was unjammed, and the radio was fixed. I suspected our family truckster was becoming the dealership mascot. They tried everything and could not repair the dreaded hitch.

Finally, as I went to check on my car the fifth time in, the manager called me into his office. He told they had put almost $2,500 worth of repairs into the car and could not figure out what the problem was. He then spoke these immortal words:

"Look," he said, "in cases like these, we fly in a specialist. If he can't fix it, we'll have to declare your car totaled." Wow! Could you imagine that? My family truckster going off to an island of unrepairable cars. This was some hitch!

As I walked out of the manager's office, I finally woke up. Was I crazy? Fixed or not fixed, the family truckster needed to go! It was off to the car dealerships for us. Before I tell you what dealership I went to, see if you can guess. Remember that our biggest problems become our biggest needs. Our biggest problem centered around dependability. What car manufacturer do you think we visited first?

It was Honda. My perception of Honda (accurate or not) was that it might not be the prettiest, fastest, or cheapest on the road, but from what I had heard, it was dependable.

As we got out of our car, a man came skipping up shouting, "You two are looking for a car!" Right—so far. Despite my attempts to break in to his sales monologue, we got the tour. This one does this, and that one does that. This one's got a "road Coke holder" and that one's got a rear windshield wiper. (I must admit, I always wanted a rear windshield wiper.) When the speech was over, out came the immortal words: "What's it gonna take to get you two in this car today?" I believe it was the first question he asked us. I mumbled, "I don't know . . . maybe a brochure."

We did not buy a car that day. We came close though. When it came right down to pulling the trigger, we backed away, just like a lot of other customers. Funny thing was, we very badly needed to buy a car that day. Unfortunately, we needed to have one sold to us.

Most people do not naturally study the true potential of the problems they live with. If they did, not only would they fix them, cost would have much less significance. It is interesting how few people, regardless of their financial status, look for the least expensive surgeon when an operation is in order. Perhaps the potential for the problem is better understood in their mind.

Many people I work with tell me this is the most difficult stage to master. I believe many of us do this quite naturally, almost unconsciously, with our best friends and those we care deeply for. The problem is that because it is unconscious, it is hard to perform on command.

The art of using developing questions is quite simple. You just have to be a little more curious with your customers. Once a problem has been established, *stop allowing your customers to run away from it!* Stay put. Get curious. For example, ask:

**"How** are you currently managing when this difficulty occurs?"
**"What** do your employees say?"
**"How** are your customers reacting to this issue?"
**"Who** else is affected?"
**"What** do they say?
**"How** do your employees feel about this?"

Key words used in developing probes are not quite as simple to track as the other probes used because the art of developing probes requires extending the customer's conversation. Sometimes this might result in the use of some of the key identifying words previously listed. However, here are some words that would be more uniquely qualified and might be of use from time to time:

| | |
|---|---|
| react | relate |
| link | affect |
| respond | feel |

Each question in its own way serves to advance the problem. A great example of this point can be illustrated in a poem called "For Want of a Nail." I carry this poem with me and, by no coincidence, this poem opens this chapter. It was written by Benjamin Franklin, not only an inventor and a politician but a poet as well. This poem represents exactly what I am attempting to teach you. Look back at the start of this chapter now and see if you can relate to its meaning.

People do not look at the impact of many of their problems. If they did, they would no longer have that problem. I identify with those who sell at a premium and have to sell "what if?" Ultimately, all they are really selling is themselves, their mind, their experience, and possibly one or two unique features. You must learn to get the customer to look down the road a bit at his problems. This is done by using developing probes, but these probes can be disturbing to the customer.

This problem can be compared to a wound. The more painful the wound, the closer the person is to doing something about it. I implore you not to rush to put a Band-Aid on this wound. Offering a solution does just that.

To me, the art of selling can be compared to a good professional fight. Think for a moment what happens in the first couple of rounds of a fight between two respectable fighters. As a fight fan, I can tell you in one word: nothing. In fight terms, the first round is often referred to as a "feeling-out round." The idea is to study your opponent and try to identify his weaknesses.

Consider what happens early in a selling situation. The research that you do is designed to teach you where you must throw your punches. Research truly is a "feeling-out round."

After a couple of rounds in a professional fight, it is not uncommon to hear a cornerman tell his fighter, "It's time to throw punches with *bad* intentions!" This tells the fighter to take what he has learned and fire more meaningful punches.

Within the analysis stage of the selling cycle, that is exactly what you are doing. Hopefully, you became aware of a couple of issues the customer was uncomfortable with. It is time for you to "throw punches with bad intentions." That is where the identification probes come in. Those questions are not as easy to answer and often disturb the customer.

Now, our boxers teach us one last critical lesson. Think about what happens when a good boxer actually lands a solid blow. It hurts the opponent. Sometimes it even cuts the opponent a little bit. I have never heard a boxer say, "Gee, I'm sorry. I seemed to have cut your eye a little bit. I'll aim for the other." I have never heard the corner people of the fighter who has landed the punch call out, "Leave him alone! Stay away from the cut!" What is communicated is quite the opposite—usually, "Stay on him! Don't let him breathe! The cut! Go for the cut!"

When the person you are attempting to persuade tells you he has a problem and your research is complete, you too must "go for the cut." You must not be squeamish. You are dealing with a customer who will wait and wait until "what if" occurs to act. Often it is too late then. If you believe in your recommendation, you must not be afraid to push sometimes.

At Xerox, within the circle of Xeroids who really know how to sell, this part of the process is referred to as "bleeding the customer." My mentor in learning how to process my selling was a dear friend named Larry Domonkos. A true Xeroid in every sense of the word, Larry once gave me this little pearl of wisdom as it relates to customers. We'll now let it speak for itself as another one of Rob's Rules:

► *If they cry, they'll buy!*

I know that may have offended some of you who are reading this, but I only ask that you continue to listen. I can assure you that I fully intend to illustrate this point in what I believe will be perceived as a more positive light. Before I do, however, take a moment to test your comprehension, and then let me finish off this questioning process with one final punch.

# TEST YOUR COMPREHENSION: DEVELOPING PROBES

Go back to the four case studies in Chapter 9. Here is your chance to test what you have learned. Write two developing probes for each scenario. Then write two developing probes that apply to the product or idea you are trying to sell. At the end of this chapter, I give you my suggestions for probes that apply to each of the companies outlined in the case studies.

## PJ INVESTING CORPORATION

1. _____

2. _____

## TO CLEAN A ROOM

1. _____

2. _____

## A TON OF TALENT, A LACK OF TRUST

1. _____

2. _____

## EVERY MOTORS, LTD.

1. _____

2. _____

## YOUR OWN SCENARIO

1. _____

2. _____

## STEP 3. IMPACT PROBES

So here we are. The customer's predicament has been methodically expanded using developing probes to illustrate better the true size of the problem. The customer has walked through his own "For Want of a Nail" with his concern as the theme. Now it's time for one last question.

With the developing probes walking the customer through the extent of the problem, you systematically refrain from leaps of logic. It would be awkward to ask this series of probes from Franklin's poetic illustration:

Seller:        **What** kind of **difficulties** are you experiencing with the nails going into the horse's hooves?" [*identification probe*]
Customer:   The nails keep breaking.
Seller:        **What** do you think the **consequences** of these broken nails could be on the kingdom? [*impact probe*]
Customer:   I don't know. I guess the horses will hop around a little bit.

Now that's what I call a leap in logic. The developing probes are designed to walk the customer through the problem. The impact probe finishes off the probing sequence and is designed to allow the customer to reflect on the overall consequences of his problems. Here is a more logical series of probes:

Seller:        **What** kind of **difficulties** are you experiencing with the nails going into the horse's hooves? [*identification probe*]
Customer:   The nails keep breaking.
Seller:        **How** often does that happen? [*developing probe*]
Customer:   About 20 percent of the time.
Seller:        **How** does this **affect** the messengers? [*developing probe*]
Customer:   Sometimes they can't get out to the troops.
Seller:        **Where** do the troops in these situations get their orders from? [*developing probe*]
Customer:   Well, uh, they don't . . . sometimes.
Seller:        **How** does this **affect** their ability to fight effectively? [*development probe*]

Customer:    Uh...well...in those circumstances...uh...it can be damaging.

Seller:    Overall, then, **what** do you think the **consequences** of these broken nails could be on the kingdom? [*impact probe*]

Do you think your friend here might be interested in looking at some alternatives now? You could be selling the greatest nails in the world. Until a customer decides he wants to fix his existing problem, your solution is of little value.

I hope this example illustrated that these probes, sequenced properly, are not as aggressive as you might have thought. The beauty of using impact probes is that they can provide you with a finishing point. It would serve no purpose to ask another impact probe after the last question. This would be the equivalent of having a boxer follow his opponent to the mat during a knockdown and continue to throw punches.

In short, the identifying probes start the questioning sequence. The developing probes help to evolve the problem and clear the way for the impact probes.

As you can probably tell, I believe it is easier to learn this process by focusing on key words. Previously I have had you focus on (and highlight) key words for open and closed question techniques. I have also had you focus on (and highlight) key words for identifying probes. Here are some key words to focus on when using impact probes:

| | |
|---|---|
| consequences | results |
| impact | effects |
| ramifications | outcome |
| repercussions | backlash |

Now I want to take you back to the Jolles family truckster. What if we had been asked some questions earlier on? Let's start with some background probes from the research stage:

"**What** type of car are you currently driving?"
"**Who** typically drives the car?"

**"Who** rides in the car?"
**"Where** is the car now?"

That last question might raise a red flag or two. Now it's time to turn the heat up on the Jolles family a little bit and begin to analyze this situation, starting with an identifying probe:

"You mentioned your car is in the shop. **What** sort of **difficulties** are you having with the automobile?"

That would get things going, but it would tell you only what the customer already knows. I want to turn the heat up some more and use some developing probes to dig around:

**"How** often does this hitch occur?"
**"What** sort of warning do you get when this happens?"
**"How** fast are you typically driving?"
"You mentioned you take this car on longer trips. **What** are some of the more dense traffic patterns like?"
**"Where** do the children sit?"

Time to finish this first problem off with an impact probe:

"Mr. Jolles, **what** would be the **consequences** of this hitch occurring on a high-speed road in a tight traffic pattern?"

Oh, you don't like that question, do you? Maybe a little below the belt, huh? Selling starts with believing in your product. You see, the Jolles family walked into that dealership just like many of your customers: We were not looking past the noses on our faces.

You may find some of the questions offensive. Each of us has our own style, but I warn you that until a customer decides to "fix" an existing problem, your wonderful product is of little concern. Shame on me for not buying a car that day. Shame on the salesman for not having the knowledge or the courage to ask more developing and impact probes to help me see the true size of the problems I had.

I did not look at the potential of my problem. I certainly will not tell you I am a fearless person. If you pressed me about what my greatest fear in life was, I would tell you it would have to be the fear of something happening to my children. *I was driving a dangerous car around with my children buckled into the back seat.* If you asked me what I was waiting for, I would not have been able to tell you. Could you imagine living with a tragedy to your children that you could have avoided? I can't.

Assisting someone to look at the potential ramifications of his problems can be painful. I understand this dilemma. Fortunately I am *customer centered.* I know what customers go through within their decision-making cycle. Fact: Customers typically are symbolically rolling the dice, hoping their problems do not get worse. They will come to you when they can't stand it anymore. Sometimes this means rolling the dice and losing. You have two choices: wait for the problem to explode or discuss the problem's exploding. I care about my customers, and so does this Rob's Rule:

► *I would rather help a customer avert a catastrophe than help clean one up.*

I hope the point has been made. To help you to understand, my illustrations were disturbing and my analogies a bit graphic. It was crucial, however, to give you the logic to understand this sequence of probes and the wisdom to use it. I did promise you that I would explain how to view this stage in a more positive light. Now I will.

## A POSITIVE PERSPECTIVE

Until now, I have not provided you with what I would call the most positive slant to this most difficult task within the analysis stage. In the past, I never felt this was necessary. This is the way Xerox taught me to sell, and that was good enough for me. If occasionally a couple of salespeople were uncomfortable with the explanation for what I was recommending, I felt they were simply missing the point of my message. Well, thanks to a talented author, a well-known insurance company, and a well-known genius, I have learned there really is more to this message.

First, the author. I owe a great deal of thanks to John Gray, who wrote *Men Are from Mars, Women Are from Venus,* which discusses relationships and the many differences between men and women. When the book first arrived in my house (via my wife), I was not particularly interested in what John Gray and his book had to say. This point of view was exacerbated by my wife's good intentions. The book was preached to me morning, noon, and night.

The book remained an annoyance until my wife began reading to me from a chapter called "Mr. Fix-It and the Home-Improvement Committee." In this chapter, Gray talks about a type of man whom he refers to as "Mr. Fix-It." I will summarize a couple of the points he makes. First, most men have a tendency to want to fix things all the time. As he puts it, "A man's sense of self is defined through his ability to achieve results."

In selling, we are guilty of teaching salespeople this same point. This would be okay if we were also careful to teach salespeople how to listen attentively and not be in such a hurry to offer solutions.

The second, and most important, point that John Gray makes is that men's obsession with fixing things also applies to fixing the feelings of women. He states, "A man tries to change a woman's feelings when she is upset by becoming Mr. Fix-It and offering solutions to her problems that invalidate her feelings."

After hearing that, I immediately thought back to one discussion I had with my wife, an art teacher. On this particular day, she had come home from school looking discouraged and said to me, "I had the most difficult day. I had one seventh grader who was way out of line. When I went to the chairman of the department, I felt I got very little support."

As Mr. Fix-It, I already had the solution, answering, "You did, huh? Well, here is what you do. First, you tell that little punk seventh grader that if he steps out of line one more time, you and he will talk it over with his parents. As far as the principal is concerned, schedule a meeting with him, and let him know you were displeased with his help. Anything else you need?"

I remember how this particular conversation ended. My wife was frustrated and she let me know about it. "Will you *stop* trying to fix everything all the time?" she said. "Ask me questions about it! I don't want you to fix it; I want you to just listen."

What do you say to that logic? John Gray is right on target. It is a conversation that goes on in many homes. What he might not have known is that this conversation goes on in many selling situations as well. Let's forget about applications to men and women. When customers tell you that they have problems, aren't you just as guilty in assuming the Mr. Fix-It role and dumping out solutions?

I believe that a common thread that links successful salespeople is the desire to see themselves as the customer's friend. I hope you see your customer as your friend too. If you do, let me ask you this question: How do you communicate with your friends? I'll throw a scenario your way and see how you would respond to it.

A good friend comes to you one day and wants to talk. Your friend tells you he is having difficulties on the job. It has gotten to the point that he is finding it hard to concentrate. I doubt that your first reaction would be to fix it, saying, "I think you should quit!" That is not how a friend helps another friend. I assume you ask him, without thinking, to tell you more:

"**What** kind of **difficulties** are you experiencing?" [*identifying probe*]
"**How** long has this been happening?" [*developing probe*]
"**What** are the **reactions** of the other employees?" [*developing probe*]
"**Who** else is **affected**?" [*developing probe*]
"**What** are the overall **ramifications** regarding your ability to be productive?" [*impact probe*]

The probing sequence effectively persuades, but wait, there's more! I think you do this naturally when you are being a decent friend to another person. Remember that in a selling situation, you are typically talking to someone who will "acknowledge" he has a problem. The challenge is to get him to do something about it. This is what friends do for friends!

• • •

Now for the lesson learned from the insurance company. My thanks this time to go Aetna Insurance Company. Quite inadvertently, this company taught me another lesson about my own selling process. Aetna had signed up for Xerox sales training, and I flew off to pilot the training in Aetna's Hartford, Connecticut, facility. I had studied the company, its customers, and the features it had to offer. With my own insurance background, I felt I was pretty well prepared to knock them dead with the sales training I had to offer.

What I did not know was that Aetna had already been though some earlier training with Xerox. About six months prior to my training, the division I was scheduled to work with had gone through a three-and-a-half-day quality program offered by Xerox. This training taught them, among other things, how to process their problem solving through a model called the Problem Solving Process (PSP).

As I maneuvered my way through the probing sequence I have taken you through, I was feeling rather good about the class's progress. We had talked about "bleeding the customer" and other analogies. I was kind of pumped up that day as I found myself shadow boxing to illustrate my point. Then, from nowhere, came a rather harmless question. "Isn't this process a lot like the Problem Solving Process we learned six months ago?" a student asked.

It isn't often that I am caught for a loss of words, but I found myself struggling with this one. What made this particularly embarrassing was that I had been a certified quality trainer for Xerox. I had even attained a level 3 certification, which meant that I not only taught the program, I taught others to teach the program and certified them to be quality trainers as well!

In all my years as a trainer for Xerox, I never had bothered to compare the two processes. I even took careful measures to keep them apart. When I taught quality, I ate, slept, and lived quality. When I taught people how to sell, that was my obsession. For the first time, I was asked to compare the two models, and guess what I found out? This person was absolutely right!

The Xerox PSP teaches some highly practical points that discipline your approach to fixing things right . . . the first time. To do this, you are first taught that you must carefully identify a problem. This problem must be clear and controllable by the group. So far, so good.

The most important lesson of problem solving is then hammered home. When most of us problem-solve, as soon as we identify the problem, we desperately want to solve it. Everyone wants to be the hero, the one with the brilliant idea. We are so ready to fix it that we are ready to bust. We can see nothing but the solution, and we go with that solution. Then, sadly, as soon as we implement our solution, we begin to wonder why we did not think of other solutions. How often have you put in a flower bed or purchased a product, only to realize soon after that there was a better, easier way? You wonder to yourself, "How did I not see the solution? It seemed to be right in front of my nose."

The answer that is carefully taught, within the PSP, lies in the second step: After you have identified a problem, you should not get anywhere near a solution. Instead, you examine that problem. I have taught people to use tools like fishbone analysis, cause-and-effect analysis, and Pareto analysis, all with the intent to help them to understand the problem better. Once the problem is carefully inspected, the solution becomes much clearer. It is the most basic and important lesson I learned in quality training.

As I compared the quality model and the selling model that day, I simultaneously taught and learned a valuable lesson. When using the probes taught within the analysis stage, you are really taking the customer through an intelligent process that mirrors a highly successful approach to problem solving.

I have never forgotten the lesson Aetna taught me that day about my own process. As a salesman, I always believed I was a problem solver. Thankfully, Aetna taught me I was a better problem solver than even I knew I was.

Finally, I would like to tell you what I learned from one of the most brilliant men who ever lived. Albert Einstein was a problem solver. He also believed in the lessons learned within problem solving. One of my favorite quotes, attributed to Albert Einstein, will stand as another Rob's Rule:

▶ *You can't solve a problem from the same consciousness that created it.*

What a tremendous message! In fact, "studying the problem" is what you are attempting to do as a problem solver within this stage of the selling cycle. It is your job to ask these questions. You are paid to help fix things right . . . the first time. Studying the problem from every possible angle and questioning early assumptions will ultimately elevate you as a salesperson in customers' eyes.

When you take a moment to put into perspective the purpose of the probing sequence, it is a logical step that many people apply when they problem-solve. Some associate this portion of the process with what is called "second- and third-level questioning." This simply implies the logical approach to digging deeper within your questioning. Well, it's okay with John Gray, Albert Einstein, and Aetna. The benefits of this stage in selling are clear. It's okay with me too.

## THE CASE FOR POSITIVE PROBING

I have tried to keep my promise, and let you see the logic of the analysis stage from a more positive perspective. If you look at the examples I have provided within the chapter, I do not think you will see any question that is too far out of line. Still, no matter the logic and no matter the cause, the questions within the probing sequence can be disturbing to the customer.

I have been asked and have had some healthy debates regarding the possibility of showing *value* through my questions as opposed to consequence. "Is a cigarette smoker unaware that he will feel healthier if he stops smoking?" "Is an alcoholic oblivious that his quality of life will improve if he stops drinking?" Consider this Rob's Rule:

▶ *When changing a person's behavior, consequence is more powerful than value.*

That's my story, and I'm sticking with it! Think back on most of the decisions you have made recently. Did you buy that last car because you had an irresistible urge for that "new car smell," or was it because you could no longer put up with the problems of your existing car? Did you buy your last home because you just had to have new kitchen appliances, or was it because you were fed up trying to endure the problems in your old house? I rest my case. Sort of.

I can't totally ignore the argument to probe for value. In 1992, I conducted a sales training pilot. The first bank "I worked with" was Barnett Bank. The training site was outside Clearwater, Florida. One of the first exercises I put these salespeople through was an activity that focused them on their customers. They were to outline their typical customer. What I heard began to soften my stance "regarding" the validity of probing for value sometimes.

Their typical customers were widowed women in their eighties. I did not think a sermon on "throwing punches with bad intentions" and "bleeding customers" was going to be appropriate here. So the probes we discussed that day dealt with improving their customers' ability to travel. Our developing probes were geared to finding ways to improve these customers' ability to be better connected to their grandchildren and maintaining their independence. The moral to the story? Consequence is still stronger than value . . . but I will never again say never.

# TEST YOUR COMPREHENSION: IMPACT PROBES

Once again, go back to the four case studies in Chapter 9. Here is your chance to test what you have learned. Write one impact probe for each scenario. Then write one impact probe that applies to the product or idea you are trying to sell. At the end of this chapter, I give you my suggestions for probes that apply to each of the companies outlined in the case studies.

## PJ INVESTING CORPORATION

1. _____

TO CLEAN A ROOM

1. _____

_____


A TON OF TALENT, A LACK OF TRUST

1. _____

_____


EVERY MOTORS, LTD.

1. _____

_____


YOUR OWN SCENARIO

1. _____

_____


# SOME FINAL THOUGHTS

What you have read is crucial when engaging in the art of persuasion and selling. Here are a few final thoughts to keep in mind when using this technique.

## DON'T LEAD THE WITNESS

Sometimes when using these probes, you have to be careful not to pump your questions out too quickly. Typically this is due to the overuse of closed questions. Watch a good court trial someday, and you will see what I mean. An exchange that illustrates this point would sound something like this:

Prosecution:  **Didn't** you, in fact, know exactly what you were doing when you went down to the basement?

Defense:  I object, your Honor. The prosecution is leading the witness!

Judge:          Objection sustained.

Prosecution:    Fine. Tell me, please, **why** you were in the basement.

Watch out for using too many closed questions, and you will most likely reduce your chances of leading the witness.

## WATCH YOUR MANNERS!

Make no mistake about it. This step of the selling cycle has you walking a fine line between helpful and obnoxious. If you are not careful, you will find yourself telling the customers what their problems are:

Seller:   It makes your company look pretty bad when you are late on those deliveries, doesn't it!

No customer would put up with too many of those questions. This leads me to one of my favorite Rob's Rules:

► *Never call a customer's baby ugly!*

This does not mean the customer can't call his baby ugly! The questions are designed to let the customer decide. This question from the seller would be a better alternative:

Seller:   **What** effects do late deliveries have on your company's image?

## CONTAIN YOURSELF

So there you are. You have sunk your teeth into a customer problem, and like a doberman, you won't let go. The customer is beginning to squirm, and you smell blood. *Be careful.* Now you must watch out for the little things.

I have been on calls with salespeople who have been so excited with the progress of their questioning that they had trouble containing themselves. You are treading ever so delicately on strong emotions. Now is *not* the time to show your joy with the newfound skills you have acquired!

Watch your body language, watch your tone, and, for goodness sakes, watch your facial expressions. The probing sequence can be traumatic, and your ability to mimic the expressions of your customer sincerely will serve you well.

## WATCH OUT FOR THOSE NEEDS

When analyzing concerns, customers from time to time will begin to talk about needs. Your first reaction may be to join them in this conversation, but I recommend that you resist. There will be a time and place to talk about needs, but to discuss them now often is a tactical error.

I remind you that many customers will freely talk about what they need. The problem is that they are not fully committed and will often stall when forced to make a decision. These are probably the very same needs they have told anyone else who will listen for the past couple of years. Unfortunately, they have never really made a commitment to fix the problems. Until they do, your discussion, albeit a pleasant one, will have little to no effect on actually persuading this customer to take action.

There is some good news to this situation. Ask yourself, "Why do they have that particular need?" In your studies so far, I attempted to point out to you that needs don't come from heaven. They are born from problems. Most customers will not tell you they need something if they are already satisfied with what they are currently receiving.

When a customer introduces a need within the probing sequence, all you have to do is gently back this need up to its source, the problem, like this:

Customer: Oh, and I thought of one more thing. I want to make sure whoever I end up giving my business to provides me with top-notch service.

Seller: I see. **What** types of **challenges** have you been experiencing with your service to date?

Sometimes customers may tell you they have had no problems, but they have a particular need because they are accustomed to that particular need. If that is the case, they will tell you so. More often than not, however, the introduction of a need provides a perfect cue to get back in there and probe away!

## WATCH OUT FOR (TOO MANY) LOW BLOWS

I want to take you back to the boxing analogy for a moment. Most of the great fighters occasionally throw a low blow. Now you and I both know that this honorable champion would never throw a low blow intentionally . . . or would he?

When a low blow is thrown, you can usually count on a consistent series of events. The moment it happens, the referee, if he sees it, steps between the fighters and yells, "Time!" He then looks at the offending party and yells, "That was low. Keep 'em up! You do that again, and I'm gonna take a point from you." He then looks at the boxer who absorbed this low blow and asks, "Are you okay?" With a wince and a gulp, the boxer answers, in a slightly higher voice, "Yeah, I think so."

Like clockwork, the boxer who threw the punch extends his gloves, and, looking remorseful, waits for the other boxer to touch them with his. In boxing, this is the equivalent of a handshake. Additionally, the boxer who threw the punch usually looks into the other boxer's eyes and says, "Sorry." The fight then resumes. No points were taken away and there are no apparent hard feelings.

As the boxer who threw the low blow backs away, he usually begins to survey the damage. Although he might have been sincere when he muttered, "Sorry," he most likely was also muttering, "but I'll bet you felt that now, didn't you?"

Sometimes you have to ask difficult questions that might put the customer on the defensive. Let me illustrate this point using those automatic door locks that I featured in the research stage.

If you recall, the question was asked, "**Where** do you typically drive your car?" That question was asked to begin to position this feature. Now assume the customer stated that occasionally he drives to less-than-safe sections of town. Here might be your questions that would follow after you complete your research:

Seller:     You mentioned earlier that occasionally you drive to less-than-safe sections of town. **What concerns** do you have with regard to safety when you do that? [*identifying probe*]

Customer:   Well, I try and remember to take precautions. In the rare instances that I forget, I suppose I put myself in some danger.

Seller:     **What** percentage of the time do you think you might forget? [*developing probe*]

Customer:   Maybe 10 percent of the time.

Seller:     **Who** is generally with you? [*developing probe*]

Customer:   Usually my wife. Sometimes the children.

Seller:     **What** would be the **consequences** if, on one of these rare occasions, someone tried to carjack your vehicle? [*impact probe*]

I know, I know. You probably think that last question was a little nasty. I'll call it a low blow if you like. You would probably never ask that question . . . unless you believed, without reservation, in your solution.

A low blow? Maybe. But consider this story. I spent most of my life in the great state of Maryland. I grew up there. I went to college there. I got married and had kids there. I have a lot of Maryland pride. My state of Maryland, however, was in the news a couple of years ago for one of the most heinous crimes I can remember. This story was known nationally, so you may remember it too.

A woman was getting ready to take her child to his first day of nursery school. The husband actually filmed her loading the child into the car. He also inadvertently filmed the animals who would moments later carjack this vehicle two blocks away. The child was thrown from the car and mercifully was not seriously injured. The woman was dragged almost a mile and killed.

I have children, and I have a wonderful wife, all of whom I love very much. If I could spare someone even the remote possibility of such a tragedy, I would. Low blows? Think of the alternatives.

You must be deeply convinced of the truth behind your actions. If you believe in your solution and display enthusiasm for the truth as you perceive it, this technique of selling will serve you well.

## TRY THE "AND" METHOD

I ran a two-day seminar in Birmingham, Alabama, once and was taught a wonderful lesson on how to use developing probes. As I was waiting for my plane for my flight home, one of the seminar participants came up to me. He was quite courteous as he expressed his gratitude for what I had taught him. Then he taught me about his "and" method of selling.

He told me that the "multiple" steps within Customer Centered Selling were going to be a lot of help to him, and he was committed to using the process. He then told me he was going to miss the process he was using because, with only one step, it was easier to remember. When a customer is talking to him about his or her concerns or problems, the seller's favorite approach was simply to reply with the word *and*. Here is an example:

Seller:     **What** sort of **challenges** do you have tracking your investments? [*identifying probe*]

Customer:   I am often too busy to watch them on a regular basis.

Seller:     **And?** [*developing probe*]

Customer:   Well, uh, sometimes I'm not sure how well these products are doing.

Seller:     **And?** [*developing probe*]

Customer:   I suppose that puts some of my decisions at risk.

Seller:     **What** would be the **consequences** of not staying on top of these investments within your portfolio? [*impact probe*]

I am not saying the "and" method is right for everyone, but I will say this: It has a home in the analysis stage within the probing sequence. If you are having difficulty using developing probes, you might want to remember our friend in Birmingham and the simplest sales process I ever heard of.

## THINK BEFORE YOU PROBE

The probing sequence located in the analysis stage is powerful. What hurts will be fixed. What hurts a lot will be fixed first. When you probe customer concerns, you are heavily influencing customer needs.

Call me old-fashioned, but I do not typically probe heavily what I can't fix. Ethically, I will not ignore these concerns, and if I believe they should be critical needs for the customers, I will recommend someone else who can help them better than I can. This, however, is usually not the case. By not probing these customer concerns, they will most likely, down the road, convert into "nice-to-have" items. The problems I do fix well, I will probe heavily. They will then become "need-to-have" items. The moral to this pointer is, "Think before you probe."

## THINK IN THREES

One of the most commonly asked questions remains, "How many of these disturbing probes are enough?" I wish I could answer that question definitively, but it is not easy. I would look at the customer's body language and facial expressions, and listen for verbal signs of persuasion like, "That's why I want to make a change," or "I am absolutely fed up." Still, customers can say the darndest things, and not mean it.

I am therefore going to give you a definitive answer. As a rule of thumb, especially for the first and second problem you probe, I advise thinking in threes. After the problem is identified, ask at least three more questions that will develop and show impact. Once you have done a credible job here, a harmless identifying probe usually sends the customer into a conversation where he begins to develop his own problems and literally bleed himself.

## THINK OF YOUR CHILDREN

The psychology of this stage in the selling cycle should be more familiar to you now. If you have children, for instance, you have probably already learned these lessons in persuasion from time to time.

When you tell a child (who habitually keeps a messy room) to clean up his room, you are actually offering a solution prematurely. If the child even bothers to obey "your orders," most likely the room will be messy again the next day. Not only has change not been initiated, there may even be resentment in the mind of the child. I see this as a classic selling situation. A good friend of mine once gave me this little reminder, so let's add it to our Rob's Rules:

▶ *A person convinced against his will is of the same opinion still.*

I try very hard with my children (and customers) to have the patience to let them come around to my position. Using the probing sequence, I begin to plant the seed for alternatives. If a child does not see the messy condition of his room as a serious problem, why would you think your demands would create any permanent change?

Ah, but if this child feels it's *his* own idea, and senses urgency as well, we are now *creating* change. Your conversation might go something like this:

Parent:   **What** kind of new friends have you made in school this year? [*background probe*]

Child:    I'm kind of hanging out with the same old crew—Fred, Louie, and Squirrel—although I have made a new friend.

Parent:   **How** do you think your new friend will like your room if he sees it like this? [*identifying probe*]

Child:    They'll like it. My friends like me for me.

Parent:   I see. **What** if your new friend has a neat room and likes neatness? [*identifying probe*]

Child:        Okay, I guess in that case I would just not really show him my room.

Parent:     **How** do you think your friend might **feel** if you don't show him your room? [*developing probe*]

Child:        Well, it would make it sort of tough to be good friends.

Parent:     **Who** else does this new friend hang around with? [*developing probe*]

Child:        Ted Weedamyer. I hate that guy! He'd be the kind of guy who would move in and steal my friend if he could!

Parent:     So **what** do you think the overall **consequences** are of this room's not being clean enough to have your friend over? [*impact probe, game, set, match!*]

Note that I have not even touched on a solution . . . yet. The goal of this stage is simply to allow your customer (or child) to see the problem as large enough to want to warrant a solution. By no means am I able to take 100 percent of the problems I sense in research and move them through this sequence. There are always going to be unanticipated variables. Nevertheless, 75 percent of the time we can draw some blood.

## ONE AT A TIME

I hope that you have a clear understanding of the sequence of probes used throughout this stage. I now want to make sure you understand how each probing sequence relates to one another.

As you might recall, my research shows that most people will not begin to initiate change based on one problem, even if that problem is fairly severe. I will assume, therefore, that when you reach the analysis stage, you are working with at least two different problems. It would not be logical to probe them together like this:

Seller:       **What difficulties** are you experiencing with your inventory? [*identifying probe*]

Customer:  Sometimes our forecasts are off.

Seller:       I see. And **what challenges** have you had with your distribution? [*identifying probe*]

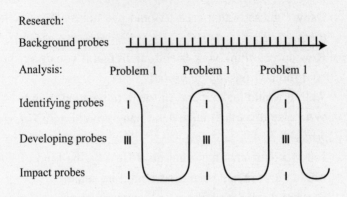

Instead, remember that once a problem has been acknowledged in the customer's mind, you must stay put and continue probing on that specific problem.

I want to leave you with one last visual reminder to help you understand this point better. Notice in the diagram that the arrow goes horizontally for the research stage. This is to indicate the concept of staying put in this stage even if problems are brought up by the customer. Once that first stage is complete, the vertical lines indicate the development of one customer problem at a time.

Well, that's it. The steps contained within this stage are more difficult to implement than you might think. Still, with hard work and repetition, the process will become "muscle memory" before you know it. Now it's time to see the fruits of your labor.

# SUGGESTED ANSWERS TO TEST YOUR COMPREHENSION: IDENTIFYING PROBES

Given the four scenarios, here are the identifying probe answers I suggest. See how closely they resemble the answers you gave. Do not worry about the difference as they relate to style. Watch closely for technique instead.

## PJ INVESTING CORPORATION

1. **What challenges** do you encounter when making large investment transactions?

TO CLEAN A ROOM

1. When you lost that school paper you mentioned earlier, **what** sort of **difficulties** did that create for you in school?

A TON OF TALENT, A LACK OF TRUST

1. **What** kind of **frustration** have you experienced in the past when you have not been given leadership roles on projects you felt you deserved?

EVERY MOTORS, LTD.

1. You mentioned that each time you have taken your car in for repairs in the past, you work with different personnel. **What** sort of **obstacles** does that create when you have to discuss previous service work?

Look over these probes as well as your own, and put them through the test:

- Is the probe an open question?
- Does the probe contain the strategic adjectives that support your intent?
- Does the probe allow the customer to paint the picture?

# SUGGESTED ANSWERS TO TEST YOUR COMPREHENSION: DEVELOPING PROBES

Given the four scenarios, here are the developing probe answers I suggest. The first step of the probing sequence, identifying probes, is in italics above each response. See how closely these developing probes resemble the answers you came up with.

PJ INVESTING CORPORATION

What challenges do you encounter when making large investment transactions?
1. **How** long does this take?
2. **What** else could you be doing with this money?

TO CLEAN A ROOM

When you lost that school paper you mentioned earlier, what sort of difficulties did that create for you in school?

1. **How** often does this happen?
2. **How** long did it take you to redo the assignment?

### A TON OF TALENT, A LACK OF TRUST

What kind of frustrations have you experienced in the past when you have not been given leadership roles on projects you felt you deserved?
1. **How** often has this occurred?
2. **What** effect has this had on your morale?

### EVERY MOTORS, LTD.

You mentioned that each time you have taken your car in for repairs in the past, you work with different personnel. What sorts of obstacles does that create when you have to discuss previous service work?
1. **How** many different people are involved within this process?
2. **Who** is held accountable in the event of a dispute?

Look over these probes as well as your own, and put them through the test:

- Is the probe an open question?
- Does the probe continue to expand the customer's concern?
- Does the probe allow the customer to paint the picture?

# SUGGESTED ANSWERS TO TEST YOUR COMPREHENSION: IMPACT PROBES

Given the four scenarios, here are the impact probe answers I suggest, below the first two steps of the probing sequence, identifying probes and developing probes. See how closely these impact probes resemble the answers you came up with.

### PJ INVESTING CORPORATION

What challenges do you encounter when making large investment transactions? How long does this take?
What else could you be doing with this money?
1. **What** are the overall **ramifications** of these delays on your ability to maximize your investments?

## TO CLEAN A ROOM

When you lost that school paper you mentioned earlier, what sort of difficulties did that create for you in school?

How often does this happen?

How long did it take you to redo the assignment?

1. Overall, **what impact** did that have on your opportunity to do other, more fun, things?

## A TON OF TALENT, A LACK OF TRUST

What kind of frustrations have you experienced in the past when you have not been given leadership roles on projects you felt you deserved?

How often has this occurred?

What effect has this had on your morale?

1. So **what** do you feel have been the **repercussions** on you as an employee?

## EVERY MOTORS, LTD.

You mentioned that each time you have taken your car in for repairs in the past, you work with different personnel. What sorts of obstacles does that create when you have to discuss previous service work?

How many different people are involved within this process?

Who is held accountable in the event of a dispute?

1. **What** are the **consequences** regarding the future liability of the people who work on your vehicle?

Look over these probes as well as your own, and put them through the test:

- Is the probe an open question?
- Does the probe contain one of the key impact adjectives that support your intent?
- Does the probe allow the customer to paint the picture?

# THE CONFIRMATION STAGE

## GETTING PAST THE FIRST DECISION POINT

Take calculated risks. That is quite different from being rash.

*—General George S. Patton*

**SELLER**

**A** t this point in the selling cycle, things begin to get a lot clearer. If the probing sequence has been performed properly, the customer should not only be ready for change, but there should be a sense of urgency to make this change.

The entire confirmation stage should not last over sixty seconds. Still, this stage of the selling cycle should not be ignored. The most traumatic stage of the cycle is almost behind you. There are only three quick steps to go before moving on to customer needs.

## STEP 1. TEST UNDERSTANDING

Earlier in this book, I mentioned that there are only three ways to communicate with people: listen, ask questions, or make statements. All of the

Xerox studies, as well as my personal experience, have validated the importance of the first two. So far within the process, you have seen a disciplined commitment to ask many, many strategical questions. Asking questions is of little value if you do not listen to the answers. Now it's time to prove yourself as a listener.

In this first step, your listening skills are on display. The conversation to this point may have lasted somewhere in the neighborhood of ten to fifteen minutes. A lot has been talked about. Background information drifted into some of the more disturbing questions within the analysis stage.

Testing your understanding within this step is not intended to play back all that has been gathered through your probing questions. This confirmation is focused solely on the concerns that have been discussed most recently. It is unnecessary to give a detailed summary, which might agitate the customer. Your "test understanding" might sound something like this:

Seller:   Well, I think I have a pretty good handle on your concerns up to this point. From what you have told me so far, it sounds as if the service you have been experiencing has not been what you expected, the product is somewhat labor intensive, and the documentation has not been as helpful as you would have liked.

Notice in this example that you do not see a "life history" review, simply a brief summary. The whole first step should be reduced to a couple of sentences and last only a few seconds.

## STEP 2. "ANY OTHER CONCERNS?"

Here is a classic, no-brainer step that has more value than most people realize. The customer at this point has just had a rather traumatic sequence of probes that has finished with your summary of what has been discussed. I have no crystal ball to tell you whether you have missed something. What an excellent opportunity to check your work.

In addition to checking your work with the use of this simple closed question—"Any other concerns?"—there is a psychological reason for this question. When people are stuck in the acknowledgment stage of the *decision cycle,* they often vehemently resist change. The more someone preaches a solution, the harder they work at defending their situation.

You may know of a couple, for instance, who are unhappy together, but unwilling to make a change. If one of the partners does say something negative about the other, it will probably be limited in scope. Ask if there are "any other concerns," and you will probably not only be told no, you will be given a whole bunch of excuses as to why the other partner's behavior is really "not that bad."

Strangely enough, when you speak to this same friend again, once he has decided to end the relationship, his tune changes a bit. Ask him now if there were "any other concerns" and you will most likely get a different answer. Your friend will now tell you of trivial, less traumatic events that still contributed to his change. I have had friends who have told me, during the aftermath of a relationship, that the way their partner brushed their teeth in the morning "really got on my nerves!" That's funny; they never said anything to me about it earlier.

When you go through the steps that lead up to this harmless question, your situation is a bit different. You earned this customer's trust by initially not asking about problems. You started slowly, and let your customer paint the picture regarding his particular difficulties. The size and scope of the problems are a bit larger in your customer's eyes now. Watch what will happen when you simply ask, "Are there any other concerns?"

If there are any, you will hear them now! Little things, like, "I never liked where their delivery person parked their truck" or "I hate the ridiculous music they play in their waiting room," may now come out of this customer's mouth like a shot.

The question now is, What do you do? This is a strategic decision you must wrestle with. My suggestion is this: If you think this customer is still somewhat touch-and-go about making a decision to look for a change, jump on it. Follow the new problem you have just identified through the probing sequence from development to impact. However, if you feel this customer is heavily leaning to looking for a change (consider comments, body language, facial expression, other obvious buying signals), think twice. My recommendation is to write the customer's concern down, get ready to solve this problem in the next stage, and move on. There is no need for overkill here. The good news is that you will not have long to wait to see if your hunch was correct. It is time for your first trial close.

## STEP 3. COMMIT TO CHANGE

At last, it's time to check your work. You have worked quite hard to enable you to ask this one question: "Are you committed to making a change?" You are about to see just how successful you were in the previous stages of probing.

Recall that the most difficult decision a customer makes within his decision cycle is whether he wants to fix an existing problem. This is the decision point that hangs most customers up, and this is the decision point this step monitors for you.

As with the previous step, use a closed question strategically to confirm that this decision point has been crossed. Other than the one example above, here are some more examples of this first, and most significant, trial close:

Seller:   Would you like to look at some alternatives?

OR

Seller:   Do you think it would be worthwhile looking at some solutions?

OR

Seller:   Do you want to fix it?

In my mind, this is a question that can't miss. If the customer says yes, you have just been given the green light to move forward. The most difficult and challenging aspect of selling is now behind you, and the process is ready to continue. If the customer says no, I have some bad news—for the customer. You will address this as an objection (see Chapter 19). After fully understanding why the person does not want to move forward, chances are you will have to move back to the analysis stage once again.

The good news for you is that the customer will not interpret this as a step back. Remember: You have been in the confirmation stage for less than a minute. To move back here and continue probing is really not that awkward. What would be awkward is to move through this decision point, perhaps even to your final recommendation, and then be faced with an objection. Now the customer would sense a backward movement from you. I have seen this occur on calls I have monitored and actually heard frustrated customers saying, "Haven't we already been through this?"

This step represents your first trial close. Trial closes are not designed to trick or fool the customer. They are designed to allow you, the seller, to check your work. The biggest benefit to trial closes is their ability to flush out objections. I am not a mind reader. I typically feel pretty sure a customer will commit to change if I have done a good job probing his concerns. Now is my chance to see just how well I did.

You must not be timid about asking the question regarding a commitment to look for alternatives. Although it does represent a major decision point in the seller's mind, the customer will not interpret this question as a setup or a trick. That makes me happy, because it is *not* a setup or a trick. I simply want to know if the customer is ready to move on.

With the use of this trial close, you should also get an idea of how committed to change your customer is. Watch and listen to your customer very closely here. If you have been successful in your probing sequence, you should now hear a sense of urgency from your customer. For instance, I would be thrilled to hear a customer respond this way:

Seller:      Would you like to look at some alternatives?
Customer:   Without question! That's exactly why I called you here today.

This response is not wishful thinking. When you have done a good job throughout the probing sequence, this type of response is actually quite typical. On the other hand, if you do not do a good job probing the customer's concerns, you might get a comment like this:

Seller:      Would you like to look at some alternatives?
Customer:   Yeah, I guess so. I hope whatever you have in mind doesn't cost a lot.

That does not sound like a heavily committed customer to me. This customer is basically telling you to expect objections to price as well as a lack of urgency to seek a solution.

The amazing thing about this stage in the selling cycle is the precarious nature of the corresponding decision cycle the customer is grappling with. This decision to "fix or not fix" on the customer's part is often emotional. Without feeling a sense of urgency, customers can vacillate around this crucial decision point. It happens all the time. Recently, I got a first-hand look at it happening to me.

I was driving my six-year-old Volkswagen Cabriolet. I had recently given my wife my annual, "I'm going to get rid of this car," speech, when it finally happened. At a traffic light, I noticed a little bit of smoke coming from under my hood. My nose began to flare (not a pretty sight), straining to detect that telltale smell. It wasn't good.

More and more smoke was billowing up from the front of my car, and I shot across the first decision point. No more whining. This was the sign I was looking for. It was time to look for solutions!

My mind was now racing. I would take tomorrow off and spend the day test-driving cars. I could try and pick up some magazines and do some quick reading. I could even make some calls to a couple of friends for some fast advice. Thoughts of financing and accounting flew through my mind as well. I would run the numbers by my accountant and purchase this car through my corporation. Yes! I did not know what this car looked like, but Rob Jolles was going to buy a new car!

These thoughts came flooding through quickly. I do not believe even ten seconds went by, and I felt the adrenaline rush of the upcoming major purchase. Yes! The old "ragtop" was finally history. It was settled.

At that moment, the light changed, and the car in front of me began to move. With this car moved the smoke that I had *thought* was coming from my car! In fact, it had been coming from the tailpipe of the car in front of me.

In a split instant, a grin worked its way across my face. I had been spared! It wasn't me! My car liiiives! I literally shot back across the decision point. "To heck with the new car idea," I thought. "I can get a few more miles out of the old ragtop." I was once again camping in the acknowledgment stage.

This is not an uncommon story. I hope that your mind drifted off to the many times you too have vacillated over the decision to fix a problem. It is another one of countless reasons that the probing sequence is as critical as it is.

# SOME FINAL THOUGHTS

This stage of the selling cycle, quick and fairly easy, provides you with a window to the customer's mind regarding his commitment to fix the problems. Until this commitment is made, solutions are a waste of time.

## HERE'S YOUR TRANSITION

Another strength of the confirmation stage is that it provides you with a great transition to what is to come. You will essentially be leaving the customer's problems behind, and as you will see, the transition can be difficult. The three steps located within this stage will help you to make this transition.

Something else has also happened that you might not be aware of. The famed window of opportunity has just opened, and look who seems to be in the right place at the right time? Coincidentally, there does not seem to be any competition around. Hey, lucky you!

Wait, it gets better . . . much better. Not only is there no competition around, but something tells me you will be able to do a pretty good job with the customer's needs that he is about to discover. What do you know about that?

## HOW MUCH WOULD YOU SPEND FOR THESE NAMES?

I love to be in this position. Think about where you have moved your customer up to this point in the decision cycle. Let me provide you with an analogy to help illustrate this point.

Imagine having the choice of purchasing one of two mailing lists. The first mailing list has a bunch of names on it. They represent a collection of prospects you know nothing about. They can be anywhere within their decision cycle. Chances are they have a problem, but have no intention of fixing it. Even if they plan on fixing it, you will have to hold your breath that you have the fix they are looking for. Chances of a successful sale are not good, but then again, the cost for this list is not substantial.

The other mailing list is special—a collection of prospects that I think would interest you. Here is a list of customers who have not spoken to your competition yet. As a matter of fact, I don't think they will. These potential customers feel a great sense of urgency to fix some existing problems—and here is the best part: For some lucky reason, the solutions they seek center around the particular strengths of your soon-to-be recommendation. I must warn you that this list costs a little bit more than the first, but I think it's worth it. Don't you?

Do not underestimate where you are within the selling cycle up to this point. We have some work ahead of us yet, but the tough part is behind us. It's time to put a smile back on your customer's face, and the next step in the selling cycle will do just that.

# TEST YOUR COMPREHENSION: CONFIRMATION STAGE

Once again, go back to the four case studies. Here is your chance to test what you have learned. Write out the three steps within the confirmation stage for each scenario. Then write an answer that would apply to the product or idea you are trying to sell. On the next page I give you my suggestions for each of the companies outlined in the case studies.

## PJ INVESTING CORPORATION

_____

_____

_____

## TO CLEAN A ROOM

_____

_____

_____

A TON OF TALENT, A LACK OF TRUST

_____

_____

_____

EVERY MOTORS, LTD.

_____

_____

_____

YOUR OWN SCENARIO

_____

_____

_____

# SUGGESTED ANSWERS TO TEST YOUR COMPREHENSION: CONFIRMATION STAGE

Given the four scenarios, here are my suggested answers incorporating the three steps within the confirmation stage. Check to see how closely they resemble the answers you gave. You will also notice that I have added an extra problem to each summary. Assume that each of these problems was taken through the probing sequence as well.

## PJ INVESTING CORPORATION

1. If I may, I would like to tell you what I have heard up to now. You are making some rather large transactions that are taking longer than you would like. This, in turn, is hampering your ability to maximize your investment. In addition, you have your doubts regarding the decision-making process behind the decisions being made.
2. Any other concerns we have not addressed?
3. Do you think it would be worthwhile looking at some solutions?

## TO CLEAN A ROOM

1. Let me see if I've got this straight. You not only have lost school work, causing you to repeat your homework; you're concerned about the perceptions your friends might have as well.
2. Are there any other concerns?
3. Would you like to look at some alternatives?

## A TON OF TALENT, A LACK OF TRUST

1. From what you have told me up to this point, you have frustrations with the number of assignments you have had a leadership role in, along with your own lack of advancement.
2. Do you have any other concerns that we haven't discussed?
3. Is this a situation you would like to do something about?

## EVERY MOTORS, LTD.

1. Let me see if I have this straight. At present, there are too many people involved with the servicing of your car. This affects accountability. Also, with regard to the car itself, you have some frustrations trying to readjust your seat constantly between your husband's settings and your own.
2. Are their any other difficulties you are experiencing?
3. Do you want to fix it?

Look over the answers provided, as well as your own, and put them through the test:

- Is the summary focused solely on customer problems, avoiding customer needs or product solutions?
- Is the summary short and to the point?
- Are the two questions that follow closed questions?
- Is the trial close that is used centered around the customer's decision to fix the existing problems?

# THIRTEEN

# THE REQUIREMENT STAGE

## DISCOVERING THE SOLUTION

### Don't Sell Me Things
*(Printed from a 1941 Sears sales publication)*

*Don't sell me clothes. Sell me neat appearance, style attractiveness.*
*Don't sell me shoes. Sell me foot comfort*
*and the pleasure of walking in the open air.*
*Don't sell me candy. Sell me happiness and pleasure of taste.*
*Don't sell me furniture. Sell me a home that has*
*comfort, cleanliness and convenience.*
*Don't sell me books. Sell me pleasant hours and the profit of knowledge.*
*Don't sell me toys. Sell me playthings to make my children happy.*
*Don't sell me tools. Sell me the pleasure and profit of making fine things.*
*Don't sell me refrigerators. Sell me the health and better flavor of fresh foods.*
*Don't sell me tires. Sell me freedom from worry and low cost per mile.*
*Don't sell me plows. Sell me green fields of waving wheat.*
*Don't sell me things. Sell me ideas, feelings, self-respect, home life, happiness.*
*Please don't sell me things*

People don't care how much you know, until they know how much you care about them. At this point in the selling cycle, once again the temptation is to want to offer solutions. The problem is that *you* are the only one who knows what the customer needs. The art of selling requires leading your customer to these needs and allowing him to feel as if he has discovered the solution. The requirement stage will permit you to do just that.

The timing of this stage within the selling cycle varies. For most customers, this stage will not take long. For more analytical customers, this stage can be a lot more extensive.

Within the decision cycle, the customer quite naturally wants to begin figuring out what it will take to fix his existing problems. The seller must parallel that position and work with the customer to determine what these requirements would be. To do this, the seller needs to go through three simple steps.

# STEP 1. LIST AND CONFIRM NEEDS

It must seem as if it took forever, but now you get to talk about those infamous "customer needs." This can sometimes be more difficult than it sounds. There are two problems you must try to avoid. The first centers on the dictation of needs to the customer. It would be inappropriate, for instance, to "list and confirm" needs this way:

Seller: I now know what you need. You need the following. First, you will need better service. Second, the way I see it, I think you want better documentation supporting what you are purchasing.

The problem with making a statement like this involves the perception of ownership. This list of needs no longer sounds like the customer's. It sounds like *your* list of needs! Once again, selling requires taking an idea, planting it in the customers' mind, and making them feel as though they thought of it. You must avoid the temptation to dictate to the customer what it is he needs.

The second problem is the complete opposite of this first one. On the one hand, you must try not to dictate to the customer what it is you think he needs. On the other hand, you should try to avoid any influence regarding this list of needs. Take a look at this example:

Seller:    So let's fix it, shall we? What is it you think you are look-
           ing for?

Nope. That will not do at all. You have worked too hard to open the door that wide. The key to this step within the requirement stage is to lead the customer gently with closed questions. These questions are designed to test and confirm information, and they work beautifully right here. These questions also will do a good job influencing the customer's needs to be described the way *you* want them to be described.

Here is an example that attempts to walk right down the middle of the two previous examples and guide the customer's needs:

Seller:      With regard to the service issues, are you looking for a com-
             pany that is more customer centered in its approach to work-
             ing with its clients?
Customer:    Yes, that's correct.
Seller:      Good. Let me take that down. Now, with respect to your other
             issue, it sounds as if whoever you choose had better provide
             you with easy-to-understand documentation. Am I right?
Customer:    Exactly. I want to know precisely what I have gotten my sales
             team into.

The techniques used here are not that difficult. As you can see, however, there is a subtlety involved when you try to get the customer to take ownership. This list will be vague and somewhat unfocused. That's all right for now. Later, in the next stage, the list of needs will be fine-tuned.

# STEP 2. "ANY OTHER NEEDS?"

The second step within the requirement stage is to make sure the customer has no other needs to address. Hopefully, through your probing sequence within the analysis stage, the customer now has a feeling of urgency. Within the requirement stage, this feeling of urgency changes to a feeling of euphoria. "At last," the customer thinks. "I'm finally going to fix this thing."

Do not be surprised to find more needs bubbling out of your customer. Add them to the list. This is his list after all, not yours. That said, be aware of a minor problem that could occur here.

When I first started to use this selling process, from time to time I would get thrown by the harmless little question, "Any other needs?" How, you ask? Well, often my customers would come up with other needs. Wonderful. Occasionally, they would come up with other needs I could not fulfill. Not wonderful!

There is some exposure here. Customers may come up with needs you can't address with your recommendation. Nevertheless, this is a risk worth taking, for a couple of reasons. First, the whole basis of Customer Centered Selling revolves around customers' needs. It would be hypocritical to avoid this step with the intention of evading this risk.

That reason alone forced me to continue to check for needs within this step of the requirement stage. Since I forced myself to continue to ask this question and react to the potential consequences, I learned another valuable lesson behind the significance of this step: The worst-case scenario involving this step is actually a benefit. When a customer brings up a need, you are really faced with two alternatives: The customer can bring this need up now or later, while you are actually recommending a solution. Given those two choices, I would much rather confront it now.

Think like a customer for a moment. When you are being shown a solution, how do you react? Let's say I was showing you a car, with a blue exterior and gray cloth interior. It happens to be the only blue-gray combination I have. While I am showing you this car, you ask if you can get the blue car but you want a lighter interior than gray. When I ask you what you like about a lighter interior and try to tell you the benefits of a darker interior, my motives become quite obvious. You think to yourself, "He's saying this because he doesn't have a lighter interior." For customers who like to stall (and that's most customers), you have just given them a reason to stop the process.

When this harmless little question about "any other needs" is asked, there is no car (or solution) in front of the customer. When I ask you what you like about a lighter interior or tell you the benefits of a darker interior, my motive is to find out more about your idea. Sometimes I can rename this need. Sometimes I can put the concerns with this need through the probing sequence. Sometimes I can channel it off as an objection. Sometimes I can just leave it alone, place it on the list, and deal with it later. The next step within the requirement stage will help me out here. The bottom line is that my chances are much better if I flush out this problem now rather than later.

I hope I presented a compelling argument. Believe it or not, of the hundreds of companies I have worked with, there have been two or three that have chosen to implement every step of the process *except* this one. It remains a puzzle to me, but I must be customer centered as well, and my job is to design what the customer wants and provide my recommendations to assist in this design.

## STEP 3. PRIORITIZE NEEDS

The final step within the requirement stage is intended to create a priority among the customer's needs. Unlike the other two steps within this stage, this step will seldom, if ever, create any difficulty or controversy. Yet this harmless little priority task has the potential to pay big dividends to you, the seller.

Theoretically, you have used your probes within the analysis stage to let the customer see the potential impact of many of his problems. You did not stop at the first problem, but continued to plow through two or three other concerns. You have even transferred those problems to needs and added a few more needs to this list. Are you willing to bet on which of these needs is the most significant? I would rather allow the customer to do this for me.

What you are really doing is allowing the customer to give you his "hot button," or most important need. By some strange coincidence, I am going to arrange my proposal, or demonstration, in the same order.

Think how you would feel if you were looking for a house, and the most important feature to you is the neighborhood. You may have had a burglary hit a little close to your old neighborhood, and it transferred over as your most important need. That is your obsession, and that is what you want.

Now here I come, your friendly realtor. I happen to love the fact that the house I am listing has a brand-new kitchen with the highest-quality appliances. By the way, as your friendly realtor, I love to entertain and would kill for such a kitchen. The neighborhood is nice too, but wow, what a kitchen! Think how weak my recommendation would be if I were to explain it to you this way:

Seller:   This house is a gem, a real gem! It has walk-in closets, which you will not find very often in older homes. It has a two-car garage, a finished basement, and is situated in a nice neighborhood. In my opinion, however, the best feature of this house is definitely the kitchen. It was just recently remodeled, and terrific new appliances were installed.

When you prioritize a customer's needs, you eliminate the possibility of this happening to you. If the customer in this example were to prioritize his list as "neighborhood, basement, kitchen, closets, and garage," that is exactly the order I am going to use in my recommendation later in the selling cycle. Prioritizing the customer's needs takes the guesswork out of the order of your solution.

Quite inadvertently, I stumbled on another benefit to establishing a priority. I was wondering if customers would object to having to go through this step and was surprised with what I found. Customers not only did not mind going through this quick step, they seemed to like it! I have never had a customer say to me, "Hey. Do you have to know me this well?" In fact, I have noticed that almost the opposite is true. Most customers seemed to enjoy this step and they seem to take more ownership in their ultimate solution. Often they want to talk more about their particular need, and this step seems to help. As for me, I very much like sitting back and hearing my customer talk about a need that happens to be a key strength within my potential solution.

There is one final benefit to this step, and it may be the most important reason of all. You have worked hard through your probing to get the things you do well onto this list. When you prioritize, it will be no coincidence to see your strengths rated first, second, and third. Remember also that "nice-to-have" items will be on this list. These are items you may be able to address, just not as well. Finally, there may be items you can't address with your ultimate solution. These may be represented by items that appeared when you asked, "Anything else?" and you chose to leave them alone.

It is natural for customers to stall. With that in mind, you are making it a whole lot tougher for them to do this when you have a prioritized list of criteria. There will be more to come on this issue when you read Chapter 19, about how to handle objections.

## SOME FINAL THOUGHTS

When I teach people how to use Customer Centered Selling, the most difficult concept they struggle with is the probing sequence within the analysis stage. The most confusing stage is this harmless little requirement stage. It may not appear confusing to you from the surface, but let me leave you with a few final words of advice.

### WATCH OUT FOR REDUNDANCY

The biggest complaint I hear centers on this particular theme: "I feel as if I keep repeating myself from the confirmation stage into the requirement stage." This is, without a doubt, the most frequent complaint I hear in all my seminars.

It is critical to remember that within the confirmation stage, you are discussing only customer problems. Within the context of selling, I define the word *problem* as "a statement of dissatisfaction by the customer." This is what you are dealing with in the confirmation stage.

The requirement stage flips these problems into needs. Now the conversation has become more positive, and the criteria for a solution are established. Once again, within the context of selling, I define the term *need* as "a want or desire by the customer." These needs are signaled by certain words. Here is a list of phrases associated with customer needs:

"I want . . ."
"I would like . . ."
"It would be nice to have . . ."
"What we are looking for would be . . ."

It would be great to have a customer walk in and tell me these things, but more often than not, when I have earned the right to be "listing and confirming needs," I will get my customers to agree to these needs using phrases like those just listed.

Here are three combinations of examples to show you what can go wrong, and why. First, I'll show you what would happen if you were unable to shift out of problems into needs from the confirmation stage to the requirement stage. I will pick up this example from the first step within confirmation. The key words that signal each stage are in boldface type:

## Confirmation Stage

Seller:        Let me see if I have everything straight here. From what you have told me so far, you are **unhappy** with the runaround you have been receiving and with the overall customer support. Is that correct?

Customer:    Yes, that's right.

Seller:        Is there anything else?

Customer:    No, that's it.

Seller:        Would you like to look at some alternatives?

Customer:    You bet!

## Requirement Stage

Seller:        All right, you are **not satisfied** with the runaround and the customer support.

Customer:    Yes!

Seller:        Is there anything else?

Customer:    No. I told you that already.

Seller:      Oh, well, how would you prioritize these concerns?

Customer:    Geez, can we move off the concerns already!


Pretty weak, yet it happens all the time when people are learning the system. Equally troublesome is when the seller brings needs into the confirmation stage. Once this is done, the requirement stage is again a redundant annoyance.


## Confirmation Stage

Seller:      Let me see if I have everything straight here. From what you have told me so far, **you are looking** to eliminate the runaround you have been receiving and improve the overall customer support. Is that correct?

Customer:    Yes, that's right.

Seller:      Is there anything else?

Customer:    No, that's it.

Seller:      Would you like to look at some alternatives?

Customer:    You bet!


## Requirement Stage

Seller:      All right, **are you looking to** eliminate the runaround and improve the customer support?

Customer:    Yes!

Seller:      Is there anything else?

Customer:    No. I told you that already.

Seller:      Oh, well, how would you prioritize these needs.

Customer:    Geez, can we move on already!


This example was just as bad as the first. I am sorry to have shown you so much that was wrong, but it is the most common problem. Now let me show you the way it *should* flow, starting once again from the confirmation stage. Notice the boldface words in each section indicating "problem" within the confirmation stage and "need" within the requirement stage:

## Confirmation Stage

Seller:        Let me see if I have everything straight here. From what you
               have told me so far, you are **unhappy** with the runaround you
               have been receiving and the overall customer support. Is that
               correct?

Customer:      Yes, that's right.

Seller:        Is there anything else?

Customer:      No, that's it.

Seller:        Would you like to look at some alternatives?

Customer:      You bet.

## Requirement Stage

Seller:        All right, **are you looking** to eliminate the runaround and
               improve the customer support?

Customer:      Yes!

Seller:        Is there anything else?

Customer:      No, that's it.

Seller:        How would you prioritize these needs?

Customer:      Well, I would probably say improving customer support
               would be number one and eliminating the runaround would
               be number two.

Now that's not too hard, is it? The key is to watch your words, and you
will have a much easier time keeping the two stages apart.

## ADD SERVICE TO THAT LIST

I assume that anyone who chooses to read this book and commit to the
study of selling is customer centered—that is, focused on the customer's
needs and providing top-notch service. With this in mind, let me contradict
a point I made earlier. I wrote that the list of needs is the customer's, not
your own. Now I want to add something of mine to that list: service.

Hopefully, way back in your use of background probes within the research stage of this process, you asked the customer about service. If the
customer's response was that service was not up to par, I have no doubt that
you now know what to do. The analysis stage has its first candidate for the

probing sequence. From there, this problem transfers into a need within the requirement stage, and you now are setting yourself up nicely to offer a solution, which will be coming up soon.

During your early questioning, however, what if you found out that service *was* up to par? You even asked questions on a deeper level and found out this customer is truly happy with the service he is experiencing. You cannot create a problem that does not exist. But add it to the list of needs anyway. By adding service you will not forget to sell yourself when it comes time to make your recommendation. When you sell, you must remember it's a package deal. Product is what you represent, and service is you!

This may come off a little stylish, but here is an example of how I will add service to the list of needs. This statement follows the second step of the requirement stage ("Any other needs?"):

Seller:      Is there anything else you need?

Customer:  No, that's it.

Seller:      Well, *I* would like to add something to this list if it's okay by you. Earlier, you told me you are very satisfied with the level of service you are receiving. I would assume that whatever solution you decide on, you will want service as good as, if not better than, what you are currently receiving. Is that right?

Maybe I'm just lucky, but I have never had a customer tell me, "No, service just isn't that important. Leave it off the list." I once again warn you: This statement reflects my personal style. However, adding service to the list is *not* a question of style. It is a necessity.

## WATCH YOUR LANGUAGE!

Keep in mind throughout the requirement stage that you are speaking the customer's language. That means no specific feature names.

Your friendly Xerox sales rep, for instance, may refer to a specific need as "duplexing." That is the Xeroid's language. The customer's need would be to "copy documents on two sides." That is the customer's language. The better the job you do at watching your language, the greater the success you will have in humanizing your ultimate solution. Once again, it becomes a question of watching the words you use around the customer.

Now you have a list of needs that is starting to look a lot like the solution you are preparing to recommend very soon. What a coincidence. . . .

## TEST YOUR COMPREHENSION: REQUIREMENT STAGE

Go back to the four case studies. Here is your chance to test what you have learned. Write out the three steps within the requirement stage for each scenario. Then write an answer that would apply to the product or idea you are trying to sell. On the next page, I give you my suggestions for each of the companies outlined in the case studies.

### PJ INVESTING CORPORATION

_____

_____

_____

_____

### TO CLEAN A ROOM

_____

_____

_____

_____

### A TON OF TALENT, A LACK OF TRUST

_____

_____

_____

_____

EVERY MOTORS, LTD.

_____

_____

_____

_____

YOUR OWN SCENARIO

_____

_____

_____

_____

# SUGGESTED ANSWERS TO TEST YOUR COMPREHENSION: REQUIREMENT STAGE

Given the four scenarios, here are my suggested answers incorporating the three steps within the requirement stage. See how closely they resemble the answers you gave. Notice that I have added an extra problem to each summary. Assume that each of these problems was taken through the probing sequence as well.

## PJ INVESTING CORPORATION

1. Let's fix it. Right off the bat, it sounds to me as if whoever you choose to do business with needs to speed up the transaction process. Are you also looking for more documented research justifying the recommendations being made?
2. Are you looking for anything else?
3. So I can get a better handle on the recommendation that needs to be made, how would you prioritize this list of needs?

## TO CLEAN A ROOM

1. Are you looking for a way to organize the smaller objects within the room better? It sounds to me as if you want to eliminate any chances of misunderstandings from the friends you don't know as well too. Is that correct?

2. Anything else we haven't planned for?
3. Given these two needs, what would be your top priority?

## A TON OF TALENT, A LACK OF TRUST

1. All right, let's see if we can work together and lay out some solutions that might appeal to you. From what I hear you saying, one very important need is to play a major part in the projects you are assigned. Is that correct? In addition, it seems as if you are getting frustrated with where you are in the company and you want to become a serious candidate for advancement. Is that right?
2. Is there anything else?
3. Now I assume all that has been listed is critical. How would you prioritize this list of needs?

## EVERY MOTORS, LTD.

1. Let's turn our attention to fixing these concerns. Are you looking for more consistency and accountability in the people who work on your car? With regard to the car itself, it sounds as if whatever car I end up recommending should have special features designed for multiple drivers. Is that correct?
2. Is there anything else you would be looking for?
3. I want to make sure that whatever I recommend fits exactly with what you are looking for. With this in mind, how would you prioritize this list of criteria?

Look over the answers provided, as well as your own, and put them through the test:

- Does the "confirmation of needs" allow the customer an opportunity to take part in the creation of this list?
- Does that list of customer needs avoid the use of any product or feature names?
- Does the list contain only needs and no problems?
- Are your questions closed questions?
- Is a there a priority established?

# THE SPECIFICATION STAGE

## LOCKING OUT MISUNDERSTANDINGS . . . AND THE COMPETITION

No man would listen to you talk if he didn't know it was his turn next.

—E. W. Howe

**W**ith the belief that you must be customer centered to establish a true working relationship with your customer, you take on the added responsibility of looking out for the needs of your customer. Because this process often parallels that of a consultant, the specification stage becomes important to both seller and customer.

This stage is important to the customer mainly because of the vulnerability he displays within the decision cycle. As you recall, the only stage within the decision cycle that can often be overlooked by the customer is the measurement stage. This leaves the customer with a vague list of criteria and exposes him to less than ethical salespeople.

The specification stage is important to the seller for different reasons. When customers are unclear in communicating their buying criteria, they often expose the salesperson as well. Companies like Xerox, which have "no questions asked" guarantees, run the risk of replacing products due to misunderstandings between the salesperson and the customer if this stage is not addressed. The good news is that typically this is a quick and easy sequence of steps to accomplish.

# STEP 1. TRANSFER CRITERIA TO SPECIFICATIONS

This first step reflects another lesson I learned from my Leadership Through Quality education while working for Xerox. Within this training, I was taught how to follow what is called a quality improvement process (QIP). This process teaches employees of the corporation how to work within systems that already function well. "If it ain't broke, fix it better" is a motto I believed in, and this portion of the quality training spoke directly to this philosophy.

The QIP encompasses a ten-step system to improve what is already working. Teaching this process contained a detailed simulation that forced participants to work with suppliers, internal customers, and external customers.

Within the simulation, the participants were to gather customer requirements and transfer these requirements to specifications. This represents a step within the QIP. The groups that did a good job forcing their "customers" to define the requirements better did much better within the simulation. Those that did a poor job within this stage supplied their "customers" with faulty products and failed with the simulation.

Consistently I would hear the participants moan, "It wasn't our fault since our 'customers' were unclear in defining their requirements." Well, what do you know! The customers were unclear, and imagine, they did not blame themselves for that lack of clarity. How unusual! I don't know of many customers who will blame themselves when they are unclear with the salesperson as to their requirements. What complicates this issue even more is the fact that this represents the weakest stage within the decision cycle. It was a great lesson in quality, and an equally great lesson within selling.

I have always been led to believe the customer is always right. When it comes down to finding fault with a customer's lack of clarity relating to customer requirements, the *salesperson* should be held responsible every time. That's what we get paid for: asking the right questions.

It is the norm, not the exception, to hear customers speak in vague generalities. Look at your own examples if you completed the Test Your Comprehension section of the previous chapter. If you did not complete this section, look at my answers. This lack of clarity does not make the list of needs wrong. It does, however, make that list of needs incomplete.

This lack of clarity exposes your customers to other salespeople as well. You have worked so hard. Why would you want to invite your competition into this sale? I can't tell you the number of times I would hear a Xeroid come back from a sales call, ecstatic over the list of criteria. "Oh, I've got this sale!" he would announce proudly. "Just look at this list of needs. Quality, service, and speed. I'm in, baby!"

Well, maybe I am little naive, but I can't imagine a salesperson from Canon or Sharp saying to the customer, "Oh, darn it! It's that need for service again. Well, we are pretty good at the other two on that list."

No, I don't see this scenario playing out that way. I think you are more likely to hear, "Uh, service? Uh, yeah, uh, we're into service. As a matter of fact, we are very much into service. Why, uh, we even won an award once in service. Yeah, and it said we were number one. Yeah, that's the ticket, number one!"

To illustrate this point further, look at the difference between a Hyundai and a BMW. Both have automatic transmissions, both have air-conditioning, and both have decent pickup. So why would one car cost about four time more than the other car? Ah, that's where specifications and measurements come in.

So you want a car with pickup, do you? How fast is fast? You want a good air-conditioning system, huh? How cold is cold? Allowing your customer to answer these questions not only keeps out other, less ethical salespeople, it helps you to assist the customer. Without these questions, maybe

I am assuming things I should not. Maybe I am selling this customer too much.

Once I was working with a Xerox customer who was looking at replacing her copier. She mentioned she wanted a copier that was "fast." I asked what she considered a fast machine, and she asked me why I needed to know and what the difference was. I said about a quarter of a million dollars. She then answered my question!

I hope I have been able to show you a need for this first step in the specification stage. The solution is a simple one: You must ask your customers to define what they are now looking for. This can be done in one of two ways. The first way is to use open questions and let the customer do the work. Look at everybody's favorite example, service:

Seller:     You mentioned you were looking for better service. How do you define better service?

Customer:   By better service, I mean I want to make sure that when I call your office for assistance, I either get immediate help or a call back within fifteen minutes.

After asking a question like this, it is important to display good listening habits and write down what the customer has to say. If it is still unclear, continue to probe.

A second technique that can be effective when assisting customers in clarifying their criteria is to use closed questions. The value of a closed question is that you have more influence over the customer's response. Let's take that same service example. Every company addresses better service in its own way. Perhaps your company addresses this issue by using computers to safety-check its merchandise. In this example, you will see the use of a closed question to direct the customer response better:

Seller:     Let's touch back on service again for one moment. By better service, I am assuming you are referring to getting merchandise delivered properly and without error to cut down on all that wasted time you were referring to. Is that correct?

Customer:   Yes. I don't want to be calling for service all the time.

I sometimes refer to that technique as the "grabbing the bull by the horns" approach, but sometimes you have no choice. The customer criterion is vague, and you don't want to take the risk that his definition will not directly match your own. Your choice may depend on how well you did earlier in the cycle, focusing your probing sequence around your strengths. Either way, the responsibility is yours to transfer those requirements over to specifications, clear up any misunderstanding, and reduce both seller and customer liability.

## STEP 2. COMMIT TO SPECIFICATIONS

The second step within the specification stage represents a great opportunity for the seller. The decision-making criteria have been established, and now it is time for a little more commitment from the customer.

Step 2 represents a tremendous opportunity for the seller to obtain the second of four major commitments from the customer. Up to this point, you have already obtained one commitment from the customer. Using your first trial close, you asked the customer within the decision stage if he wanted to "fix" his existing problems. Now that the criteria have been established, there is "nothing else" the customer is looking for, and his needs have been carefully measured. This is a spectacular time to commit the customer to these specifications. Here are some examples:

Seller:   Will you be basing your purchase decision on this list of criteria?
OR
Seller:   You mentioned earlier that you wanted to fix it. Does this fix it?
OR
Seller:   Is this what it's going to take to make you happy?

None of these questions is designed to be aggressive. They are designed to smoke out any objections the customer might have and to insulate you in the event your customer may want to stall a little bit and add some criteria to that list later.

# SOME FINAL THOUGHTS

The specification stage is not a difficult stage within the selling cycle. If customers would only do a better job within their *decision cycle*, we might not even need this stage. Unfortunately, this stage is often forgotten, as is understanding where the customer is in his cycle, and major disputes are created. Here are some final thoughts to assist you in working effectively within this stage of selling.

## YOU CANNOT MEASURE EVERYTHING

One of the major reasons this stage within the selling cycle can be a little tricky centers on the lack of clear-cut rules. You have to listen to the customer. You have to make a determination as to whether the criteria you and the customer create are clear. You also have to make sure the criteria begin to define the solution you have in mind. In either case, not everything can be measured.

For instance, assume that within the requirement stage, the customer told you he can't afford payments of more than $100 a month. That is a measurement. Unless you feel this is unrealistic, it is unnecessary for you to ask the customer later to measure this for you.

## WATCH OUT FOR ANALYTICAL PEOPLE

I now have to amend a general theme I presented within this chapter. On a few different occasions, I told you that this stage should not take long. This is especially true when you now realize that "you cannot measure everything." Well, there is one exception to the rule: When you work with analytical people, this stage may slow down to a snail's pace. Analytical people are detail oriented and inquiring in nature—for example, accountants, economists, statisticians, and government workers (or so I have been told). Anyone whose nature centers on precision is often considered analytical.

This type of person is often offended by generalities. You will not have to worry about remembering this stage because, lest you forget, he will remind you. Be prepared to slow down in this stage and do not rush this customer. If you do a good job here, without the analytical customer's prodding, your stock as a salesperson will go up dramatically in his mind.

## SELL PARANOID

This last point might sound a little unusual: I recommend you "sell paranoid." Assume there is always a competitor lurking around the corner preparing to meet with your customer. Understand that no matter how effective you are at using the skills I teach you or anyone else teaches you, no one closes 100 percent of his customers on the first call. This means competition.

With this in mind, I ask you to beware. Do not underestimate the power behind influencing a customer's criteria to resemble the strengths of your product. The specification stage allows you to create specifications that your competition can't match. You are literally helping the customer to define his or her needs better around the specifications of your strongest solutions!

## TAKE A SHOT AT THE OBJECTION OF PRICE

Have you ever wondered how and why Xerox wins so many government accounts? I can assure you it's not price. We all know that the government is forced to do business with the least expensive vendors, so I ask you again: How does it get these accounts?

The answer is simple: Xerox gets in early and creates specifications that no one else can match. Then it is the least expensive vendor! If you do a good job within this stage and the probing sequence within the analysis stage, you will be working to head off a price objection before it is even voiced.


If you perform this stage effectively, you should be able to understand the customer better, reduce the chances of misunderstandings, and eliminate competition. With benefits like those, I recommend you take the one to two minutes necessary to accomplish these steps.

# TEST YOUR COMPREHENSION: SPECIFICATION STAGE

Once again, go back to the four case studies. Here is your chance to test what you have learned. Write out the two steps within the specification stage for each scenario. Then write an answer that would apply to the product or idea you are trying to sell. Remember, not every need is measurable, so one measurement for each example will be adequate. On the next page I will give my suggestions for each of the companies outlined in the case studies.

PJ INVESTING CORPORATION

_____

_____

_____

_____

TO CLEAN A ROOM

_____

_____

_____

_____

A TON OF TALENT, A LACK OF TRUST

_____

_____

_____

_____

EVERY MOTORS, LTD.

_____

_____

_____

_____

YOUR OWN SCENARIO

_____

_____

_____

_____

# SUGGESTED ANSWERS TO TEST YOUR COMPREHENSION: SPECIFICATION STAGE

Given the four scenarios, here are my suggested answers incorporating the two steps within the specification stage. See how closely they resemble the answers you gave.

PJ INVESTING CORPORATION

1. With regard to speeding up your transaction process, are you looking to shave that down to about a day? Tell me more about what you are looking for in the area of research.
2. Is that what it's going to take to earn your business?

TO CLEAN A ROOM

1. In looking at cleaning your room, are you talking about removing all visible clutter?
2. You said you wanted to make a change. Is that what it's going to take to make that change?

A TON OF TALENT, A LACK OF TRUST

1. What's your definition of a "being a major part" of the projects you are assigned?
2. Is that what it's going to take to make you happy?

EVERY MOTORS, LTD.

1. You mentioned accountability. Are you looking for one responsible party as opposed to many?
2. Is that it? Is that what you are looking for?

Look over the answers provided, as well as your own, and put them through the test:

- Does this list of customer needs avoid the use of any product or feature names?
- If the customer's need was quantifiable, was there a measurement established?
- Does the trial close take the form of a closed question?

# FIFTEEN

# THE SOLUTION STAGE

## PUTTING YOUR PRODUCT KNOWLEDGE ON DISPLAY

Of the best leader, when he is gone, they will say: We did it ourselves.

—*Chinese proverb*

Finally, the time has come to talk product. The solution stage represents your first opportunity to display that dazzling product knowledge you were led to believe was so important. Well now, you "product heads," here is your time to shine.

This stage brings to mind the feeling a football team must have when they are first and goal from the one-yard line. It should not be hard now to just punch it in! Unfortunately, many salespeople lose sight of important skills that are necessary to avoid fumbling the ball. You have worked too hard to give it up here.

The solution stage is not a difficult stage within selling. What it does require is discipline. Discipline to stick with the skills that allowed you to arrive here. Discipline to tie your product recommendation carefully to the customer's needs. Discipline to present your product in a way that allows your customer to understand the recommendation you are making.

# STEP 1. COMMIT TO SELLER

What book would be complete without a little bit of controversy? Here comes mine. I am going to reintroduce you to a trial close that I am willing to bet you have heard before. What's more, I am also willing to bet you don't much care for it. Another term for the "commit to seller" is "precommit." No matter what you want to call it, here is what it sounds like:

**"If I am able to offer a solution that addresses this list of criteria to your total satisfaction, would there be any reason why you would not give me an opportunity to earn your business?"**

That might be a bit too civilized. Try this one on for size:

**"If I can recommend a solution that addresses your needs, would you buy it from me?"**

Does it look familiar now? If you are one of the many who do not like the sound of this trial close, you are not alone. Many people bristle when they even hear those three words, "If I can . . ." All I ask is that you give me a moment to explain its relevance. Then you may make up your own mind.

First, let me see if I can explain why you do not like this trial close. It makes you think of the stereotypical salesman with the plaid jacket. It sounds shifty, loaded, as if I am trying to pull something over on you. Sneaky, slimy, unethical, and deceptive. Does that cover it?

I happen to be a big fan of this trial close, for a number of reasons. Let's start with the perception issue. One of the reasons you may feel the way you do is because of where this trial close often turns up. There you are, walking to the sales floor with your significant other, and out pops

Salesguy Sam with a big grin. Without the benefit of even a "hello," you hear those dreadful words, "Hey, if I can . . ."

"Oh, no, it's a sales trick," you think, and you back away.

Perhaps the biggest problem with this line is its positioning. Unlike your other experiences, I am not coming from left field with this line. You see, I listened to you in the research stage. I asked you more open questions than you are accustomed to and allowed you to explain yourself to me.

I asked more difficult questions in the analysis stage but allowed you to paint the picture and let you see the impact of many of your problems before they became a crisis through my probing sequence.

I displayed good listening habits as I took notes and then summarized what I had heard in the confirmation stage. You told me there were no other concerns you were experiencing, and then you said you wanted to do something about it.

In the requirement stage, we worked together in a consultative manner, listing what it was that you were looking for. After making sure there were no other needs, we even prioritized your list.

Together we tightened that list and came up with measurements to your needs in the specification stage. You even told me at that time that you not only wanted to fix your existing situation, but that list represented what you would fix it with.

Now I simply want to know whether, *if I can recommend a product that addresses your list of criteria better than anyone else, you would buy it from me.* This line does not come from left field. I earned the right to ask you this question! Sometimes it is not the phrase that offends you, but rather where that phrase is positioned.

Another problem with this trial close is the unfortunate misunderstandings that many have regarding the *real* reason it is used. When I sold insurance for New York Life, I had a manager who meant well but did not understand the precommit phrase, "If I could ___, would you ___?" When I objected and said to this manager I thought this might instigate an objection, he looked at me with "a wry smile" and said, "Oh no, don't worry about that. The customer probably won't even hear this phrase."

Won't hear it? When I first used this phrase (out of position of course), it was like hitting my customers over the head with a two-by-four. They not only objected; they objected loudly. My manager would ask me if I was using that trial close, and I would not hesitate in answering with a lie: "Yes, sir!"

It was not until I was trained to sell by Xerox that I came to realize the value of this phrase. My trainer taught me about this trial close but immediately told me not to worry; most of the salespeople he worked with did not use it. My manager told me the same thing. But something strange had already happened to me. Once I had learned how people make decisions and how to influence that process, I realized the power of this trial close.

It was the classic case of everyone looking for the wrong solution. Everyone at Xerox kept telling me that using this line would probably elicit an objection. Even I remembered thinking to myself while selling my whole life policies, "Yes, ladies and gentlemen, if they have an objection, I am going to hear it right now."

Then it hit me. What would be wrong with getting an objection now? Would it be better if I laid out my entire solution "rather than" heard this objection? Would "the objection" somehow magically go away? No! Not only would it not go away, it would lead me to another Rob's Rule:

► *Trial closes are designed to elicit objections, not avoid them.*

The wrong solution? You bet! At this point in the sale, you have to ask yourself just how sure you are that the customer has no more objections. I would rather ask my customer, and this trial close will do it.

Sometimes I want to cut through it all and just ask the customer if he has a brother-in-law in the business or if he is not the real decision maker. This trial close is the next best thing. You can avoid it if you like, but remember something: The next time you work hard for a customer, I mean *really* hard for a customer, and you not only don't get the business but you find out you were *never* going to get the business, think about me and this controversial little phrase. I believe you will save yourself not only frustration but time as well.

The commit to seller will help you to avoid customers who are not serious about a solution. I am not one who likes to give others my best ideas, only to see someone else profit by their implementation.

# STEP 2. RECOMMEND SOLUTION

There appear to be no hidden objections, and it is finally time to recommend a solution, or what I call FABEC statements, an acronym that is perfect here. Too often salespeople begin to spew too many facts, obsess on the wrong benefits, and generally make a mess here. A little discipline using this acronym, and you will have no problems. FABEC means: feature, advantage, benefit, explanation, and confirmation.

F stands for *feature*. There is typically a name to whatever you are recommending, and now is the time to let your customer know what it is. I have intentionally avoided features so far, but here is your chance to shine. You have been speaking the customer's language up to now. It is time to speak your language. Here are some examples of customer needs translated to seller's features:

| CUSTOMER NEED | SELLER FEATURE |
| --- | --- |
| Protection of purchase | Money-back guarantee |
| Copying on two sides | Duplexing |
| Better protection in bad weather | Antilock brakes |
| Quicker investment of principal | Sweep account |
| Protection for minor injuries | First-dollar accident rider |

Do not forget to start with the feature or features that address the customer's most important criteria and stay in that prioritized order, and naming your solution should not present any real problems.

A stands for *advantage*. Often there are "nice-to-have" advantages to the features you are recommending. These advantages do not directly address the customer's need, but you might feel remiss in not mentioning them. For instance, your customer might want a pair of glasses that do not slip down his nose. The feature that you show him is the Optigrab Nose Inducers, which will keep glasses from slipping down the nose. But wait. They are also lighter than most other glasses and will keep his glasses from leaving red marks on the side of his nose. That my friends, is an advantage. The customer did not ask to see this, but it represents a "nice-to-have" feature.

B stands for the *benefit*. This is the most important part of the FABEC acronym because it represents what the customer is really buying. The benefit is the specific value to the customer. So far, your customer knows the name of what you are recommending, and something nice about it. The benefit is your opportunity to tell your customer why you have chosen this feature.

The benefit links your solution directly to the customer's needs. Benefits are crucial and too often forgotten by salespeople. Too bad, because benefits, not the feature, are what your customer is using to base a decision on.

Customers do not buy features, they buy benefits. Let me explain this point with a story. I conducted a seminar in Reno, Nevada. The audience I was speaking to was a group of almost 500 polygraph examiners. You might be wondering why an insurance agent who mutated into a "Xeroid" would be talking to a bunch of polygraph examiners, but it did make sense. Polygraph examiners' expertise is gaining confessions, not testifying in court. I felt the selling process I had learned would be of help and I gave it a shot.

About ten minutes into my talk a man stepped up to the audience microphone and fired this shot my way:

"We have heard some of your talk now and I'm confused. You are a copier-jock. You sell copiers. We sell death. We sell life behind bars. Why don't you try and sell me that!"

Well, I must tell you, I have never been fond of being called a "copier-jock." This gentleman walked back to his seat, with pats on the back by some of his buddies. When he was seated, I looked at the gentleman and fired back:

"I do not believe you are selling death or selling life behind bars. I believe you are selling the chance for this person to get off his shoulder a burden that you and I can't even imagine. I believe you are presenting a chance for this person's spouse to try and make a future for herself. I further believe that you are selling the opportunity for this person's children to go on with their lives as well. I do not, however, see you selling death anymore than I see myself selling copiers."

At the conclusion of the seminar, this same gentleman was the first to greet me and to tell me how much he learned and could apply to what he did.

A salesperson needs to focus on benefits or the real reason why you are making a recommendation. Benefits do not represent the "nice to have" ideas, they represent the "need to have" ideas.

Using the the Optigrab Nose Inducers example as the feature, an advantage might be their ability not to leave marks on your nose, but the benefit is the most crucial element: they will keep the glasses from slipping down the customer's nose. That is what they told me they wanted this feature to do, and that makes it the benefit of this feature!

The "E" in "FABEC" stands for explanation. This addresses the next logical question from the customer: "How does it work?" It is my hope that you will be able to give the customer a feature, an advantage, and a benefit in less than thirty seconds. The explanation may take a bit longer, depending on the nature of your solution, the personality of your customer, your time frame, and other external factors. The explanation is something I have no way to gauge without knowing about your product. Then again, I would think the explanation is something you are pretty adept at. It is getting to the explanation that requires the tactics I have been describing.

Watch your customer's body language, and keep a lookout not to overdo it here. I do not want to burst your bubble, but even after the most gifted explanation, there is a good chance your customer will forget what you taught him before he even gets home. Not to worry. If you keep your feature, advantage, and benefit crisp and to the point, he will not forget them, and that's what he is really basing his decision on anyway.

C stands for *confirmation*. After each feature, advantage, benefit, and explanation, you have a wonderful opportunity to make sure your customer is comfortable with your solution. All you really need to do is ask, and that is where the confirm comes in.

Sometimes the explanation can get a little long. A lot is riding on your customer's acceptance of your solution. It is a simple step, and it is a fast step. Here are some examples of how you can confirm each element of your solution:

Seller:   How does that sound to you?
OR
Seller:   Do you think that will address this particular need?
OR
Seller:   Does that look good to you?

And so on. Listen carefully to your customers, and often, after your explanation, you will hear them say things like, "I like that" or "That looks great." You do not have to follow this up with a confirmation of your own! Remember: It's not a straitjacket; it's just a process.

If I am working from a proposal or a flip chart, I have always liked to cross out or place check marks by each item as it is confirmed by the customer. I feel this is psychologically powerful, but it is a question of style. What is not a question of style is the use of tight FABEC statements for each recommendation within your solution. These statements will allow you to communicate with your customer better and make a stronger case for your solution.

# SOME FINAL THOUGHTS

Sometimes I feel a little guilty going over ways to improve your techniques within the solution stage because it often represents an area that salespeople feel most comfortable with. I hope I was able to show you a valuable and necessary trial close and a logical approach around which to structure your solution. Now here are a few final thoughts.

## DON'T FORGET THE MAGIC WORDS

When you are using the skills outlined within this chapter, draw on a couple of magic words as often as possible. It is amazing how powerful the words "you said" can be. These magic words can vary from "you said" to "you mentioned," and from "you told me" to "you had told me." The intent, however, does not vary. These words gently remind customers that these are *their* words, not yours.

I strongly recommend their use whenever possible within the solution stage. These magic words seem to fit best when going over benefits within your FABEC statements because the benefits link directly to the customer need. Using these magic words will also force you to focus on what your customer has said, and not necessarily on what you have said. Perhaps now you can see how critical it is for you to continue to "let the customers paint the picture" and tell you *their* problems and *their* needs. It certainly would be embarrassing to be involved in this exchange:

Seller:     Another reason that I mention this feature is to address your need for quicker service, which you said was important.

Customer:   I never said that was important. You did.

Seller:     Well, uh, one of us said it, ha, ha . . . ha.

## IT'S OKAY TO BE OPINIONATED

See if this scenario sounds familiar. You are ready to make a purchase. The salesperson has had some difficulty listening and asking questions, but you maintained your composure. Occasionally you were even able to interrupt the dissertation covering aspects of the product you are totally uninterested in, to ask a question or state a need. Finally the solution is presented. It comes down to a choice of product A, B, or C, and you make the fatal mistake of asking for a recommendation:

Seller:     . . . and it does this and it does that.

Customer:   So which would you recommend?

Seller:     Oh, sorry, I can't do that.

Customer:   Why not?

Seller:     We're not allowed to.

Customer:   WHY THE %*&# NOT?!

If you have not picked it up from this example, this happens to be a pet peeve of mine. What a bizarre irony: When the *customer* should be speaking, the *salesperson* will not stop talking; when the *salesperson* finally should be speaking, the *customer* will not start talking. For goodness' sake, be opinionated! Often, that is exactly what the customer is paying you for: your professional opinion. Sadly, the only way to get opinions out of some salespeople is to ask them what their selection would be if the product was for them.

I recently tried this while considering the purchase of a CD player. After the CD speech ended, I was finally able to tell the salesperson my specific needs, which brought my options down from ten products to three. I tried to sneak one by the salesperson and asked for his recommendation, but he was too cagey for me and told me he could not do that. I asked him which he would buy, given my buying criteria, and he gave an opinion. I told him, "Fine, that's the one I'm buying." Amazingly enough, he seemed perturbed while writing up the sale, somewhat disgusted by my tactic!

It is not okay to dictate customer problems or customer needs in previous stages of the selling cycle. It is okay to be opinionated when it comes time to recommend a solution. And now is the time. It is even okay to show some enthusiasm for the recommendation you are making. Which approach would you prefer as a customer preparing to make, in your mind, a major decision:

Seller:   I think this feature is pretty good and should take care of your first need.

OR

Seller:   I think this feature is outstanding and will definitely take care of your first need.

We have had our discussion regarding belief in your product. I will assume the recommendation you are making is one you believe in. Do not be shy in letting the customer hear this. Remember, the customer is often battling a fear of change. If you are not excited and opinionated about the solution you are recommending, why would the customer be?

## PLEASE, DON'T OVERDO IT

When providing recommendations within the solution stage, carefully explain your product. Lord knows, I have taken enough shots at the sacred product knowledge cow, so I won't be more critical. Well, maybe just one more suggestion: Please, don't overdo it.

When I went out shopping to replace the old family truckster my wife was driving, we stopped by Volvo one day. The whole Jolles family was in attendance (to Volvo's delight) as we started to look at the station wagons. Just as the salesman began lecturing us on the "Story of the Station Wagon," one of the smaller Jolles members had to visit the Volvo family bathroom. Off went my wife and children, just as the salesman shifted into a conversation on safety.

At the time, one feature my wife and I were looking for was a passenger-side airbag. Other cars we were looking at had this feature. With Volvo representing itself as the leader in safety, I was quite surprised when I heard Volvo did not. I asked why and was given this answer: "The driver-side airbag is smaller and closer to your face. Therefore, it requires less force. The passenger-side airbag is larger and farther away. Therefore, it requires more force. We at Volvo have not perfected this feature, and until we do will not place it in our cars." Made sense to me. I appreciated his honesty.

When my wife returned, she asked about the airbags. I started to explain it to her and then decided it might be better if the salesperson explained it instead. Unfortunately, the explanation was a little different the second time around and went something like this: "Well, Mrs. Jolles, as I told your husband, the driver-side airbag is closer to your face. Therefore, it requires less force. The passenger-side airbag is larger and farther away. Therefore, it requires more force. A majority of collisions occur between 35 and 40 miles an hour, which deploys the airbags. When these airbags deploy, that explosion can be somewhat violent. Quite frankly, Mrs. Jolles, the passenger-side airbags have been ripping the noses off the dummies!"

My wife looked at me horrified as I looked at the salesperson with a puzzled expression of my own. "Did you have to tell her that much?" I thought to myself. The thought of this turned us both off, and we quickly headed for the door. Both of us had strange dreams that night; noses was the common theme.

I am a firm believer in the old KISS model: "Keep it simple, Stupid!" Analytical customers often require a great deal of explanation. The rest of the world does not need as much. Read your customer, choose your words carefully, and if you have a passenger-side airbag, watch your nose.

## USE THE "COMMIT TO SELLER" TRIAL CLOSE

You probably knew I was going to take at least one more shot at getting you to use the trial close within the solution stage, so here goes. You are exposed to this trial close in various forms all the time. You have just come to accept it and are not even aware of it.

Take a doctor, for instance. Many of us go for a second opinion when our doctor recommends major surgery. Let me ask you this. When is the last time your doctor presented you with a choice: "I am going to look you over and then provide you with my opinion. If you like my opinion, I would like you to pay me. If not, don't worry about it. No payment is necessary."

Salespeople basically work free until a customer agrees to make a purchase decision. Many professions, like the medical profession, get paid regardless of whether a customer likes their recommendation. As a salesperson, you earn the right to use this trial close. I believe it is more than fair to ask a customer for a commitment, assuming that what you recommend provides everything the customer is looking for.

## ONE THAT GOT AWAY

One final lesson: The solution stage represents a far less important stage within selling than most people understand. The sale is typically won or lost well before you present your recommendation to the customer. Keep this stage, along with all that product knowledge, in perspective.

I love to think back on many of the larger sales I made for Xerox within training, as well as my insurance days at New York Life. I have always felt fortunate, and at times a little lucky. "That does not mean I sold every client I ever met." Here is the story of one that got away because I was unable to make the argument effectively and put the solution stage in perspective.

One of the pioneer home shopping shows, QVC, contacted Xerox to inquire about sales training. I was put on the account and made my first call. Before I could get out my first question, the customer need was clearly spelled out. QVC did not really want "sales training" per se. What they were looking for was training for their on-air personalities in recommending products. The decision maker had heard about the use of features and benefits within copier recommendations and wanted that part of the process taught to his staff.

My strategy was simple. Following my own model meant backing this decision maker up and "going to school" regarding how QVC operates. Although the customer was outlining a specific need, QVC was somewhat unsure of what else it wanted or how to proceed. I had never watched one of these shopping shows before, so part of my education meant tuning in and studying the show. What I saw amazed me.

I chose to watch a show that was devoted to tools because I wanted to be able to understand and relate to the product. I had remembered the decision maker wanted me to focus on the telephone calls that were being taken and thought an education in features and benefits would maximize the effectiveness of these calls. Most of the calls went something like this:

| | |
|---|---|
| Personality: | Hi there. You're on the show. |
| Caller: | I am? Well, I just want to say, I love the show. |
| Personality: | Hey, thanks. So you're getting yourself a new saw! |
| Caller: | Yes, sir. I'm getting one for my son too. |
| Personality: | Well, that's great. They make wonderful gifts. |
| Caller: | Yes, sir. I'm excited! I've been looking for one of those beauties. |
| Personality: | You should be. You and your son are going to love that saw. Hey, thanks for calling. |

Do you see anything wrong with that call? I do. When you study how people make decisions, you begin to study selling from two perspectives: the seller's and the customer's. When you look at who is calling, you quickly become aware that these customers are in the investigation stage of their decision cycle. The personality's conversation is actually lined up nicely and appealing to other customers in that stage of the decision cycle . . . and that is exactly what is wrong with this call.

Appealing to customers in this stage of their decision cycle allows this show to touch the obscure percentage of people who are a hair away from pulling the buying trigger and making that decision. The pitch for the product should get the customers' attention. The telephone call conversation does absolutely nothing to add to or detract from the other viewers' decision. But what if this conversation was a little bit different? What if this conversation was used to touch the real masses of customers who are in the acknowledgment stage: those customers who are not totally happy with what they have but are not willing to do anything about it.

You now know how people usually make decisions. You have learned that these customers' problems will not be resolved until they appear large enough in the customers' mind to warrant a solution. I am aware that some people are literally addicted to these shopping shows and will buy based on impulse, but then again, those people will buy regardless of telephone conversations. These are the layups that do not require a salesperson's touch.

Obsessing on the solution as QVC does merely reinforces the small percentage of customers who are ready to buy. I looked at that electric saw. I thought about the tree house that I just built. The tree house, like many other home owners' projects, started out as an exciting labor of love. It did not end that way.

When I was a child, my dad had the largest, loudest, meanest electric saw on the planet. Back then, nobody wore goggles or took any other wimpy safety precautions. I vividly remember holding the wood (usually the short end, I might add) as sawdust flew. The fear I had from the deafening noise of the saw was exceeded only by my concern that the dull blade would jam and violently seize up as I held the wood, trembling. Don't get me wrong. It was time spent with my dad, and I would not trade that for anything. But, boy, did I hate that saw!

I constructed my kids' tree house all by myself. I did not own an electric saw, although I would readily acknowledge a problem in not owning one. I cut each pressure-treated piece of wood by hand. It made the project take weeks instead of days. It blistered my hands and hurt my arms. I worked alone because I was crabby and miserable. That was not how I planned on completing this project.

That tree house experience took me through my acknowledgment stage within the decision cycle and moved me to a decision. Soon after the tree house was built (and with my one good arm), I went out and bought "an electric saw."

My pitch to QVC was simple. They could pitch the product all they wanted, but I recommended they use the telephone calls to touch the roughly 80 percent of customers in the acknowledgment stage. People do not call and buy a product if everything is perfect with the product they have. My recommendation was to have a conversation relating to the problem these customers are fixing—the problem the vast majority of viewers can relate to. The conversation would sound something like this:

| | |
|---|---|
| Personality: | Hey, there. You're on the show. |
| Caller: | I am? Well, I just want to say I love the show! |
| Personality: | Well thanks. So you're buying the saw. **What** are you using now? [*background probe*] |
| Caller: | I have an old saw that I have been thinking of replacing for years now. |
| Personality: | **What** kinds of **difficulties** were you experiencing with that old thing? [*identifying probe*] |
| Caller: | It has seen better days. It doesn't seem to have the power it once did. |
| Personality: | **How** did that **affect** the jobs you were using it for? [*developing probe*] |
| Caller: | It was slow, and sometimes it would jam up and chew up the wood. |
| Personality: | Oh, my. **What impact** did this have on your overall projects? [*impact probe*] |

I believe this type of conversation would affect a lot more viewers than the previous one. This dialogue aims itself at a much larger population and avoids a discussion covering only the solution. To avoid a repetitive pattern, the probe sequence could be taken in a positive direction as well. Questions revolving around future projects, saving time, and money would work nicely.

I may not have done as effective a job selling as I had hoped, but to this day, I remain convinced this approach would have been more effective. When QVC balked at the proposal I put together on behalf of Xerox, it was I who recommended they not be trained in learning to present only bene-fits. Ethically, I could not do it, and I killed the deal based on my belief that we would be taking money to teach a process that would be of no help.

Learning to provide solutions to customers should not represent a difficult job for you, the seller. What can be difficult is respecting the *decision cycle* a customer goes through, allowing that cycle to lead both customer and seller to the solution.

Now, with the solution presented, explained, and confirmed, it is time to see just how effective you have been. The end is in sight. It is finally time to close.

## TEST YOUR COMPREHENSION: SOLUTION STAGE

Once again, go back to the four case studies. Here is your chance to test what you have learned. Write out the trial close used, and a FABEC statement based on one of the two recommendations you would make for each scenario. Then write an answer that would apply to the product or idea you are trying to sell. On the next page, I give you my suggestions for each of the companies outlined in the case studies.

PJ INVESTING CORPORATION

_____

_____

_____

_____

## TO CLEAN A ROOM

_____

_____

_____

_____

## A TON OF TALENT, A LACK OF TRUST

_____

_____

_____

_____

## EVERY MOTORS, LTD.

_____

_____

_____

_____

## YOUR OWN SCENARIO

_____

_____

_____

_____

# SUGGESTED ANSWERS TO TEST YOUR COMPREHENSION: SOLUTION STAGE

Given the four scenarios, here are my suggested answers incorporating the trial close and a FABEC statement used in your solution. See how closely they resemble the answers you gave.

## PJ INVESTING CORPORATION

1. If I can show you some solutions that address the list of criteria that you came up with, would there be any reason that you would not go with my recommendation?
2. Let's take a look at some ideas I know you will like. First, you wanted to speed up your transaction process.

**Feature**

- I think our Instant Invest program will satisfy that need and then some!

**Advantage**

- With this program, you will notice right off the bat a reduction in the time-consuming paperwork that bothers so many customers.

**Benefit**

- The most important reason I recommend it, however, is the speed of the program, which was critical to you.

**Explanation**

- Once you place a call to our office through our new computerized system, the Instant Invest program allows your deposit to be credited in less than twenty-four hours. This will meet your requirement of a two-day turnaround, which you had mentioned earlier.

**Confirmation**

- How does that sound?

## TO CLEAN A ROOM

1. If I can show you a way to accomplish that change, will you promise to keep this room clean?
2. Well, I think I have a great solution for you and I'll tell you why. You told me

that your most important need was to find a way to better organize your things.

**Feature**

• I recommend plastic storage boxes.

**Advantage**

• One advantage to plastic storage boxes is that they are easy to stack, taking up minimal storage space. This will be nice when you move out on your own but still want many of your belongings with you.

**Benefit**

• However, the most important reason I recommend these boxes is that you told me that you wanted to organize better some of the smaller objects in the room and easily be able to find things when necessary. These boxes will do both.

**Explanation**

• Let me tell you how they work. The plastic boxes are clear so you can see exactly what's in each box, from any angle. That keeps you from having to tear open boxes while searching for small objects.

**Confirmation**

How does that sound to you?


A TON OF TALENT, A LACK OF TRUST

1. If I can come up with a solution that addresses everything you said you were looking for, will I have your commitment to act and follow through?
2. I believe I can help you to achieve these goals.


**Feature**

• We have a training program, Interpersonal Skill Development, that I think would be a great fit for what you are looking for, and I'll tell you why.

**Advantage**

• First, this program offers you skill advancement credits. I know you didn't ask about this, but it certainly wouldn't hurt your internal résumé.

**Benefit**

• But that is not why I am recommending this program to you. I am recommending this program because it teaches key skills that become necessary building blocks to make you more effective in leadership situations. This will send the right signals to senior management, who assign these leadership roles.

**Explanation**

- Let me tell you a little more about the program. The course not only teaches you more about the way you communicate personally, but how others communicate as well. This allows you to communicate better with the groups you lead and work more productively.

**Confirmation**

- How does that sound to you?

EVERY MOTORS, LTD.

1. I hope when you see how we at Every Motors handle this list of needs that you came up with, you will become another satisfied customer.
2. To begin, let's take a look at your top need, your request for accountability from one person.

**Feature**

- At Every Motors, we have a system that we are very proud of, called our Customer Connection program.

**Advantage**

- An advantage to this program that many customers appreciate is its ability to speed up the entire servicing process.

**Benefit**

- However, the best part of this program speaks directly to your most important criterion. The Customer Connection program provides you with one, and only one, individual who remains responsible for the entire service procedure involving your car.

**Explanation**

- Once you purchase your car from us, we will immediately introduce you to the person who will be representing you within this program. He is a tenured employee who has been trained in all aspects within this industry, from sales to service. He will be your contact, no matter what the issue, and he will give you the accountability you said you were looking for.

**Confirmation**

- How's that for a match!?

Look over the answers provided, as well as your own, and put them through the test:

- Is the commit-to-seller trial close given?
- Is the feature chosen appropriate given the customer's need?
- If an advantage is offered, does it represent a "nice-to-know" element of the feature?
- Does the benefit recommended address the customer's specific need?
- Does the explanation of the solution contain a reference back to the customer (e.g., "you said")?
- Is a confirmation given at the end of each recommendation?

# THE CLOSE STAGE

## EARNING THE RIGHT TO CLOSE

When we give it our all, we can live with ourselves—regardless of the results.

*—Anonymous*

**O**ne of my first memories as a neophyte salesperson is with closing the sale. It seemed as if everywhere I went and every corner I turned, I kept hearing the same thing—from managers, peers, grizzled vets. Over and over again, "The close is the easiest part of selling." I heard it so often that I believed it without question—that is, of course, until I got in front of my first customer. All of a sudden, the close did not seem so easy anymore. As a matter of fact, the close was downright difficult.

Once the rhetoric wore off, I realized I was clueless when it came to

215

closing. I'd been told that it "is the easiest part of selling," but unfortunately, that was where my education ended, making the close one of the most difficult steps for me to implement.

# THE MANY MYTHS OF CLOSING

The whole concept of closing brings with it many myths, perpetuated by old schools of selling that placed such a heavy emphasis on this particular stage of selling. I also believe many salespeople, like myself early on, are sometimes a little intimidated to challenge the conventional methods of selling.

Well, I am not. I would like to offer some arguments that might surprise some of you, but I will back up my claims with facts, not opinions. It's the twenty-first century, and time to do away with some of these ridiculous myths.

## MYTH 1:  FOLLOW THE ABC'S OF CLOSING:
##          ALWAYS BE CLOSING.

Interesting statement. If it said Always Be *Trial* Closing, I might agree. But that is not what this myth refers to. It refers to the belief that the more you ask for someone's business, the better chance you have of getting it. This is categorically false.

Please don't get me wrong. This theory was not always false. There was a time when orange leisure suits were in style. The problem is, customers have gotten a lot smarter, and your bombardment of closes will not assist you in closing. As a matter of fact, they can work against you.

A few years ago, Xerox commissioned a study looking into this exact issue. The results were astounding. To begin with, a line began to emerge, once again, right around $100. Each time a salesperson attempted to close on items that cost less than $100, the chances of gaining a commitment increased by 4 percent. (This might explain your weakness when shopping in a mall and caving in on a small purchase.)

Once the price of the commitment rose above $100, something astonishing happened. If customers were not ready to buy, they began to withdraw . . . quickly! If the response to the salesperson's close was "no," the chances of gaining a commitment from the customer immediately fell by 24 percent. That's one in four.

Why? A lot of it has to do with ego. Many customers feel that once they have said "no" to something, to say "yes" later would indicate they had been weak or manipulated. There is a kind of power to saying "no" to a salesperson. Sometimes the customer is left thinking, "I said 'no' and I'm not letting some fast-talking, smooth salesperson change my mind. I said 'no' and I'm sticking with 'no'!"

Ego also has a lot to do with a second problem related to the concept of closing, and particularly to a key theory relating to negotiating skills. As many preach (but few follow), the most basic approach to negotiation is for both customer and seller to feel they have each achieved the results they were looking for. This is a win-win solution. When a customer says no to a seller while closing, both parties immediately adapt a negotiation stance. Unfortunately, neither party is in a position to give a whole lot.

The customer digs in, not wanting to feel manipulated into saying yes. The salesperson digs in, not wanting to take no for an answer. Someone is going to lose and give in, and neither party wants to be the one. It becomes obvious that by accepting this myth of "always be closing" you are taking an unnecessary gamble. Fortunately, the solution is simple and will be covered within the close stage process.

## MYTH 2: THERE ARE A THOUSAND EFFECTIVE WAYS TO CLOSE, AND EACH IS GOOD IN ITS OWN WAY.

There are a thousand books on the topic of closing, and many claim to have a thousand ways to close. That part is true. Unfortunately, the word *effective* is what I have trouble with.

Don't misunderstand me. There are plenty of seminars and plenty of trainers who offer programs that cover the "tricks of a closing." this very subject. As a Xerox sales trainer, I had been recruited almost annually by these con artists. The money was great. If only there wasn't this little word called *ethics*. I mention ethics because the mere fact of obsessing on closing demonstrates a total lack of sales skill knowledge. You earn the right to close, and ask a customer for a commitment. Why in the world would you want to spend an entire day learning the "tricks" of closing? I would rather spend an entire day learning how to get to the close.

Look closely at this snake oil, and what you will really find are a couple of legitimate closes sandwiched within a number of closing con games. Within these "thousand" closes are hundreds of closes that all begin to look alike. The reason for this is that they *are* all alike. To this day, I refer to trainers who teach these seminars as "trainers who have gone to the dark side." Rest assured, I will never do it.

There are not a thousand ways to close. There are about ten legitimate ways to close a sale. Of that ten, I am partial to about four. Of the four, I will show you one approach that I recommend.

## MYTH 3: YOU DO NOT NEED TO CLOSE TO GAIN A COMMITMENT FROM THE CUSTOMER.

Not true. You *do* need to close to gain a commitment. I believe salespeople are probably the easiest people to sell. We have empathy for what the seller is going through. In many instances, I even assist a seller to get my business. It is not that I am such a nice person; I just want to buy the best product for my needs, and if the salesperson does not know the process, I will help the person . . . to a point.

You see, I do not feel as if I am that different from most other customers. In the end, I will do just about everything I can to help the seller—everything, that is, except ask me for my business. This is where I draw the line. I need to be asked!

That is my opinion, but I am not alone. Going out on sales calls with countless salespeople selling all different kinds of ideas. There seems to be a nervous sort of fumbling just as the final commitment is ready. This is often the result of not having a set selling process and trying to listen for ridiculous "buying signals."

It is ludicrous to risk all your work on vague "buying signals." Trial-close your customer in the three strategic spots within the selling process along the way, put in the four-step approach I will show you, and worry no more.

## MYTH 4: THE ONLY THING WORTH CLOSING FOR IS THE CUSTOMER'S BUSINESS.

If I agreed to this one, I would shoot down any credibility I might have established. It is just not true. When closing, the goal is to close for the highest realistic level of commitment. Period.

This is not to suggest that this highest realistic level of commitment might not benefit from a little creativity on your part. After my insurance days, I still considered myself an expert within the legal profession vertical market. There were no lawyers I was aware of who made decisions of consequence without taking these decisions to the partners' meetings on the second Tuesday of each month. This was clearly communicated by the decision influencer during our first meetings.

Closing for the "business" would have been insulting. However, this is not to say I could not be a little creative within the level of commitment I sought. I always asked if I could sit in the reception area during these meetings. When the topic of office equipment came up, I offered to act as an information source. This idea was consistently met with comments like, "That won't be necessary." I would always tell them I was used to night work from my insurance days, and I had plenty to do and would appreciate the opportunity.

Seventy percent of the time, I was allowed to sit outside the meeting. I wasn't out there for long because I was brought into the meetings almost 100 percent of the time. Often the buying decisions were made based on my ability to address objections my decision influencer would not have had a prayer of answering without me present. Even the reception area was useful. It was easy to concentrate on my work because I never saw another salesperson waiting with me.

Be creative when determining what you can close for when working with customers. You will probably get a good idea of what you can expect during the opening stages of the selling cycle.

One last point. I have attempted to keep this process as generic as possible, allowing you to relate the art of selling not only to products and concepts, but parenting, managing, and any other issues that require persuasion. I mention this again because not all solutions require the exchange of money. If money is required, it usually is flushed out during the commit-to-seller trial close and is placed on the list of needs. Wherever it falls within the customer's criteria is exactly where it should fall within *your* recommendation. If it is his third criterion, it should be recommended third.

In the rare (and I mean *rare*) instance that money is not raised as a buying criterion in the requirement stage, it often still remains an important issue on the solution stage. It should therefore be discussed after the last prioritized aspect of your recommendation is discussed. In either case, it is important that money be covered before you move into the summary close.

# THE SUMMARY CLOSE

Put the myths behind you and prepare yourself for a simple, four-step approach in an ethical manner to asking for the final commitment from the customer. The close I am about to show you is called the *summary close*. I have chosen it because, as you will see, it is a natural fit to finish off the process you have learned. There is a lot of room for personalization, and I can assure you that there will be plenty of room to stylize this close. Nevertheless, I recommend you stick closely to the four steps within the process.

## STEP 1. CONFIRM BENEFITS

The first step of the summary close is one last check with the customer. (Now you can see how this particular approach to closing got its name, because this confirmation requires you to touch lightly on the benefits.)

Most salespeople do not understand how powerful this last confirmation can be. Let me show you what I mean. Read this next statement, stop, and without reading any further, try to anticipate what the next step of this process would be:

Seller:   Don't you agree that by moving forward with the recommendation I am making today, you will be speeding up your turnaround, improving your quality, and getting the level of service you said you were looking for?

What would you think my next question to you would be if you answered yes to this question? Sounds to me as if somebody is getting ready to ask for a commitment. No one would dare answer yes to that question if they did not intend to go ahead with your solution. That, my friends, happens to be the biggest strength of the summary close.

If there is an objection, the customer is going to push back. It does not make me happy to hear a "no" here, but if I do, so be it. If the customer says "no" and gives me an objection, it does not put me in the best of moods, but at least I am not battling my customer's ego as well as the objection. I didn't ask for his business. I merely asked if my solution did everything the customer said he wanted it to do. It is off to my objection tactic, and I will give it my best shot.

If the customer says yes, I am a happy guy. Why would you hesitate now? Through your trial closes, the customer has now agreed to the following:

- "I want to fix my existing situation."
- "That's what it is going to take to fix my existing situation."
- "If you can do this for me, I will buy it from you."
- "I agree your solution gives me everything I was looking for."

There are never guarantees, but I would feel pretty confident at this point and would consider my chances of getting this business extremely good.

What most people do not realize about the summary close is that by confirming the benefits, you are actually trial-closing the customer. That summary packs quite a psychological punch.

You might be interested to note that when I learned this close in training at Xerox, this first step was presented as simply a way to make the transition to asking someone for his business. What I learned through using this close and observing it was that this step forced out any remaining objections and confirmed my position within the close. Folks, I call that a trial close.

## STEP 2. ASK FOR COMMITMENT

Well, what do you know! At last, it's time to ask for the final commitment. I made a promise when I started this book, as I do in my seminars, that closing would not be hard. With the confirmation of benefits of step 1 out of the way, I believe I have kept my promise. This should no longer be a difficult step. It is amazing how easy closing really is when you have earned your right to be here.

Notice my choice of words for step 2: "ask for commitment." With respect to closing myth 4 ("the only thing worth closing for is the customer's business"), the operative word here is *commitment,* not *business.* Your strategy here should be to close for the highest realistic level of commitment.

How do you ask for commitment? My recommendation is to do it as simply as possible. Remember that you no longer have to play games like, "My pen or yours?" This is now a natural step, and the customer expects you to ask, so do it!

Some salespeople have favorite pens, lucky pads of paper, even superstitious places to eat before a big appointment. (I know because I have a whole slew of superstitious quirks.) An understanding of these superstitions and quirks is often found within the closing approach many salespeople choose. In other words, if you have a favorite closing line, go ahead and use it. The summary close merely provides a structure within which you can use your favorite technique.

There are many techniques used in asking customers for commitment. For instance, a popular approach is called *assumptive,* because it assumes that a commitment has been made. Unfortunately, this approach does not have the best reputation, because of where it is used. When you shake a salesperson's hand, and he asks you in the first three sentences, "Would you like to take delivery on that item today?" you recoil. But it is not a big deal to ask someone that same question after going through the steps of the selling cycle and answering the four trial closes before this question is asked.

Another popular approach used in closing is the *alternative* technique, especially useful if there are multiple variables involved. An alternative approach would sound something like this:

**"Would you like to start with just the business account, or would you prefer to include the household account as well?"** [*alternate*]

I am almost embarrassed to tell you the approach I use when asking a customer for a commitment, but here goes. It is referred to as a *direct* approach to commitment. It is not fancy, but I save fancy for more important places within the model.

**"I would love to have your business."**

Imagine, you have read this book up to this point, only to be enlightened by those seven words. The point is, these words are of little consequence when you have properly followed all the other steps allowing you to be here.

The way you ask for a commitment from your customer often has two important variables. First, you must know what your highest realistic level of commitment is, and tailor your close around that commitment. Second, you must be true to your own style, and find the approach that is right for you.

## STEP 3. DISCUSS LOGISTICS

With a commitment in hand, you must stay focused and finish this sale off correctly. The only thing left to do is to work out the logistics to implement the sale you have just made—for example, items like delivery, training, and follow-up. It certainly would not be appropriate for you to rush out without completing this portion of the call.

As process driven as I am, when I work with customers and teach them this process to sell by, I usually do not touch this part of their process. It would be inappropriate for me to run around and dictate to you how to handle the logistics of your sale. That part is usually intact, and if it is not, it is an issue you would resolve immediately.

I would make the correction of any implementation issues a priority because of the next stage that awaits the customer within the decision cycle. I do not want to add to any buyer remorse if I can help it.

I hope you are comfortable in actually implementing solutions, and the logistical part of this step will not throw you. Remember, the smoother job you do demonstrating your ability to implement, the better your customers will feel making their commitment.

## STEP 4. REASSURE THE CUSTOMER

One of the pleasures I found in working to create Customer Centered Selling was adding this last step to the close. It has never been an official step within any process I have taught in the past, but it sure is part of *my* process.

Some of you might be wondering if I am carrying this "Customer Centered thing" too far. I know I certainly learned that once you have the customer's check, pack up your briefcase and GET OUT OF THERE! I would tend to agree *if* it were not for this little thing called the reconsideration stage that all customers go through.

I remember the one (and only) time I went skydiving. The instructor said something that sticks in my mind to this day. He said that most people who think about skydiving never act on the idea because they are faced with 51 percent fear and 49 percent curiosity. He went on to tell us that the only reason we were there to jump was that we were motivated by 51 percent curiosity and 49 percent fear.

Closing can be emotional. Often the customer is faced with similar percentages, only now curiosity is replaced with need, and the fear is fear of change.

I have to admit myself that although I felt it was a good idea to reassure the customer, I never really pushed that hard to get others to do it— until I spoke at the Baltimore Hostage Negotiation Seminar. A comment that day changed my tune.

It was a large seminar of about a thousand participants. There were hostage negotiators, SWAT team members, police officers, and rescue professionals. If they carried a badge, they were there. Occasionally I suggest to groups that they might want to reassure their customers after a commitment has been made, and today happened to be one of those days.

After I made my suggestion, a police officer walked up to a microphone to address the audience:

Mr. Jolles, I happen to agree with your suggestion. Two months ago, I was on the phone communicating with a suspect for almost forty hours. It took me twenty hours, and I got the children out of the house. It took me ten more hours, and I got the wife out of the house. Ten hours later, I was able to get the suspect out of the house. However, as you put it, my highest realistic level of commitment was getting this person to come out, but with his gun. My last words to him were, "Just go slow."

The suspect stepped out of the house onto the porch. I moved up the driveway slowly with the SWAT by my side. The suspect looked out, he looked back, he looked out, he looked back. Then he blew his head off.

I spent forty hours on the phone with this person and can tell you that this was not the kind of person who intended to come out and put on a show. It was an emotional moment. He changed his mind. I always wonder, to this day, if I could have handled this differently. I wonder, if the last words out of my mouth had been, "You are doing the right thing. I will be here every step of the way and everything I promised you will happen, I can assure you," whether that could have saved his life. I believe it could.

This was an emotional moment within the seminar. I never again made this step to the closing process optional. Just in case you are curious, these are the times your local sales trainer inserts an emergency break. The room was just a little bit heavy at the time the tension was high, and the audience needed air.

The message is clear: Your customer will reconsider and will wonder.

People fear change. I am also assuming that the solution you recommended may very well cost this customer more, not less, than he is already paying. Give customers something to think about when they reconsider. Let them hear your voice in their mind telling them, "The hard part is over. Now comes the part where I get to prove to you just what our company can do. Congratulations. You made a wise decision."

## SOME FINAL THOUGHTS

Now that the "big, bad close" is finally on the table, I hope that you can see how the close truly can be the easiest part of the sale. It does not mean the close stage should be any less important than the other stages of the selling cycle. It does mean, however, that it is simply one of many logical steps within the process of persuasion.

With the summary close now broken down into four manageable steps, I hope this portion of selling no longer gives you unnecessary anxiety. Here are some additional ideas to add polish to what I hope will be a stellar finish to your sale.

### WATCH YOUR TONE

By tone, I am referring to not just what you are saying, but how you are saying it. Up to now, I have discussed only the words used in closing. There is a lot of emotion involved when a customer makes this final decision, and much of it is affected by the way you say things.

Marshall McLuhan once performed a study that shed a great deal of light on this issue. He studied the emotional side of communication and its impact on us all. His study focused on the question, "Emotionally, what is more important: what you say or how you say it?"

The results were significant. He found that a mere 7 percent of our message is affected by the words we use; 38 percent of the message is affected by body language, movement, and other nonverbal cues—all nonverbal cues *except* facial expression. He felt that would be significant enough to remain in a category by itself. He was right. He discovered that a staggering 55 percent of the emotional impact of a message is affected by facial expression! Together, facial expression and body language—the "how"—are responsible for 93 percent of the emotional impact of a message. When you ask someone for his business, this is an emotional moment.

These numbers should not be surprising. Think back on your childhood. I can certainly remember being told to do something and blandly muttering, "Okay, I'll do it." What followed was an occasional kick in the rear. As if in shock that I had been found out, I would protest: "What was that for? I *said* I would do it!" We can all remember those famous words that followed: "It wasn't what you said. It was how you said it."

The moral of this message, as it relates to closing, is to watch your nonverbal cues, particularly your facial expression, when you are asking customers for a commitment. If you look unsure, they will feel unsure. If you look confident, they will feel confident.

Another area to be careful about is your selection of words. Your request for commitment should be short and to the point. Remember that you have just finished your product recommendation, which allowed you to go over your solution point by point. There is certainly no need to go over features or long-winded explanations of your recommendation again.

## START WITH THESE THREE WORDS

When you really look at what gives salespeople the most difficulty in closing, what you see might surprise you. You would think it would be "asking for commitment" or "maintaining confidence," but that is not the case. The most difficult aspect of closing for most who sell is the transition to the close.

Salespeople frequently have difficulty winding up the sale because they are uncomfortable moving into the close. Let's assume you are prepared to use the three trial closes located within the Customer Centered Selling process, so knowing when to close is no longer a problem. The problem now centers around how to guide your customer into the close smoothly.

My suggestion is to move into your close with your choice of the following three-word transitions:

Seller:    Don't you agree . . .

OR

Seller:    Wouldn't you agree . . .

Starting your close in this manner also makes your restatement of benefits more of a question. This will allow you to combine the listing of benefits and confirmation all in the same sentence.

Starting your close with one of those two simple transitions accomplishes two tasks: Not only are you moving smoothly into your close, you are simplifying the summary close as well. That's *my* kind of transition.

## HANDLE THE TRANSFER

One of the biggest objections that many salespeople face is the transferring of the customer's account from one company to another. The most frustrating aspect of this objection is that rarely will the customer voice his concern. Instead, the objection is usually vague and unclear.

Customers have difficulties because they are uncomfortable with telling their existing salesperson they have decided no longer to do business with him. No wonder this can be awkward. Often the customer feels guilty. Although there is most likely no real attachment, there is at least a history that has been perpetuated by one or two obligatory lunches each year.

My suggestion to you is to try to feel out in the research stage how attached your customer is to his current salesperson. Take note of it, and if you sense an attachment, try this line in your "ask for commitment" within your summary close:

Seller:    I would be more than happy to handle all the transfer procedures with your existing sales rep.

Using this committing question within your close addresses the potential objection before it is even voiced. Why not take an active approach and eliminate any embarrassment your customer might feel? This will not only reduce the chances of fighting a vague objection, it will aid in putting your customer at ease.

## THERE IS NOTHING ELSE!

There are many ways to move from step to step within the Customer Centered Selling process. Your choice of transitions will ultimately depend on your personal style. In the close stage, however, my recommendation is to be cautious. When you use a transition like, "Don't you agree . . ." you are not exactly presenting the customer with an open question. I am not even sure if I could call this transition a closed question. This recommended transition appears more like a stranglehold question!

"Don't you agree" does not provide a whole lot of options for the customer. It is rather difficult for your customer to say no, and that is no accident. You have earned the right to ask for your customer's commitment. *You* must agree this is a fair question. Customers fear change, and, as you have probably learned from your own buying habits, they welcome an opportunity to stall.

There is no need to hem and haw. There is nothing else. It bothers me a great deal when I'm working with a salesperson who has meticulously worked his way to the close and then takes the pressure off the customer. Here is a classic exchange:

Seller:     Don't you agree that buying this product from my company not only will provide you with the service you are looking for, but give you a greater return as well?

Customer:   Well, uh, yes.

Seller:     Great! Is there anything else?

When a customer agrees that you have addressed all of his needs, *do not* challenge the customer to think of anything else. Look him in the eye, and go for it!

## PRACTICE, PRACTICE, PRACTICE

When all is said and done, one of the best ways to display confidence and conquer the close is to practice. This is necessary to avoid any show of tension on your part. Too much is riding on how these closing words come out.

You would think that most salespeople would practice their technique for asking a customer to make a commitment. Not true. I venture to guess that at least 80 percent of the salespeople I have worked with have had no special approach to closing or favorite line used to ask for a customer's commitment. Ironically, of salespeople I have polled, at least three people will tell me they have a favorite pen or a favorite pad of paper for every one who tells me they have a favorite way to close.

The solution? Write it out and practice it. I am not a big fan of scripts, but there are exceptions to the rule, and here is one of them. I am really referring to the transition into the close and the actual words used in asking for a commitment.

You don't need to reinvent the wheel each time you ask for your customer's commitment. The process does not change. You merely need to practice what you believe are the most natural words for you.

## PICK UP THE PHONE

The next issue that needs to be dealt with when discussing the aspects of closing is a sensitive one. I am not going to ask you what you do when you make a sale. Rather, I want to ask, What do you do when you *do not* make a sale?

Chapter 19, designed to assist you in handling objections, is right around the corner, and I expect it will be of great value. However, no matter how talented you are as a salesperson, no one has a 100 percent closing ratio, so the question remains: Assuming you have done all that you can do, whether over the telephone, face to face, or in a letter, what happens after the rejection?

I recommend one last telephone call. This call is in no way designed to convince the customer to give you one more chance. The customer is going to be wary of any potential "sales tricks," so be cautious as to how you word what I am about to say.

I recommend that you use this call to thank the customer for the opportunity to work for his business. Remind him that you intend to be in your business for a long time to come, and ask what you could have done better so that you can improve. Finally, ask the customer if it would be all right to call on him in six months (or whatever else you feel is a reasonable period of time relating to what you sell) to follow up on his account.

Making this call also helps to give you a head start the next time you call on this same customer. By establishing a follow-up time, you have essentially defeated your most difficult nemesis: the person at the front desk, known as a "screen," whose job it is to keep salespeople away from "decision makers."

Do not think that a letter can accomplish what this telephone call does. It does not. Everyone sends an informal note to the customer, but rarely does this customer get the kind of call I have been describing. It takes courage and will earn you respect in the customer's eyes.

You are perhaps the biggest beneficiary when picking up the telephone and making a call to the customer. No one wants to address this point, but it needs to be acknowledged:

▶ *Rejection is the silent killer of many salespeople.*

Rejection takes its toll on us all and probably does more to keep people out of selling than any other factor. Most salespeople are competitive in nature, and no matter how long you work in the selling business, "no" still hurts.

What is amazing about asking a customer what you could have done differently to have earned his business is his response: "It wasn't you." I have used this process for years, and these are the three words I almost always hear.

Many salespeople will tell you that it does not matter to them whose fault the loss of a sale is, but do not believe them. It is a blow to one's ego to lose, and it hurts. It is surprising how good it does feel to hear that it was nothing that you did personally.

What follows is really crucial. Was it a misunderstanding? Clear it up on the next call. Was it price? Work on your analysis stage probing sequence (and learn how to handle price in the objection handling chapter). Most important, this is not the time to fix it. No matter what it is, work to never make that same mistake again, but trying to fix it now is a waste of time and will only upset the clients more. It's over.

Picking up the telephone and calling the customer after you have lost a sale can be one of the most difficult calls you will ever make. The rewards, however, far outweight the negatives. The feedback you receive will be far better than any that a sales trainer like me can offer. This newfound respect from your customer, feedback, and a head start for the next time you meet with this client would not be possible by simply writing a letter. When you do make that call, don't forget one last thing: Make sure you listen.

## GO OUT ON THE TOWN

As I finish this section dealing with closing and coping with rejection, here is one final word of advice: Keep things in perspective. The close brings out a lot of fear in many salespeople because it represents the moment of truth: whether your idea will be accepted or rejected. Your reaction to winning and losing should not be all that different.

As a salesman myself, I am highly motivated by reward. When I make a good sale—I mean a *good* sale—I like to celebrate. This often means a trip to my favorite restaurant or eighteen holes on a warm day. These rewards are sweet because they symbolize victory.

These victories are not the only time I reward myself. When I work very hard on a good sale and lose, having done everything that I could do, including maintaining my discipline within the sales process, I still take myself out for that special meal.

Maybe this is just a simple case of losing the battle but winning the war. Most people I know have little trouble winning. The trouble emerges when they lose. When you lose, my suggestion is to pick yourself up, dust yourself off, ask yourself what you would do differently given the chance to do it again, and get it behind you. Lobster works for me every time.

North Carolina's Dean Smith, one of the most successful college basketball coaches in the history of the sport (and coming from a Maryland Terrapin alumnus, that's not easy to admit), said it best: "If you make every game a life and death proposition, you're going to have problems. For one thing, you'll be dead a lot."

•  •  •

There is no real secret behind the art of closing. There is no need to obsess on closing or to fear closing. Earning the right to ask customers for a commitment by following logically their *decision cycle* should provide you with all the confidence you need. Don't forget that your trial closes test your work along the way, and closing will be a mystery no more!

## TEST YOUR COMPREHENSION: CLOSE STAGE

Once again, go back to the four case studies. Here is your chance to test what you have learned. Write out the four steps within the summary close for each scenario. Then write an answer that would apply to the product or idea you are trying to sell. On the next page, I give you my suggestions for each of the companies outlined in the case studies.

### PJ INVESTING CORPORATION

_____

_____

_____

_____

### TO CLEAN A ROOM

_____

_____

_____

_____

### A TON OF TALENT, A LACK OF TRUST

_____

_____

_____

_____

**EVERY MOTORS, LTD.**

_____

_____

_____

_____

**YOUR OWN SCENARIO**

_____

_____

_____

_____

# SUGGESTED ANSWERS TO TEST YOUR COMPREHENSION: CLOSE STAGE

Given the four scenarios, here are my suggested answers incorporating the four recommended steps within the summary close. See how closely they resemble the answers you gave.

### PJ INVESTING CORPORATION

1. Wouldn't you agree that by allowing our company to handle your investing needs, you are going to be getting everything you said you were looking for?
2. When would you like to arrange for your first transaction?
3. I will leave you with these brochures, and we'll get started by . . .
4. Mr. Bracken, the hard part's over. Now comes the easy part: allowing us to

prove to you that your investment needs are in good hands. Thank you for your trust.

## TO CLEAN A ROOM

1. Don't you agree that by cleaning up your room once and for all, you're going to be able to find things easier and be better organized?
2. How about starting right now?
3. Let's start by going to the store to pick out your boxes. How about a Daddy inspection once a week so I can help you to stay on top of it?
4. Danny, I think you're going to love the change you have agreed to make. I'll certainly be here to help you out along the way. I love you, pal!

## A TON OF TALENT, A LACK OF TRUST

1. So, with the added training you're not only going to be in better shape gaining the leadership roles you wanted, you'll be taking quicker steps to advancement. Do you agree?
2. There is a course starting next month and one the following week. Which one would you like to sign up for?
3. We'll start by contacting the personnel office to make your request known. Then we'll . . .
4. You know, I think you are going to love the training as well as the doors it potentially may open. I'm looking forward to having you on the team and being your manager.

## EVERY MOTORS, LTD.

1. Do you agree that buying your car from our dealership will not only provide you with the staff accountability you desire, but the key automobile features as well?
2. I would love to have your business.
3. Let's step over here and go over some financial information.
4. I just wanted to congratulate you on a wise purchase decision. You are going to love that car and our dealership as well. Thank you for your business.

Look over the answers provided, as well as your own, and put them through the test:

- Is there a question confirming the benefits of your solution?
- Is the committing question short and to the point?
- Are the questions used close questions?
- Is there a positive finish to the summary close?

# SEVENTEEN

# THE MAINTENANCE STAGE

## RESTARTING THE PROCESS

Character is the ability to carry out a good resolution long after the ex-
citement of the moment has passed.

—*Cavett Robert*

With the sale complete and the customer committed to your solution, the process is by no means finished. Quite the contrary. The process is actually fairly close to starting all over again. Respecting the steps within the maintenance stage will improve your chances of being there when the process begins again.

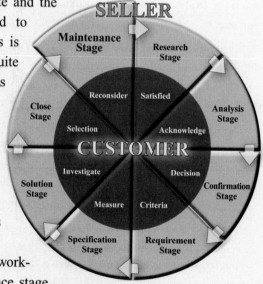

There is no magic to working through the maintenance stage.
If your selling process was effective, the real
key is to remain disciplined in your approach to monitoring your sale.

Remember, if you are not watching your customer, someone else probably is.

Creating a process around the monitoring of your sale is not easy. Here the solution you sold heavily affects your follow-up and your approach to the maintenance of your customer.

With this in mind, I offer three final steps within the selling cycle that are fairly generic and should apply to whatever solution you and your customer have agreed to.

# STEP 1. REVIEW LOGISTICS

Working with salespeople and finding out how they follow up with their customers, I found surprising similarities in how they went about monitoring their customers. Two of the three steps within the maintenance stage were being implemented. The problem was that this first step was not one of them.

If you look back within the close stage, you may recall that one of the last steps you completed dealt with the discussion of logistics. This represented the first real promise you made to the customer. I truly believe that your success often depends on your taking care of what many may perceive as "the little things." Here is an example of what the first step would sound like:

Seller:   It is a pleasure to meet with you again, Ms. Johannsen. I believe it has been about a month since you made your purchase from my company. Nancy, I am anxious to hear how successful this solution has been for you, but I would first like to hear how we did implementing this program. Was the delivery made on time? Were our people courteous? Was the training we provided adequate?

There are only really two scenarios that may occur when you revisit a customer and review the logistics. The first, and hopefully the more common, one would be to hear that everything was handled fine. This will certainly promote a feeling of goodwill and get the meeting off to a good start. These questions demonstrate a real commitment on your part to satisfy the customer completely.

The second scenario is not as pleasant. For a moment, assume that the implementation of your solution did *not* go well. I am not going to tell you that you won't be blasted by the customer with your questions here because you will. What I will tell you is this: Your customer will go a whole lot easier on you if *you* are the one to bring this topic up.

Of the salespeople I watch, 99.9 percent want to start their follow-up immediately with customers by asking about their solution. It is natural to want to hear how well your idea is working, but think for a minute: Imagine how rude it appears to the customer for you to be gloating about your great solution when the customer is stewing about the rude treatment received during the delivery of product.

Regardless of the scenario, I have never had a customer appear in the least bit put off by my questioning. You should be the one to initiate this conversation so you will be in position to check your solution. Your first follow-up call is a "can't miss" maintenance step that will certainly add polish to your professional approach to customer care.

## STEP 2. REVIEW THE SOLUTION

With your review logistics step behind you, it is time to see just how well your solution is working. Hopefully, the solution you recommended was a sound one, and this portion of the maintenance stage will flow smoothly. This is not to say that it is now time to abandon the selling process that got you here, however.

It would be a waste simply to ask the customer, "So what do you think?" You sold this solution based on an agreed-on, carefully measured list of needs. Start your review right there:

Seller:   I'm pleased that everything went smoothly from the logistical end of this purchase. Now let's talk about the solution itself. Your most important need was to be able to understand better the investment products you were purchasing. Has the documentation we have been providing you met with your expectations?

One by one, and in order of priority within the review solution step, I recommend you check with your customer. Be prepared to address possible objections and sharpen your listening skills. Considering that the customer committed to a solution that most likely was influenced by your particular strengths, I would not anticipate major problems—but you never know. Nonetheless, I would still rather be the one taking the heat and working to resolve these concerns with my customer. My only alternative is for my competition to do it for me. Something tells me my answer will be a better one.

## STEP 3. REVIEW THE CHANGE

Customer satisfaction is my ultimate goal during the maintenance stage. That's my story, and I'm sticking with it. However, this stage also represents a golden opportunity for the seller in two different areas.

First, by constantly monitoring your customer's situation for any change you are staying on top of any potential problems that may appear on the horizon. Remember that one of the best ways to create change and sell this customer in the first place is to find one thing, just one thing, that the current salesperson did not find. Putting that one thing through the probing sequence may very well have accounted for your sale. Being proactive in your approach to change may spare you the loss of your customer.

The second benefit of reviewing the change with your customer relates to the cyclical nature of the process you have learned. Change that may seem insignificant to the customer may allow you the opportunity to begin the selling process once again. A seemingly insignificant change, like the addition of office staff or the expansion of a customer's business, represents the kind of change you and your product line dream of. Into the research stage we go, *background probes* being launched, and away we go.

## SOME FINAL THOUGHTS

The maintenance stage represents a rare opportunity for the seller and customer to sit back and analyze the solutions, as well as future needs. Assuming all has gone well, the mood is usually relaxed. However, as with most other stages within the selling cycle, there are some subtleties that need to be addressed.

## TAKE IT SERIOUSLY

Too often I see salespeople caught up in such a frenzy to make the sale that they lose the discipline required within the maintenance stage. This stage within the selling cycle really boils down to trust: Can the customer trust you and your company?

Always take this issue seriously because the consequences of broken trust are grim. Once trust is broken, reputation is sure to suffer. And, as many of you have found out in your own lives with people you have cared about, once trust is lost, it is nearly impossible to gain it back again.

Maintain your discipline and continue to work with the customers you sell. It may not mean immediate gain financially, but it's the right thing to do. Do it for your customers who trusted that they not only bought a solution, they bought you as well. If not for your customers, do it for yourself. If not for yourself, do it for the rest of us who are selling and working to clean up a sometimes tarnished image within the selling profession.

## GET THOSE REFERRALS

If I have not convinced you to work hard to make sure your customers are satisfied within the maintenance stage because it's the right thing to do, let me try appealing to your sense of greed. Although I vowed not to attempt to offer prospecting advice, I can't resist a quick discussion covering the use of referrals.

In my mind, for most who sell, referrals are the best source of future prospects. There is little controversy here. If there is a controversy, it would center on when to ask for these referrals. I know you will not be surprised to find I have a rather strong opinion on this issue.

The question is whether you should ask for referrals in your close or when you come back to follow up with your client. I have always felt blessed to have sold for two companies that were highly respected within their industries. I knew the hardest part of my job was to sell the products. Once they were sold, I never questioned the products or service from either

New York Life or Xerox. They would deliver. But if I had no intention of returning or felt my solutions would be less than adequate, I probably would have asked my customers for referrals in my close. Waiting first to deliver a policy, a fax machine, or a training program that I knew would meet my customer's expectations allowed me to keep my first promise with the customer. To me, this represents an ideal time to ask for referrals.

Whether you ask for referrals during the close stage or the maintenance stage is up to you. You *must* ask for them, however. This is not debatable. *When* to ask for referrals is debatable, and I have given you my opinion. In either case, these referrals will most likely turn out to be some of the easiest prospects to weave into the Customer Centered Selling process.

## WHO DO YOU KNOW . . .

Many salespeople will not argue about the issue of whether to ask for referrals. Asking for referrals begins to resemble closing a customer. Both share the same battle cries: "It's easy," and "Just do it."

There is, however, a right way and a wrong way to ask for referrals. I would guess that 95 percent of the salespeople I work with use the wrong way, probably because of the way it is taught. We tell salespeople to go out and get referrals, but we forget to tell them how. Here is the standard, classic referral approach:

Salesperson:     I just wanted you to know how much I appreciated working with you. I intend on staying in this business for some time to come and would appreciate any help you could provide. Do you know of anyone else I could talk to that would need my services?

There is nothing inherently disturbing about this example. Given the percentage of salespeople I hear this from, I would venture to guess this probably resembles the type of request that you would make. The only problem with this approach is that the results are extremely limited.

Let me tell you what customers typically say when asked for referrals this way, and see if this sounds familiar to you:

Customer:    Gee, let me think for a minute. Well, I can't come up with any names right now, but if you leave me your card, I'm sure I will come up with a name or two.

Does this exchange bring back some memories? What a shame the customer can't think of any names for you. What makes this most frustrating is, I am assuming, he truly wants to provide names. The problem is, you didn't help him.

Think for a moment, and try to remember the last good-size party you attended. During that evening, you came in contact with maybe thirty different people. How many of these people came up and asked you if you knew where to buy some life insurance? How many of them asked you for the name of a good copier salesperson, an accountant, a realtor, or a lawyer? All those potential clients just waiting to talk with you. How could you fail? To think, you came in contact with all those people, and you could not provide a salesperson with one referral!

Sometimes when I look back on my New York Life training, I am not sure I am as kind as I could be. They did not teach me many skills I felt I should have been taught; however, they did teach me how to get a referral. I can assure you that New York Life *never* taught us to ask a customer if he knew of anyone who needed insurance. What New York Life taught was much more helpful than that. New York Life taught me to ask, "Who do you know?" This simple little statement helped me net some of my most successful referrals.

Rather than asking customers if they knew anyone who needed insurance, I was taught to break that statement down a bit. Here is a series of questions that would do just that:

"I just wanted you to know how much I appreciated working with you. I intend on staying in this business for some time to come and would appreciate any help you could provide."
"Who do you know who just got married?"
"Who do you know who just had a baby?"
"Who do you know who just bought a house?"
"Who do you know who just started a business?"

The answers to these questions are an insurance agent's referrals. You would be amazed at how many customers who can't think of referrals *can* all of a sudden start spitting out names. The questions vary depending on what you are selling, but the concept does not. Break your questions down, and help your customers to help you.

In case you are tired of excuses and would like some *real* referrals from your customer, give them a helping hand. Ask them, "Who do you know?"

## BREAK YOUR RULES, NOT YOUR PROMISES

In sales, we often get caught up emotionally in the drive to close a sale. During this process, promises are made. Assume that these promises are made in good faith. For just a moment, I would like to look at what happens when some of these promises are broken.

Breaking a promise to a customer is inexcusable and obviously makes customers unhappy. TARP (Technical Assistance Research Programs) provides a dramatic picture of what happens when customers are unhappy.

The average unhappy customer will tell about eleven to twenty other customers of their displeasure. That should concern us all. One of the most common reasons customers state they are unhappy with salespeople, surprisingly enough, is not necessarily related to whether the solution works. Customers state they are unhappy because of promises that were made between the salesperson and themselves that were broken.

One way of avoiding this issue lies within the Customer Centered Selling process. When you work with the customer to develop decision-making requirements and then transfer those requirements into specifications, misunderstandings can often be avoided.

This is by no means a guarantee. No matter how hard you try, misunderstandings occur. The question then becomes, What next? One of the key deciding factors in awarding Xerox the Malcolm Baldrige Quality Award was the company's reaction to a product that did not work properly. In my mind, this is often the true test of a company's commitment to its customers.

In meeting these commitments, sometimes rules have to be broken. I was inspired by an article I read about Southwest Airlines and how it views this issue. Its philosophy centers on keeping promises even if that means breaking some rules. The story dealt with a pilot whose plane had pushed back from the terminal for an on-time departure. As the plane was beginning to move toward the runway, the pilot saw a passenger inside the terminal frantically waving his arms, pleading with the pilot to return. The airline rules were straightforward: "Once the airline door is closed, the airplane is considered gone." That was the rule.

The pilot chose to break the rule. Pulling the airplane back into the terminal took all of five minutes. In doing so this pilot broke the rule but saved a passenger. Interestingly enough, the pilot was not reprimanded in any way by Southwest Airlines for his actions. Coincidentally, when it comes to airline preference, Southwest Airlines seems to be at the head of the pack in survey after survey.

Paying attention to your customers is critical to achieving long-term success. TARP would support this belief as well. Certainly problems will occur from time to time between you and your customer. What amazes me are the numbers provided that support the quick repair of these problems. TARP statistics state that when a customer is unhappy and the problem is then repaired, 60 percent of these customers can be saved.

Saving over half your customers who are unhappy is an appealing thought, but the news gets even better. TARP goes on to state that if the problems are repaired quickly, the percentage of customers saved jumps to 95 percent!

As many of us learned early and chanted often, "Rules are meant to be broken." Well, this might have represented a belief in a more rebellious stage of life, yet in this portion of the selling cycle, perhaps this should be our motto once again. You need to consider reason and logic, but when it comes to keeping a customer happy and avoiding broken promises, consider breaking the rules first.

The maintenance stage represents an opportunity to ensure customer satisfaction and potentially increase selling opportunities. The three steps suggested touch lightly on a game plan for you to follow. A lot of the follow-up you perform will depend on what you are selling and to whom you sell it. Despite these issues, plan your time wisely, and never underestimate the power of the customer care that is a major theme of your movements within this stage.

# TEST YOUR COMPREHENSION: MAINTENANCE STAGE

Once again, go back to the four case studies (Chapter 9). Here is your chance to test what you have learned. Write out the three steps within the maintenance stage for each scenario. Then write out answers that would apply to the product or idea you are trying to sell. On the next page, I give you my suggestions for each of the companies outlined in the case studies.

## PJ INVESTING CORPORATION

_____

_____

_____

_____

## TO CLEAN A ROOM

_____

_____

_____

_____

## A TON OF TALENT, A LACK OF TRUST

_____

_____

_____

_____

EVERY MOTORS, LTD.

_____

_____

_____

_____

YOUR OWN SCENARIO

_____

_____

_____

_____

# SUGGESTED ANSWERS TO TEST YOUR COMPREHENSION: MAINTENANCE STAGE

Given the four scenarios, here are my suggested answers incorporating the three steps within the maintenance stage. See how closely they resemble the answers you gave.

## PJ INVESTING CORPORATION

1. I am anxious to go over some of the programs we set up, but first I would like to make sure you are satisfied with the way you have been treated so far.
2. Fine. Now let's go over how these funds are performing.
3. Have there been any changes that relate to your investing that have occurred since we last met?

## TO CLEAN A ROOM

1. Wow! I can't believe it's been a month. I want to hear how it's going with you, but first I want to make sure I've done my part in the promises I made to you.
2. That's great, and thank you. I've really tried to get out of your way on this one. Now, how are boxes and other ideas we came up with working out?

3. What changes, if any, have you experienced since we set these ideas into motion? Did anything change since we started the big clean-up?

## A TON OF TALENT, A LACK OF TRUST

1. It's good to sit down and meet with you again. I am looking forward to hearing all about the training you attended, but first I want to know how the logistics worked out. Was the program itself organized properly?
2. Now tell me about the course itself.
3. Have there been any changes with you or your work group since the last time we met?

## EVERY MOTORS, LTD.

1. Nice to see you again. I am very much looking forward to hearing about your car, but first I would like to hear what our report card looks like, starting with how well we handled ourselves with the execution of this purchase.
2. Wonderful! How is the car running?
3. Have there been any changes that would relate to the business we have performed since our last meeting?

Look over the answers provided, as well as your own, and put them through the test:

- Does the first step avoid talking about solutions and focus on implementation instead?
- Is there a question that relates to the agreed-on solution?
- Is there a question that relates to customer changes?

PART III

# THE
# SUPPORT

# EIGHTEEN

# THE OPENING TACTIC

Barriers are invitations to courage.

*—Anonymous*

**A**s the shampoo commercial once pointed out, "You only have one chance to make a first impression." When opening up a sales call, that one chance usually boils down to about forty-five seconds. These are precious seconds; handle them carefully.

You might ask why you are learning this process at the end of the sales model rather than the beginning. After all, you use the opening tactic at the beginning of your sales call, not at the end. To answer this question, think of the opening as a kind of topic sentence. For those of you who have forgotten, a topic sentence is intended to act almost like an overview of the paper you are writing. Also think back to the agonizing hours you spent in school trying to write these topic sentences. Your English teacher told you that once the topic sentence and opening paragraph were written, the rest of the paper was easy. Your teacher was *partially* right.

Now I'm going to tell you something your high school English teacher did not tell you. The reason that you agonized over the writing of this topic sentence is this: It's difficult to tell someone what you are going to tell him when you don't know what you are going to tell him! I finally learned it's a whole lot easier to write the paper and then go back and create the opening. At this point, I know exactly what I am going to talk about and how I am going to talk about it.

The rationale for holding the opening back until the end of the model is the same. You now know the body of the paper, which, for you, are the steps within the Customer Centered Selling model. Now you are in position to connect where you will be going and how you will be getting there and provide an overview for your customer.

The opening tactic I will be showing you is flexible and can be applied to the opening of any call. The verbiage will change, but the process will not. For the purposes of this chapter, however, I will be mainly tracking a cold call (initial call) appointment because it is the most difficult opening to manage. The rejection rate is extremely high, and if I can make you comfortable in this stage of the selling cycle, the rest of the opening scenarios will not be difficult. From time to time, I will refer to other opening scenarios that are not cold calls, to show the flexibility of this model. At the end of the chapter, in the Test Your Comprehension section, I provide a variety of openings aimed at sales calls in different stages.

Sometimes when I work with Jenes teams I refer to the opening tactic as the "search for the magic pill." This is how many view the opening tactic, so I will deal with this topic first. Many salespeople believe that some simple words, much like a magic pill, will allow them to see all prospects, no matter how cold the prospect might be. There ain't no such pill. However, there are solid strategies that allow you the best opportunity to speak with a customer. When working with the opening tactic, remember that the intent is to work within the odds and play the best odds possible.

Let's face it. If you can't get past the opening, the Customer Centered Selling process is useless.

With the opening tactic put in perspective, let me show you the simplest approach I know to get customers to allow you into their lives.

## STEP 1. INTRODUCTION

The first step is basic. Telling a customer who you are and what company you represent is not rocket science. Surprisingly enough, there are a few factors to keep in mind nevertheless. For instance, how much do you want your customer to know? Perhaps you are the largest dealership in the area. You could make this part of your introduction. I am not so sure I would make it part of mine. *Customer Centered Selling* teaches you this important Rob's Rule:

▶ *The most powerful benefits are the ones customers discover on their own.*

You could tell your customer of your company's size. I would rather get my customer to *want* a large dealership first.

Some salespeople tell me they envied my position as a salesman who represented Xerox. It is wonderful talking to customers cold and having them recognize my company, and I will not for a moment tell you I did not cherish what the name Xerox did for me as a salesperson. I will tell you, however, that this name did tip my hand a bit; that is, the moment I said the word *Xerox,* my customers knew a lot about me. For instance, they knew of the quality Xerox represents. They knew of the high cost Xerox also represents. Any and all possible objections my customer might have to Xerox and the Xerox solutions I would be providing were fair game.

When I sold for New York Life, I did not have to tip my hand as much. Selling group health insurance allowed me to broker with many companies. Although I usually sold New York Life, I did not lead with this company. This allowed me to operate more as a consultant than a company representative.

When you are taking a true consultative approach to selling, as Customer Centered Selling provides, it is more advantageous to you, the seller, not to tip your hand as to your solution within your opening. In some situations, this cannot be helped, but even in a worst-case scenario, take it easy and don't go into too much detail about how wonderful the company is that you represent. Using the Customer Centered Selling process will help to influence what your customer ends up needing. These customer needs should revolve around whatever your company specializes in.

# STEP 2. INITIAL BENEFIT STATEMENT

An initial benefit statement fills a very important need in the customer's eyes. It provides the customer with a WIFM, the acronym for "What's in it for me?" the single most important element of any opening.

To understand an initial benefit statement better, you need a quick lesson in human psychology. The simple truth is that most people in this world are greedy. Now this statement comes from Rob Jolles, one of the most optimistic people you will ever meet. Let me explain.

In the movie *Wall Street,* there's a famous scene where Gordon Gekko delivers his "greed is good" speech. I believe Gekko was right. Standing in front of a hostile crowd, he attempted to persuade a group of workers why his takeover bid was good for them. He appealed to their sense of greed. In the movie, he succeeded.

I happen to believe everyone is greedy, and I don't believe this is a bad thing. Your desire to be successful in your career is somewhat greedy, but also very necessary. Ask yourself why you bought this book. Was it because you felt sorry for me and no longer wanted my poor book to remain alone on the shelf you found it on? I doubt it (but thanks anyway). I believe you bought my book because you thought you could learn some ideas about selling to help make you more successful. Your definition of success may have little to do with money but may in fact, relate to happiness, personal satisfaction, or simply bettering yourself. I don't want to burst your bubble, but I would call that greed.

Please do not look on this as a negative comment on people. Actually, it is just the opposite. Once you understand that most people desire to be more successful, you also begin to realize how much easier they are to sell. Think of how difficult it would be to sell a widget to someone who could care less about his job, let alone about the success or failure of his purchase.

With your newfound knowledge about what is really important in an opening, look at this classic opening and you be the judge. As you read it, chant in your mind the following words: "What's in it for me, what's in it for me, what's in it for me."

Seller:   Hi there. I'm Rob Jolles from Jolles Associates, Inc., and I have
          been assigned as your new sales rep. Our company has just intro-
          duced some brand-new products. Would it be okay for me to take
          a few minutes and tell you about them today?

Well, what's in it for you? If you were dying for a lecture on product,
today is your lucky day. Otherwise this opening is most likely going to
meet with the two-letter word that most of us in sales are not fond of: No.

What if we change this opening around a bit? Here is an example with
just the first two elements of the opening tactic incorporated:

Seller:   Hi there. I'm Rob Jolles from Jolles Associates, Inc. We have
          been successful working with other companies similar to yours,
          and in many instances we have found innovative approaches to
          increasing sales.

Interested? I hope so. The challenge of writing an effective initial benefit statement is to provide just enough information without giving away
your key solution. I like to compare this challenge to what you would read
on the outside of a book jacket. I do not know of any jackets that reveal the
climax of the book; what you read on the outside of a book is intended to
entice you. Interested in finding out more about this particular topic? It
will cost you $25.95. Please pay at the front counter.

Enticing a customer with a well-worded WIFM sometimes requires a
rather creative balancing act. The example of the WIFM that I provided
just above ("We have been successful working with other companies similar to yours, and in many instances we have found innovative approaches
to increasing sales") might meet with the following reaction from your
customer:

Customer:   Wow! Sounds great. Tell me about some of these approaches!

Obviously you got your customer's attention using the initial benefit
statement. The bad news is that you may have done too good a job getting

his attention. Not to worry. Based on the example provided, if a customer were to ask what some of your solutions were that you provided, respond in this way:

Seller:     We have numerous approaches that are specifically dependent on customer needs. Rather than taking your time by lecturing you on all these approaches to training, I think you will find it more worthwhile if I can learn about what you do and how you do it. This information will put me in a position to recommend only the solutions that best fit your needs.

In other words, "I'm not telling!"

It is not a question of bad luck for most salespeople who have difficulty opening up a sales call. It is a question of appealing to your customer's desire to be more successful. Try to figure out what would be an effective initial benefit statement for your customer, and see if you don't get a few more appointments.

## STEP 3. PROCESS

Often when you appear in front of a customer as a salesperson, you are guilty until proved innocent. For instance, your customer may have last met with a salesperson who did not ask any questions and "feature dumped" (lectured you on feature after feature) on the product. It is only natural that he will assume the worst of you. This may not be fair, but it is reality.

Therefore, if the initial benefit statement is the most critical step of the opening tactic, the process is certainly a strong second. The customer needs to know in the first forty-five seconds how you intend to proceed, and that is the exact intent of the process step within your opening.

Starting in high school or perhaps earlier, most of us have heard the advice, "Tell them what you are going to tell them, tell them, then tell them what you told them." The process allows you to "tell them what you are going to tell them." The process step takes on even greater importance when you consider what you have learned through the Customer Centered Selling process. For instance, by focusing on the customer, you have learned how critical it is to listen and ask questions early on in the selling cycle. It is not possible for a customer to read your mind and understand your intentions.

Telling the customer up front that you intend to listen to him and ask questions sets a completely different tone from what most customers are accustomed to. Why would you want to keep this a secret? Here is an example of the process step within an initial appointment:

Seller:   Hi there. I'm Rob Jolles from Jolles Associates, Inc. We have been successful working with other companies similar to yours, and in many instances we have found innovative approaches to increasing sales. What I would like to do today is simply learn more about your company. All I really need to do is ask you some questions. If there is a need for some of the approaches we have been using, I will make a recommendation. If not, I will be on my way.

You are in control of the process. If you intend to take notes—and I don't know how you will be able to apply the Customer Centered Selling process if you do not—all you need to do is ask. The only time a customer gets nervous about your taking notes is when you just whip out a pad and start writing.

Guilty until proved innocent? Fine. Clear the air up front and let your customer know exactly how you intend to proceed. This will eliminate many unspoken objections and prepare the customer for an intelligent and productive appointment.

## STEP 4. TIME

The intent of this step is to provide the customer with an exact sense of how long the meeting will take. It is simple and fast, but not without controversy.

The controversy lies in the perceived necessity of this step. I'll present both views. There is a strong argument against setting time within a sales call. Many in the hallowed halls of Xerox argued long and hard to eliminate this step entirely. Their arguments were strong. They would ask, "Why lock yourself into a specific time constraint when you could potentially be shortening your own call?" It is a simple question that raises a very good point. Often you will be eliminating your own chances for a longer, more complete sales call. Argument made and understood.

The other side of the argument is even more basic. If you were to eliminate time, you would be forced to say things like, "Can I have a few minutes of your time?" Remember that the process step, preceding this step, makes the point that in sales you are guilty until proved innocent. With this in mind, you must ask yourself while you are thinking like a buyer, what does a "few minutes" from a salesperson mean to you?

Most customers will not go into detail about the last time a salesperson said "only a couple minutes" were needed. They will not tell you how they squirmed in their chairs trying to figure out a way to end the meeting. All you will end up hearing is, "Gee, we're kind of busy."

The bottom line is this: If you can't get an appointment with a customer, nothing else matters. I am not thrilled at shortening my call either, but for the more difficult calls, the most important issue is that the customer agree to meet with you. The actual length of time will vary greatly and become dependent on a few things. For example, the whole debate of time centers on the cold call or arrangements for the first appointment. This will usually be a shorter call.

Pick a scenario; it requires a certain length of time. Perhaps you are looking at a second appointment and will be presenting a solution. The time in this case may be a great deal longer. Still, as a courtesy to the customer, I recommend establishing an amount of time.

When you attend a company meeting that has been planned properly, time is most likely established and adhered to. This gives all those in attendance the feeling that they are attending a well-planned meeting. Why should your meeting with a customer not display the same type of professionalism?

Looking at the last step in the opening tactic, the question of whether you should establish a sense of time should not be the issue. The real question should focus on how much would be a reasonable amount of time. The answer will be based on where the customer is in the decision cycle, your goals within the selling process, specific solutions that you represent, and personality styles, to mention a few. As you become more and more comfortable with your product and your customers, the decision of a realistic time frame will work itself through.

# SOME FINAL THOUGHTS

The opening tactic offers a straightforward approach to starting a sales call. The importance of this tactic, however, should not be underestimated. Too much is at stake. As with many of the other steps within the selling cycle, there are a few subtleties that warrant your attention.

## CONSIDER THE DECISION LEVELS OF CUSTOMERS

When applying the initial benefit statement within the opening tactic, understand that everyone has a different decision level. Often the decision level reflects what the motivation to be successful looks like. There are three classic decision levels of customers that affect a customer's motivation within the initial benefit statement.

The first level of customers are the decision makers—those who are ultimately responsible for making the decisions. These customers are usually obsessed with one thing: making profit. No matter what you say, no matter what you do, the bottom line is usually tied to a question of profit. You should therefore gear your initial benefit statement to the bottom line—for example:

Seller:   We have been successful working with customers and finding creative approaches to increasing profit.

The second level of customers are called decision influencers—those who have a great deal of influence in making the selection decision. They have access to the decision maker and usually make a recommendation to the decision maker but do not actually make the final decision. Decision influencers usually are motivated not so much by profit but by how good or bad they may look in their decision maker's eyes. Your initial benefit statement would change to reflect this desire:

Seller:    Some of the solutions we have presented have literally revolu-
           tionized the speed and accuracy within these departments.

These successes are often perceived as successes for the person who
recommended the solution. That has a strong appeal to a decision influencer's ego.

The third and final level of customers are the end users—those who
ultimately will be using the solution you may be recommending. At Xerox,
these customers are those who actually operate the copier sold to their
company. I have found that most end users are not necessarily obsessed
with profit or looking good in the decision maker's eyes. The end users'
obsession is centered on themselves—for example:

Seller:    I think you will find that many of the solutions we could poten-
           tially recommend will not only make your work easier, but addi-
           tionally will make leaving the office at 5:00 P.M. a reality.

When preparing an initial benefit statement for your opening, consider
first who you are talking to, and aim your opening accordingly. It would be
as unrealistic for end users to concern themselves with company profits as
it would be for decision makers to concern themselves with whether an
end user gets out of the office at 5:00 P.M.

## CONSIDER WHERE YOU ARE IN THE SELLING CYCLE

The decision level of your customer should not be your only consideration.
Your actual position within the sales cycle will have a lot to do with how
you approach the use of the opening tactic as well. The wording of your
opening will change; the tactic will not.

In this chapter, I chose to focus heavily on the initial opening appointment. Many of you will not move through the entire sales cycle in one
appointment. This does not mean that you should abandon your opening
tactic for the next two or three meetings you might have with the customer.

Maybe it has been a week or two since you last met with your customer. Maybe your customer has become a little nervous. Maybe he has

spoken to his existing vendor, who was not as complimentary about you as you would have liked. You just don't know where your customer has been.

Start all your appointments by telling your customers what is in it for them. Even if the customer is excited to see you, put in an initial benefit statement. No customer is going to criticize you for being "too positive" in your approach to working with him. The issue of redoing the steps within your opening tactic also applies to process and time. Here is an example of an opening tactic for a sales call designed to recommend a solution.

Seller:    Hi, John, It's good to see you again. For those I have not had an opportunity to meet, I'm Rob Jolles with Jolles Associates, Inc. [*greeting*]

After my meeting with John, my company has put together some ideas that will have a dramatic impact on your ability to increase sales. [*initial benefit statement*]

Today what I would like to do is review the list of needs that John came up with and tell you how my company would address this list. [*process*]

This meeting should last only twenty-five minutes. [*time*]

The opening tactic is flexible and can be applied to just about any selling situation. It is not a straitjacket and can be modified according to the selling scenario. For instance, if you are convinced the customer knows your name (I advise watching that assumption), there is no need to give this customer your name again. Make sure you know where your customer is within the process, figure out what your game plan is, and develop your opening around the four basic steps.

## WATCH OUT FOR VOCAL RAPTURE

When you establish a set length for your sales call, take that time seriously. This is the first promise you have made to the customer, so often more is riding on this apparently insignificant issue than you might think.

My style has always been to take my watch off and place it on the desk where I can see it. I want my customer to understand that I too am taking this issue seriously. Too often I see salespeople fall prey to what I call "vocal rapture." The salesperson is on a roll and assumes that the customer is dying for him to continue. He begins to fall in love with his own voice. He is suffering from vocal rapture.

Do not be fooled. You made a commitment to the customer, and you need to honor it. A potential solution might be to ask this question:

Seller:    I promised that I would take only fifteen minutes, and I am just about out of time. Would you like to continue, or would you like to set another time when we can pick up on this conversation?

Hopefully you moved into your probing sequence within the analysis stage. If so, I think the customer will want you to continue. Perhaps you never even left the research stage. I still believe you earned the customer's trust. In any case—maybe I am just lucky—I have never had a customer tell me no to both alternatives outlined. Keep your promise, and avoid vocal rapture.

## WRITE IT OUT

I am not a fan of sales scripts. They do have their place, but for the most part they are too constricting. With that point made, let me offer an exception to the rule.

When you use the opening tactic, a lot is riding on these first forty-five seconds. I do not recommend searching for words here. Write out your opening, and then wordsmith it. This might take you an hour to create and might be one of the most frustrating hours of development you spend. When the dust clears, however, you will have the first forty-five seconds taken care of.

Your development does not stop here. Now you need to write out two or three more openings. One version can be used to open an appointment. Others can be created for product recommendation or even follow-up appointments. Once you have created a library of openings, you have one last step ahead of you: You must now memorize them and practice them. Say these openings so many times that they stop sounding memorized.

When it comes to using the opening tactic, practice makes perfect. Take a few minutes and choose your words carefully. These are words that will serve you well for years to come.

## KEEP YOUR SUCCESS IN PERSPECTIVE

When you use the opening tactic for a second or third appointment with a customer, chances are your choice of words will not necessarily make or break your appointment. What's at stake here is your professionalism. I have tried to tackle the initial call in this chapter and focus on the most difficult opening situations. The opening tactic will help you, but let's put your success in perspective.

I do not want to give you the impression that using the four steps within the opening tactic will magically open every door. This is not *The Wizard of Oz*, and you are not Dorothy at the gates of the Emerald City. I do not expect every professional screen to answer my opening by saying, "Well, why didn't you say so in the first place! That's a horse of a different color. Come on in!"

This is a numbers game. I speak with salespeople who tell me they are successful in about 10 percent of the initial-call openings. Great! Why not make it 20 percent? Maybe the approach you have been using has been successful 30 percent of the time. Maybe now that success will jump to 45 percent.

Using the opening tactic does not guarantee you success. But it does allow you to make the smartest decisions psychologically and play the best odds. Keep your results in perspective, and play the odds.

## WATCH OUT FOR THOSE BUZZ WORDS

Many salespeople create openings with good intentions, but they find their success is not improving as dramatically as they would like. Often their lack of success can be tracked to a few harmless buzzwords they are unaware of. For instance, when a salesperson says, "I want to tell you about . . . ," it sounds as if he is going to give a lecture to his customer. For an initial call, the salesperson should not "tell you" anything. I would prefer the salesperson "listen to you" instead. Another example is the use of the word *discuss*. Customers often interpret the word *discuss* to mean, "The salesperson is going to talk and I have to listen." I would prefer the salesperson "ask you questions and take notes" instead.

Sometimes buzz words can't be helped. Customers will not object to the words themselves; they will object to the *feelings* they elicit. This means you will not be aware of what really created the objection, which makes it a difficult objection to address. Watch your words, say what you mean, and you won't have to worry about unidentifiable objections.

Many regard the opening tactic as the most crucial part of the sales call. Depending on the scenario, they might be right. Certainly the opening represents an area where customer objections are extremely common. A well-thought-out, carefully planned first forty-five seconds can help a lot.

I offer you no magic pill. What I do offer instead is a sensible approach that provides you with the best opportunity to start your sales call with an articulate, complete process. Will you still hear objections from your customer? Oh, yes. I would prefer, however, that these objections not be a reaction to something you did wrong. With that said, it's now time to slay this beast you call an objection. The process is complete. Now let's disturb it a bit.

## TEST YOUR COMPREHENSION: OPENING TACTIC

Using the four-step opening tactic, write an opening for each of the scenarios we have been tracking. Now let's spice it up a bit. For the first scenario, write an opening for a cold call situation. In the second scenario, write an opening for a second call, picking up at the solution stage within the *selling cycle*. For the third scenario, write an opening to start a sales call positioned in the maintenance stage. Finally, for the last scenario, create an opening for a phone call to address an angry customer who has had some problems with your company. When you have completed these openings, write an opening that addresses the product you sell.

PJ INVESTING CORPORATION: FIRST MEETING

_____

_____

_____

_____

TO CLEAN A ROOM: SECOND MEETING, STARTING AT THE SOLUTION STAGE

_____

_____

_____

_____

A TON OF TALENT, A LACK OF TRUST: REVISITING THE EMPLOYEE IN THE
MAINTENANCE STAGE

_____

_____

_____

_____

EVERY MOTORS, LTD: TELEPHONE CALL ADDRESSING A DISSATISFIED CUSTOMER

_____

_____

_____

_____

YOUR OWN SCENARIO

_____

_____

# SUGGESTED ANSWERS TO TEST YOUR COMPREHENSION: OPENING TACTIC

Given the four scenarios incorporating the opening tactic, here are my suggested answers combining the four steps. See how closely they resemble the answers you gave.

## PJ INVESTING CORPORATION: FIRST MEETING

1. Hello, I am Rob Jolles with PJ Investing Corporation.
2. I have been successful working with other investors like yourself, finding creative approaches to maximizing their investment opportunities.
3. What I would like to do is to find a time to sit down and study your financial portfolio. In that meeting I would simply like to ask you some questions, take notes, and listen to you. If, in the end, there is a need for my services, I'll make a recommendation. If not, I'll be on my way.
4. Our meeting should take no longer than thirty minutes.

## TO CLEAN A ROOM: SECOND MEETING, STARTING AT THE SOLUTION STAGE

1. Hi, son.
2. I'm so proud of you for all the work you've done so far. As we agreed, I made some calls regarding the ideas we talked about, and I think when you see the stuff we can do, you're going to feel even better about making the changes we talked about.
3. All I want to do now is go over the different containers we can use and plan our next step.
4. This shouldn't take more than ten minutes.

## A TON OF TALENT, A LACK OF TRUST: REVISITING THE EMPLOYEE IN THE MAINTENANCE STAGE

1. I've been looking forward to this meeting. Great to finally sit down with you again.

2. I think if we continue to meet and monitor the solutions we agreed to, you'll not only find yourself moving to your goals faster, you'll find working here a lot more rewarding as well.

3. Today I wanted to hear how your training went and then answer any questions you may have of me.

4. Unless you have a lot on your plate, this meeting won't take any longer than fifteen minutes.

## EVERY MOTORS, LTD: TELEPHONE CALL ADDRESSING A DISSATISFIED CUSTOMER

1. Hello Mr. Adams. This is Rob Jolles from Every Motors.

2. I have been informed there have been some difficulties with your car, and I wanted you to know I can certainly understand your frustration. You put your trust in us, and you are facing this difficulty. If I can hear from you exactly what has happened, I will be able to expedite whatever solutions will be necessary and provide you with the level of service you expect from us.

3. What I will need to do is file a report, so I'd like to ask you a few questions concerning this matter.

4. This should take no longer than ten minutes.

Look over the answers provided, as well as your own, and put them through the test base on the opening scenarios:

- Is an adequate greeting given?
- Are you letting the customer know "what's in it for them"?
- Is there an overview of how you intend to proceed?
- Has there been a clear-cut sense of time established?

# NINETEEN

# THE OBJECTION-HANDLING TACTIC

Nothing got without pains but an ill name and long nails.
*—Scottish proverb*

E very time I teach a seminar, participants seem to be chomping at the bit to get to the objection handling. An obsession with the handling of objections often indicates a lack of understanding of the sales process. This is not to say that objection handling is not a necessary part of your sales training. It simply means that it is one of many tactics within your selling aresenal.

As with the opening tactic, it is no coincidence that this tactic has been saved for the end. Many of the objections a customer might offer are created by you, the salesperson, when you do not follow and respect the way people make decisions. Up until now, you have been operating in a reactive manner in your handling of objections. The objections you will be hearing now will be somewhat more legitimate. This is because now you are operating in a more proactive manner.

## WHY CUSTOMERS OBJECT

Why do customers object? I believe it is important to understand this issue because it helps to put in perspective the tactic that I will be showing you. I often sense disappointment and fear in salespeople when they face an objection. When you have a better understanding of what is making your customer object, you will be less anxious about hearing these objections.

I believe the biggest reason that customers object is fear of change. This is quite natural and to be expected. Unfortunately, this fear of change is often masked with excuses. I must tell you, though, that I have never had a customer come up and tell me he was objecting because of this particular fear. Still, this is what paralyzes many of us.

Think back to the 1992 presidential election. President Bush made many errors in his attempt to get reelected. To my mind, however, there was one very smart tactic, although implemented too late: creating a fear of change among the voters.

President Bush's advisers conceded that the president was not without fault for some of the problems that were plaguing our country. Some of those problems could have been handled differently.

Then there was this Clinton fellow. He promised change. Who knew? Maybe this change would be for the better. Then again, maybe it would be for the worse. As we were shown a picture of an empty president's chair in the oval office, we were asked, "Who do you want in that chair?" What we were really asked was, "How badly do you *really* want change?"

It was no coincidence that, right before election time, a lot of votes swung back to President Bush. When it came right down to it, people became frightened of change. They worried that, as bad as things might have been for them, with change things could potentially get worse. Here is an appropriate Rob's Rule:

► *The fear of change often outweighs the pain of the present.*

This is another reason that I stress the art of questioning a customer's problems during the probing sequence. If the customer's problems are small or insignificant, the customer's need is equally weak. If the need is weak, you no longer have to worry about price. It probably will not matter even if you offer the least expensive solution: fear of change will keep you from making the sale.

The probing sequence within the analysis stage is designed to make small differences become big differences. This helps to make the differences in the customer's mind larger. If what you are offering is only a little better than the customer's existing situation, fear of change will often stop the customer from making a change. In boxing, as well as most other sports that are viewed subjectively, you cannot just beat the champion, you must crush the champion. "The same holds true for beating the existing vendor."

Another way people object, also related to the fear-of-change theory, is simply to stall. Think about how many times you have stalled at the last moment yourself. This could have been due to a fear of change or to a host of other reasons. The fact is, you never really had an objection, you were just stalling. Stalling is quite natural and often to be expected.

# THE FOUR NO'S

Sometimes the nasty objections that customers come up with can be overwhelming, but put them in perspective. I know it seems as if there are hundreds and hundreds of reasons that customers object, but I firmly believe they fall into one of four categories.

These categories can represent rather large groupings for your objections to fit into. Let me first show you how, strategically, Customer Centered Selling attempts to head these objections off before they are ever brought up.

## "NO NEED"

Perhaps the first, and most common, reason people object is that they feel they have "no need." A "no need" objection can come out of a customer's mouth in any number of ways. Your customer might actually use those words, make up an excuse, or go to the stall tactic, but usually the objection can be traced to a feeling of no need. I have little doubt that anyone who has sold has seen his share of these objections.

The reason behind the objection should now be familiar to you because you have learned how people make decisions. The decision cycle teaches you that 85 percent of customers have no identified needs. Product recommendations and overaggressive tactics both elicit "no need" objections. The ultimate irony of this category of objection is that although it remains the most common reason that customers object, it is the easiest objection to avoid.

Remember that close to 80 percent of customers actually have problems but have not decided to do anything about them. Through careful questioning in the research stage and some gentle prodding in the analysis stage, you should be able to move the customer past the decision to fix and begin working with needs.

In the less frequent instances when customers truly do not perceive even the hint of a problem, the "no need" objection becomes much more difficult. It is my hope that the WIFM within the opening tactic will buy you some time to move into the research stage of the procession. These are steps that have been created to take care of expected objections. The objection-handling tactic will fill in if "no need" still rears its ugly head.

## "NO HURRY"

A frustrating situation that is often brought up in my seminars is probably a scenario you are all too familiar with. It goes something like this:

> Often I sit down with a customer. We seem to be getting along great. The conversation is light, and I can feel a lot of trust building between us. The customer seems very clear about his needs, and I could swear the sale is about to happen. I offer a recommendation that seems to excite the customer, and into the close I go. The customer then tells me he needs to think about what I have recommended, and everything comes to a screeching halt.

Sound familiar? Your customer might offer any number of excuses, but make no mistake about it: You are looking at a "no hurry" objection. What makes it so frustrating is that most salespeople will swear they thought they had the sale in the bag. Well, the bag has a hole in it.

Here is what needs to be done. The entire analysis stage has been created with "no hurry" objections in mind. It is human nature to stall, and the "no hurry" objection category is a classic solution for the customer. Do not be deceived by your customer's apparent signals to buy. Not only must you use the probing sequence; I strongly urge you to use all the trial closes taught as well as pay particular attention to the commit-to-a-decision trial close.

## "NO MONEY"

Ah, at last, the crux of the matter. So many salespeople fear the "no money" objection that it sometimes it seems as if it should be placed on a pedestal. Well, I do not wish to pray to this nemesis of so many salespeople. I would prefer instead to destroy the pedestal on which it has no business being placed.

I happen not to believe that customers have "no money." How many times have you "had no money," only to *find* money once you felt the need was serious enough?

Here is a classic example. At the Xerox Document University, I had a close friend who was a technical trainer for the company. He had one strange quirk: He never had any money. When I first met him, he had just bought a beautiful Porsche 914. A year later he sold the car. No money.

My wife and I would often invite my friend and his various girlfriends out for dinner. He would respectfully decline. No money. The theater, movies, drinks: It didn't really matter because the answer was always the same. No money.

My friend's "no money" problems became so bad I frequently had to lend him money for lunch. If ever there was a person who symbolized "no money," it was this person. That was until his mother became ill.

I saw my friend in the hallway one day, looking kind of shook up. I asked him what was wrong, and he told me his mother was in the hospital. He had just found out and needed to fly to Memphis later that day.

My friend was gone for three days. When he returned, he looked like a different person. He was again relaxed as he told me the good news. It turned out not to be what the doctors had feared. His mother had spent only two days in the hospital and, as he put it, was already bowling by the time he left.

I found myself relieved as well, but I was also curious about how much his airline ticket cost, knowing how sympathetic the airlines are to travelers who buy tickets with three hours' notice. I asked him and he calmly told me that Washington to Memphis had cost him $1,100.

I was still curious. I could not figure out how a person with such limited means could afford a $1,100 airline ticket. As courteously as possible, I asked, "Where did you come up with the money for the airline ticket?" He looked at me as if I had lost my mind and said, "It was for my mother!"

That experience continues to remind me that when it is important enough, we all find the money. When a problem hurts badly enough, the "no money" objection becomes less important.

Need some more examples? Who does your taxes? In case you were unaware, the IRS will do your taxes for a cut-rate nominal fee! I do not know of too many people who take them up on that offer. I also do not know of many people who look for the least expensive surgeon when they are faced with a serious medical problem.

If you have a hangnail, you might just stop at a clinic on the way home. If the problem is more serious, you probably won't be stopping at the clinic. You will pay for the best doctor you can find, even if the rates do not fall within the "usual and customary rate" charges the insurance companies have created. This may very well mean you will have to pay a significant amount out of your pocket to have your surgery. Isn't it strange how money becomes less and less important as the problem grows bigger? Perhaps now you can see how critical the skills within the analysis stage truly are.

To counteract "no money" as well as "no hurry" and "no need," the early stages of the Customer Centered Selling model are imperative. These skills are designed not only to move a customer into making a decision, but to create a sense of urgency and justify price.

## "NO TRUST"

The final category for objections is the most disturbing to me. A "no trust" objection indicates the customer is ready and willing to make a change but is not sure he wants the change to be with you. In other words, the customer is sold on the solution. He is not sold on you, the salesperson.

"No trust" objections occur because of the lack of sales training that exists in most sales industries. If all a salesperson does is dump features and solutions on a customer, it only makes sense that the customer will shop around. Why not? If all I did as your salesperson was bore you with a lecture covering my solution, why would you feel any obligation to buy from me?

Trust is addressed in Customer Centered Selling. When you carefully research a customer's business, you begin to earn trust. When you analyze that customer's business and confirm your information, you earn trust. When you not only work with a customer to understand his requirements but also spec out those requirements, you earn trust. Finally, when you articulately tie your solution to the customer's needs and close in a non-manipulative manner, you earn trust.

"No trust" objections might come up from time to time, and this is to be expected. With that said, following a consultative, customer-centered process should prepare you to earn the customer's trust and keep this category of objections from giving you any real trouble.

# FOUR STEPS TO HANDLING OBJECTIONS

Many people believe that there is a secret to handling objections. I hope that you have discovered that the secret is to learn how people make decisions and intelligently mirror that process through your selling. Just the same, objections are part of selling, and there is a four-step process for handling objections that I have found quite useful.

## STEP 1. CLARIFY

By far the most important step within the objection-handling tactic is to clarify. Do not be deceived by what appears to be a simple step. Clarification can be a challenge because it requires you to think quickly on your feet. It is a difficult step to prepare for and must be done without appearing rude to the customer. To prove this point—it's so important, I am going to offer you six good reasons why you should clarify objections!

### REASON 1. GET THE *REAL* OBJECTION

When working with objections, there is something you have to understand right up front. This point centers around Rob's Rule:

▶ *Rarely will a customer offer his real objection up front.*

People are funny about their objections and how much they will tell you—if you do not ask for more. The equally strange phenomenon is that if you do ask a few more questions, customers will tell you only what you need to know to answer their objection. Think for a moment about how many times you gave a salesperson an objection without telling him all he would need to know to answer it. For example, when a customer says, "I'm not sure this is right for me," I do not have a clue as to how to answer. When you say to a customer, "Could you tell me a little more about what is not right for you," you would be amazed at what you might hear. It is not uncommon for a customer to reply by saying something like, "Well, two years ago I bought a similar product, and it did not work well."

I don't know about you, but I would want to hear even more about what did not work well! I want to hear more because most likely once I do, I will be able to answer the objection easily. Sometimes, through a series of clarification questions, the objection will go away without my even having to answer it.

### REASON 2. AVOID ANSWERING THE WRONG OBJECTION

No matter how committed to quality and dedicated to service, companies do make mistakes. The premium companies that base their pricing on their level of detail are particularly hard hit by company foul-ups. These mistakes are often the last thing a salesperson wants to have come up during a sales call, yet ironically, it is the salesperson who most often ends up bringing these problems up.

Let me give you a scenario illustrating this problem. When a salesperson begins hearing the same objection on a regular basis, he becomes sensitized to the issue. As a customer begins to ask a question in this sensitive area, the salesperson's mind begins to race ahead and think, "Oh, no, not this objection again!"

Without listening carefully and without fully understanding the objection, the salesperson begins to trudge mechanically through his favorite response. There is only one problem. There are a significant number of

times your customer is not objecting to this sensitive area. The exchange
ends up sounding something like this:

Customer:    I must tell you before you proceed, I'm kind of concerned
             about delivery.
Seller:      Well, uh, I can explain that. In the past month, our company
             has had some difficulties in that area, but the computer prob-
             lem has been fixed and we are back to 100 percent efficiency
             again.
Customer:    I was just asking about *where* your product would be deliv-
             ered. What's this about a computer problem?

All companies have problems, but there is no need to advertise them
to your customers. Clarifying the objection will make sure that the only
problems discussed will be the ones your customer brings up.

## REASON 3. AVOID SOUNDING CONFRONTATIONAL

Another reason to clarify a customer's objection involves the perception of
you, the salesperson. Once an objection has been given, a salesperson may
snap back with an immediate response and can be perceived as confronta-
tional.

A salesperson who responds immediately to an objection creates an air
of stubbornness and insensitivity. Most people do not like to feel that they
are wrong. The quicker the response, the surer they are that you have not
been listening to them. If for no other reason than to avoid the perception
of confrontation, first clarify the objections you hear.

## REASON 4. BUY YOURSELF TIME TO THINK

This reason is a basic one, yet I can't tell you the number of times I observe
salespeople not taking advantage of this benefit. Although you can certainly prepare and anticipate objections, they can come up at any time, and
often at inopportune times. Why rush your response?

Clarifying objections allows you the time to compose yourself to respond to the objection at hand. Objections often can represent highly emotional issues in the customer's mind. A few extra moments to prepare your

response can go a long way to finding the correct words to use with your customers.

## REASON 5. SHORTEN YOUR TALKING TIME

Picture yourself in the customer's shoes for just a moment. You are looking at a rather difficult decision and trying to analyze the information as carefully as possible. You are puzzled by one aspect of this decision, so you ask the salesperson what you see as a rather harmless question. Out comes a response that just won't end. It goes on and on and on and on. You begin thinking to yourself, "This really was not such a big deal to me a minute ago, but judging by the salesperson's response, I must have hit on a key issue." Time for a Rob's Rule for objection handling:

► *The longer it takes a salesperson to answer an objection, the more credibility the objection is given.*

The reason the objection is so difficult to answer is that the salesperson does not know exactly what the objection is! Without clarification, the salesperson must verbally address everything about the objection and hope that one part of his response will touch on the customer's real reason for bringing it up.

From time to time, you may find yourself spending five or ten minutes working on a customer's objection. If you are going to spend a long time with it, make sure the majority of the time is spent listening to the customer tell you more about the objection.

## REASON 6. APPLYING THE 10 PERCENT RULE

A customer who wants to stall can come up with some very creative objections. There is little backing up these objections. Often the customer is just making up excuses.

I will not antagonize my customers, but it is amazing what happens when you ask them to "tell you more" about their particular objection. I refer to this as the "10 percent rule." I venture to guess that at least 10 percent of the time, your customer will respond with something like, "Uh, well, you see, I think you actually answered that question earlier." It is kind of hard to "tell you more" when the objection never really existed.

I do not recommend putting the customer on the spot, so I suggest you be prepared to assist him out of his predicament gracefully. Perhaps a comment relating to how confusing the topic he is addressing might be of help. I would rather help my customer to feel comfortable moving away from an attempt at stalling than breathe life into an objection that does not exist.

Let me finish by suggesting two important points. First, watch your own timing, and be careful you don't take too much time clarifying. You do not want the customer to perceive your clarifying actions as a stall tactic. Second, understand that my suggestion to clarify is not intended as a mask for questions you have no answers for. There is certainly nothing wrong with your saying, "I don't know the answer to that, but I will find out and let you know in twenty-four hours."

I hope the reasons I have given you for clarifying objections have convinced you how critical this first step is. Successful handling of this first step will make the rest of your task go much more smoothly.

## STEP 2. ACKNOWLEDGE

Assuming the objection has been clarified (and if six reasons did not help convince you, I don't know else what will), it is time to demonstrate your listening skills. It may also be time to demonstrate your empathy skills as well.

Acknowledging a customer's objection usually requires only that you confirm your understanding of the customer's concern. To acknowledge, all you need to do is recite your understanding of the customer's objection. For example:

Customer:    I must tell you before you proceed that I'm kind of concerned about delivery.

Seller:    Could you tell me more about your delivery concerns? [*clarify*]

| Customer: | Well, two years ago, we changed vendors for a brief period of time. We were promised on-time delivery, only to find out their "on-time delivery" referred solely to deliveries between 8:00 A.M. and 5:00 P.M. We often have deliveries that are after hours. |
|---|---|
| Seller: | So your concern is centered on the need for evening deliveries. Is that right?" [*acknowledge*] |
| Customer: | Exactly. |

That wouldn't be such a difficult objection to handle.

Another key benefit of the acknowledgment step is the time you will save answering objections. When you acknowledge, you gain permission to answer the customer's objection. There is nothing more frustrating than thinking you understand the objection, launching into an answer, and then finding out you answered the wrong objection. Clarifying will help get you to the right objection. Acknowledging will confirm it for you.

## STEP 3. DETERMINE THE TYPE OF OBJECTION

Assuming you now not only know what the real objection is but have also confirmed your understanding of this issue with your customer, it's just about time to answer. First, you need to figure out what type of objection you are hearing.

Two types of objections can come from your customer. The first can be called a *misunderstanding*. The second, and more difficult, can be called a *drawback*. Let's look at misunderstandings (the easy one) first.

### MISUNDERSTANDINGS

Ah, wouldn't life be grand if all objections were misunderstandings! A misunderstanding objection means just that. The customer has misunderstood something that you need to clear up. The solution is fairly simple, though not without a certain amount of danger.

When a customer misunderstands something, the problem is not so much what you say but how you say it. I have seen salespeople who react with little tact when they are able to prove a misunderstanding with a customer. In short, the customer is wrong, and the salesperson is right. If you are not careful, you will prove you are right, but the customer will not want to do business with you. You must be respectful of your customer's ego. No one likes to be told they are wrong.

I suggest that you perfect a technique that I have admired and used for years. The technique, referred to as *feel, felt, found,* works like a charm.

The *feel* portion of this technique is designed to massage the customer's ego. When you tell a customer that a lot of people feel the same way he does, you immediately eliminate the risk of harming your customer's ego.

The *felt* portion of this technique injects empathy into your response. It is one thing for your customer to hear that a lot of people *feel* the same way he does. It is even more powerful to hear that *you felt* the same way yourself!

Now you are ready for a response. The *found* portion of this technique provides your response. At this point, the answer should be an easy one, but there is no sense dropping the ball here. By explaining what you or your company have *found*, you open the way to offer your solution with the minimal amount of confrontation.

Let me show you what this technique is like in action. Say that you are talking to a customer who is concerned about whether you will personally be performing all his organization's accounting work. An objection was raised about this issue and, after clarification, you have found out his real concern is his fear of having someone less competent working on the account. You have acknowledged this concern and have determined the objection to be a misunderstanding. A "feel, felt, found" response would sound something like this:

Seller:   You know, a lot of people **feel** the same way you do. When they work with an accounting firm, they want to make sure they are getting the best service possible. In your specific case, that means personal accountability as well. I **felt** the same way when I first came to this firm. I wanted my customers to know that they could count on me to work with them on all details of their case. What we **found** was that by customers' working with the people who support me, they were guaranteed work that meets with their quality standards, and they saved money by not having to pay a higher fee every time they had a question that would not necessarily require my attention.

Using the feel, felt, found technique allows you to tell the customer gracefully he is wrong. A few caveats: First, you can use this technique only once per customer. If you use it repeatedly, your customer will begin to get suspicious. Second, never use the technique to cushion a misunderstanding that your company created. Imagine how awkward it would be to hear a customer complain about bad service from your company and to respond by saying, "Gee, a lot of people *feel* the same way you do . . ."

The key to handling a misunderstanding is tact. "Feel, felt, found" is a technique that forces just that. You do not have to use all three words. For instance, you do not always have to have "*felt* that way yourself." The most important thing is clearing the way to allow your customers to hear that they have misunderstood.

## DRAWBACK

The drawback objection is the most difficult type to handle because an objection due to a drawback is defined as something the customer is saying he or she wants but you cannot provide. Fear not. Where there's a will, there's a way!

Don't become intimidated by this type of objection. Certainly I would much prefer all my objections to be misunderstandings, but sometimes you have to work with what you get.

To paraphrase the Rolling Stones: "You can't always get what you waaant." Think back for a minute to the last house you purchased. Did you get everything you wanted? This I strongly doubt. As a matter of fact, I am willing to bet you could pay twice what you spent for that last house and you *still* would not get everything. I do not doubt that you got many of the most important things you were looking for, but nobody gets everything.

Now I am sure that you got many of your most important needs taken care of and that was how you had to base your purchase decision. I know of people who spend literally years searching for their dream house, only to find it does not exist. Even those who build are not spared this dilemma.

I mention this only to offer you strength. Your customer, just like you and everyone else, makes decisions based on all the criteria. If you believe that the solution you offer addresses all of the criteria better than anyone else, you should not feel awkward going ahead with your recommendation.

When addressing a drawback objection, after it has been clarified and acknowledged, summarize the benefits you offer versus what you cannot offer. Keeping with the house example, your response might sound something like this:

Customer:    I really want to be closer to a shopping center.

Seller:    Well, Ms. Hayes, this house is not as close to the shopping center as you would like. But I still feel very confident that this house is the best one to satisfy your needs. You see, I made this recommendation based on your total list of requirements. I guess I have to ask you this question. Which is most important to you overall: a house that is in a nice neighborhood, with good schools; that has a two-car garage, and gives you the room you require; or a home that is closer to a shopping center?

If by chance you are wondering where that customer's buying criteria came from, remember where you would be in the selling process to hear this type of objection. One of the most powerful lessons in Customer Centered Selling focuses on avoiding talking about solutions until you have earned the right.

You can't be asked whether your solution has or does not have various attributes until you first offer a solution. This will not come while you are researching a customer or while you are analyzing customer concerns. It will not come while you are confirming your understanding of these problems and will not come while you are studying customer requirements.

As you begin determining customer specifications, you may become aware of criteria you can't fulfill, but do not be overly worried. When you analyzed your customer's concerns, I doubt seriously you would have probed heavily into an area you could not fulfill. Therefore, if this need even makes the customer criteria, something tells me it will not be a crucial need.

Of course, it is human nature for customers to stall. When you are in the solution stage, and you tell a customer you can't address a particular piece of buying criteria, your customer can be a little persistent. Let's face it, your customer has found something that potentially could stop you dead in your tracks . . . or has he?

Now think back to what may have seemed like an insignificant step nestled within the requirement stage: the third step, prioritizing the customer's criteria. If you have done your job in the analysis stage, all the problems you probed transferred over to needs and, coincidentally, should have a 1, 2, and 3 by them. The one need you could not fulfill was not probed in the analysis stage and will most likely have a much lower number by it.

When restating the benefits, you are much better prepared to put into perspective what the customer can and cannot expect. I suggest you even use the number when saying, "Which is more important to you overall: getting 1, 2, 3, 5, and 6, or getting 4?" That puts things into a little better perspective now.

The only gentle reminder I would like to offer once again involves ethics. If the solution you are proposing does not address your customer's most important criterion, you have to think seriously about the recommendation you are making. The Customer Centered Selling process is designed to help you sell in a consultative manner. If your solution is not the best given the total list of customer requirements, the recommendation should not be made.

## STEP 4. CONFIRM

Have you ever battled an objection that did not seem to want to go away? You have answered the objection, sensed that the customer was satisfied with your response, moved on, and, boom! It's back again. This is the reason you learn to confirm the objections your customers give you.

Sometimes objections can take on a life of their own, hanging around almost like a bad penny. You think you have the objection answered, but ten minutes later the customer tells you, "I'm still hung up on . . ." The best way to handle this problem is to confirm that the objection has been answered. Simply check back with the customer to ensure his question has been answered—for example:

Seller:     What we *found* was that by your working with the people who support me, not only will you be guaranteed work that meets with your quality standards, you will be able to save money by not having to pay a higher fee every time you have a question that would not necessarily require my attention.

Customer:   I see.

Seller:     Does that answer your question regarding who will be working on your account?

You do not need to worry about any formality required within the confirmation step. Often a simple, "How does that sound?" or even "Okay?" will do the trick. The key is to try to get your customer to tell you that the objection has been answered.

Once you have asked a confirming question, you can count on one of two responses from your customer: The customer will, or will not, be satisfied with your response. If he is not satisfied, you might as well know now, before you move on. I suggest more clarification and possibly a return visit to the analysis stage for another taste of the probing sequence.

In the worst-case scenario you may find yourself spiraling out into a negotiation posture. This is another book in itself, but be prepared to give up something in order to get something in return. This would follow the tried and true win-win approach to negotiation.

If customers are satisfied with your response, it is time to move back into the process from wherever you left off. I will not for a minute tell you that by confirming the objection, you have guaranteed the objection will not be heard again. What I *can* tell you is that by confirming, you have psychologically made it much more difficult for the customer to bring the objection up again.

## THE SALESPERSON'S ULTIMATE NEMESIS: "YOU COST TOO MUCH!"

So there you have it. A simple, four-step process for handling objections. What more could you ask for? Plenty. When I give a sales seminar, probably the most frequently asked questions relate to addressing objections dealing with price—specifically, what you do when a customer says, "You cost too much!"

Before I tell you how to handle this nemesis, consider what you have learned so far. An objection to your cost can be handled as either a misunderstanding or a drawback, "Feel, felt, found," for instance, can work quite nicely. If you have no luck with "feel, felt, found," you could try to address the objection as a drawback. Stack the benefits on one side, price on the other, and hold your breath. I must tell you, however, I am not fond of holding my breath when I sell.

Selling for Xerox taught me how to handle price objections. As a matter of fact, I can't imagine how any Xeroid could survive without being able to handle price objections. When selling for Xerox, it is not a question of if you will hear a price objection, it is a question of when. This holds true for most other premium-priced companies.

A sobering comment I make from time to time is to stop looking for a "magic pill" and stick with sound sales tactics. For price objections, however, I recommend the use of **TCO** because it represents the closest thing to a magic pill that I have ever seen.

TCO stands for total cost of ownership, and here is how it works. When a customer says, "You cost too much," stick with the objection-handling tactic and start by clarifying. You never know when your customer could be referring to something very minor about your proposal or even some kind of insignificant rider or administrative fee. But assume that after you clarify, the response from your customer is this:

**Customer:**   Your quote is 10 percent higher than anything else we have seen.

That seems pretty clear, doesn't it? Clear for you maybe, but I have one last question to ask my customer. Using the TCO method requires just a little bit more clarifying and would sound something like this:

**Seller:**   Are you referring to the cost of purchasing this machine or owning this machine?

If that question seems a little confusing to you, you are not alone. My customer is typically confused. This does not upset me in any way because I am asking the question in the hope that my customer will ask me for clarification. The scenario consistently plays out this way:

**Customer:**   What's the difference?
**Seller:**   Well, the cost of purchasing the machine is the cost contained within the proposal I have given you, and as you say, I am 10 percent higher than any other vendor you are looking at. I do not in any way dispute that. The costs of owning that machine, however, are much more involved. These costs reflect the cost savings associated with the reduction of downtime on that machine, the cost saved in not having to take people away from their jobs to train the temps and new office personnel you spoke of. The improved quality and service that will keep that machine up and running. You see, I can prove to you that when you add all the costs associated with this purchase, this will be the least expensive machine you ever own [*confirmation*]. Isn't that what you are looking to accomplish with this purchase decision?

That, my friends, is called TCO, and it is designed to remind the customer of one crucial point: You get what you pay for!

Let me calm your fears on two concerns that might be on your mind. The first relates to the example I just provided and centers on where I happened to pluck those convenient benefits out of the air. Remember this Rob's Rule:

► *If you do not bring up product, your customer will not bring up price.*

How can a customer ask you how much something costs, or accuse you of a higher price, if you are in the research stage asking background probes? If your customer does, simply tell him you have various products with many different price options. Chances are you will not be asked, because your customer will be too busy telling you about what he does and how he does it. If you do not bring up product, your customer will be unable to bring up price until the solution stage. By that time, you should have a slew of benefits ready to unleash if necessary.

The second concern that might be on your mind relates to the product I used in my example. Not to worry. I have used the TCO approach with customers who sell tangible and intangible solutions. The TCO question to your customer is designed to be vague and elicit a response.

Here is one more example, this time with an intangible product. Many of my clients sell mutual funds. These salespeople are involved in a classic battle involving cost. On one side of the fence sit the no-load salespeople who literally are *required* to take an order-taking posture. You can purchase products, but you are not really able to get any significant advice. On the other side are salespeople who are basically selling the same product but with a 4 or 5 percent commission. At first glance, this looks like a no-brainer decision. Let's see: buy the product free or pay a commission. Decisions, decisions.

Customer Centered Selling has been a highly effective tool for salespeople in this second set. Strategically they begin to influence the need for service, advice, consulting, and proactive strategies way back in their background probes in the research stage. After you take these issues through the probing sequence in the analysis stage, these key needs begin to appear in the requirement stage. Once that happens and the loads are brought up in the solution stage, TCO comes to the rescue if an objection even surfaces:

| Customer: | A load? I don't want to pay any loads! I was told to avoid them. |
|---|---|
| Seller: | What specifically were you told about these fees? |
| Customer: | Well, I was told it is an unnecessary cost that can be avoided. |
| Seller: | When you say "cost," are you referring to the cost of starting this program or running this program? |
| Customer: | What's the difference? |
| Seller: | Well, the cost of starting this program has an administrative fee of 4 percent, and as you say, that is 4 percent higher than the other alternative you are looking at. I do not in any way dispute that. The cost of running this program, however, involves all the costs associated with this decision—for instance, the cost associated with having someone who is trained and licensed to sit down with you and go over your financial planning and the cost savings in working proactively instead of reactively to make smart decisions before there is trouble, not after. You see, Ms. Jenkins, I can prove to you that when you add *all the costs* associated with your purchase decisions, this will end up costing you far less in the long run than the 4 percent you are questioning now. Isn't that what you are looking to accomplish with this purchase decision? [*confirmation*] |

The key is to get customers to look at the total picture. A major strength regarding TCO is that it stirs memories in us all. When a TCO strategy is developed, it is natural for us all to think back on the last time we forgot this lesson—the time, maybe, when you found someone at a "bargain" to finish your basement or redo your roof. By the time these jobs were finally finished and you repaired the damage left behind—the broken promises and the corners that were cut—you were lucky if you broke even on a less-than-average job.

Sadly, this lesson in quality seems to last only between six to twelve months before we're off trying to buy something for nothing once again. You would think I would be one person who would not forget this lesson, but recently I was bitten by the "get what you pay for" reminder.

I had been looking at a pair of Rockport dress shoes and was hung up on the $110 price tag. It's not that I find that a particularly high price, but for a casual shoe, I found myself a little slow in my purchase decision. After looking at the shoes a few different times, I finally marched into a mall in Maryland and headed for my Rockports at the other end of the mall. That was my first mistake.

As I walked the length of the mall, I passed by a few men's shoe stores. I was on a mission, so none of these stores broke my stride—until I saw what looked like my Rockports in another store.

I put on the brakes and went in to the store to investigate. The shoes were mounted on a display with a mountainous background, just like the ones I had looked at before. The shoes were light as a feather, just like the ones I had looked at before. Even the name was almost the same. I'm not 100 percent sure of the name but instead of Rockport, these were called something like "Shmockport." The best part of all was instead of the hefty $110 price tag I had been looking at, these shoes were only $59! To think I was on my way to buy practically the same shoes farther down the mall for over $50 more. What luck! I bought my Shmockports, almost giddy with the knowledge that I had pulled a fast one. That was my second mistake.

The shoes lasted about two months before the black leather turned gray and the stitching eroded and broke loose, separating the top of the shoe and the sole from each other. The shoes were useless, and the Shmockport company was not interested in my customer satisfaction.

A week after depositing my Shmockports in the trash, I parked closer to the store that sold the shoes I originally wanted, went in, and bought my Rockports. Unfortunately, they were no longer $110. When you added the wasted time, fuel, and expense of my first purchase mistake, these shoes were now closer to $200. Message: You get what you pay for.

AT&T helped out all premium-priced companies several years ago when it dramatically delivered this message in its advertisements. The commercial showed what looked like a young executive in a panic in the company men's room. As he nervously fixes his tie, he mentions how he was responsible for switching the telephone systems last year, and how pleased his boss was with the fact that he saved the company some money over its previous system. Now they have found out that the system they bought is not upgradable with the changes they want to make, and they will have to replace the entire system.

As this young man continues to fiddle with his tie, he looks at the other person in the room and says, "You don't think they will fire me, do you?" With an equally nervous look, his friend replies, "Uh, no, uh I don't think they will fire you." The scene fades to black, followed by this simple message: "AT&T, the right choice."

To this day I feel that was one of the most effective advertisements ever produced. It stressed the TCO concept and the need to consider everything that goes into a purchase decision. Isn't it a shame AT&T lost its way, sucked into the silly attacks on its competition and away from its original message of quality?

Toyota provides another example of the TCO concept in action. Rather than fight a sticker battle it can't win, Toyota has tried to get customers to focus on all the elements that go into owning a car. The company's bet is a simple one. Although you may pay a few thousand dollars more to purchase a Toyota over those that directly face off against it, Toyota asks you to add *all* the costs of owning your automobile. If you add costs associated with fuel, depreciation, insurance, and service, Toyota's claim is that you will be paying less overall with a Toyota than those that directly compete with its cars. It happens to be a brilliant strategy and one that should represent the true focus of all customers.

The concept of TCO is one major reason that premium companies like Xerox survive. This is also the reason that as long as Xerox continues to deliver on its quality promises, it will continue to dominate the upper end of the markets it competes in. If you were producing a million photocopies a month, would you look for the bargain copier?

This is not to suggest that premium-priced companies are never without fault. I must say that I get a perverse pleasure in seeing a Volvo with its hood up on the side of the road. As I drive by, part of me wants to shout, "Look at your car that never breaks down now!" Still, for every Volvo with its hood up, you can count on quite a few more cars that face off against Volvo with their hoods up.

One final suggestion when battling price—an objection that should not surprise most salespeople: If you seek premium-priced solutions, you most likely will hear these objections on a regular basis. If this is the case, prepare early and arm yourself with real dollars.

Let me tell you what I mean by "real dollars." When you are applying the probing sequence in the analysis stage, most customers ultimately feel a pinch involving money, time, or image. Time and image ultimately cost money, so why not develop these customer concerns toward the almighty dollar? For example, if the customer problem you are probing occasionally offends clients, why not continue to use the probing sequence and bring that problem to real dollars?

| | |
|---|---|
| Seller: | You mentioned that the issue in question occasionally offends your clients. How often does something like this occur? |
| Customer: | Not too often. Probably about once or twice a month. |
| Seller: | What would be a conservative dollar value that you would place on the revenue generated by an average customer? |
| Customer: | I would say something in the neighborhood of $5,000. |

You can continue to probe from this point, and I hope you do. The key is, you have now quantified a customer problem to real dollars, not just discomfort. When the issue of price comes up, be prepared to reach into your pocket and bring these dollars back into the conversation. In the long run, this will help your customer to grasp a TCO concept all that much more easily.

Money and price objections can be the ultimate nemesis of many salespeople. After the probing sequence, if they even come up, you could try to "feel, felt, found" them away. If that does not work, try it as a drawback, and stack the benefits. If that approach does not work, TCO and your preparation earlier in the selling cycle should prepare you to meet any objection head on and win!

## SOME FINAL THOUGHTS

The four-step method to overcoming objections has worked well for me over the years. Still, the best approach I know of to handle objections is to study how people make decisions and respect that approach when you sell. As with the other processes and tactics I have shown you in this book, objection handling is not without its subtle points.

## LISTEN FOR THE CONFIRMATION

The confirmation step is almost as important as the clarification step. Still, if you listen hard enough, you will find on many occasions that your customer will confirm your responses to his objections for you. For instance, it is not uncommon to hear customers say, "I really like that" or "That sounds great." In situations like these, the confirmation step has already been accomplished for you. After a customer has said he likes the features you have shown him, it would be awkward to say to him, "So, do you like that feature?"

Remember once again that people, not processes, make decisions. Listen carefully, and you may very well find that many steps, including the confirmation step, will be accomplished for you by your customer.

## TREAT CUSTOMER QUESTIONS THE SAME WAY

Sometimes customers' objections can be perceived as questions. Sometimes customers' simple questions can be perceived as objections. Have you ever wondered what the difference is?

You could try to determine your customers' intent by studying their nonverbal communication, emotion, displeasure, and other difficult signals, but I think this will only confuse the issue. I have a better idea: Treat questions the same as objections.

When a customer has a question, I recommend getting into the habit of clarifying the question. This will offer you many of the same benefits that clarification did when working with an objection. After you respond to the question, confirming that the question has been answered will allow you to move on, assured that the customer's question has been addressed.

When you treat perceived objections and questions the same, you no longer have to worry about misreading your customer's intent. If what you hear is a question, your process will be interpreted as courteous. If what you hear is an objection, your process will be interpreted as professional. Either way you come out ahead.

## FOLLOW THE PARETO PRINCIPLE

No matter what company you represent and no matter how squeaky clean your reputation is, every salesperson has a few objections he hears on a regular basis. Maybe it's price. Maybe it's quality. As a sales trainer, the objections I hear about most are in the areas of follow-up.

What amazes me is how shocked and surprised some salespeople act when they hear their most common objections. I still go out with various Xerox salespeople who will get hit with a price objection and stumble through it. When the sales call is over, the salesperson will tell me how much he hates hearing that objection. My response is usually the same: "Why don't you practice a response?"

I believe the Pareto Principle follows most objection patterns. In the eighteenth century, Wilfredo Pareto made the startling revelation that the distribution of wealth seemed to follow a pattern: 20 percent of the population seemed to control 80 percent of the wealth. As Pareto put it, economic classes seemed to divide along the trivial many (80 percent of the population) and the vital few (the 20 percent of the population in control). In problem solving, the Pareto Principle basically teaches you to separate the trivial many from the vital few. In other words, following this principle, if 80 percent of the time you are hearing the same three or four objections and 20 percent of the time you are hearing countless numbers of others, would it not be worthwhile to study and prepare for the vital few?

Think for a moment, and write down your three or four "vital few" objections. Next, take a moment and introduce yourself. It's time you and your objections had a little talk. Pull out a pad of paper and write down some well-thought-out, articulate responses. Wordsmith your responses a little bit more until you feel confident about them. Finally, memorize these responses and practice them until they do not sound rehearsed.

If you spend some time studying the vital few responses rather than avoiding them, selling is a whole lot easier. Your anxiety will go down, and your confidence will go up. With the tough ones out of the way, you can set your sights on more important matters. Who knows, you might even be able to make a dent on the trivial many that remain.

## GIVE IT A NEW NAME

Drawback objections can be the most difficult objections to work with. The customer wants something you just do not offer. My question is, Do you offer something that is similar? If so, you might want to give your objection a new name.

Here is an example of what I mean. Let's say the company you work for has an 800 telephone service. Your customer is being wooed by "local vendor phone calls" and the perceived advantages. The exchange may sound something like this:

Customer:   I must tell you up front, I am interested in working with you, but I really want to make sure the person I deal with is local.

Seller:   What appeals to you about working with a local vendor?

Customer:   Well, I want to make sure that whoever I work with will be easy to get hold of, even to answer the slightest questions. With a local vendor, I feel that is easy to achieve.

Seller:   Oh, I see. You are looking to make sure that whoever you select has the ability to be reached easily and without any type of telephone charges or hassles. Is that right?

This technique is called *renaming*, and properly used, it can be very effective. Analyze when to use this tactic, and pay attention to ethics. Renaming is designed to add clarification to the customer's request and can be used to influence an objection to meet with your strengths better. This tactic is not designed to trick customers in any way. I recommend its use only when the request appears trivial and in your mind can be satisfied equally well by your approach to addressing the need.

Use this tactic wisely and with caution. I wrestled with the idea of even placing the renaming tactic in this book. It is, however, effective, and when used properly, it can be very helpful with drawback objections. Used improperly, it can be manipulative and unethical.

## DON'T BE SORRY

All companies make mistakes. The quality companies fix them as quickly as possible, ensuring customer satisfaction throughout the process. This does not excuse the mistakes made, and some customers are going to let you hear about them.

There are two major mistakes that are often made when working with objections that result from our own companies. The first mistake is to ignore the situation altogether. Not dealing with a mistake does not make it go away. Instead, the customer's anger festers and grows.

Think about the last time you were angry over a supplier's mistake. How did you react to not having someone address the issue? Even something as small as a broken button on a laundered shirt can fall into this pattern of avoidance. When you walk into the dry cleaner, you are mildly angry. You tell the person behind the counter of this mishap and are countered with, "May I have your receipt, please?"

This does not do at all! You will typically respond by getting more hostile as you tell your tale of woe about the meeting where you showed up with your shirt sleeve flopping. The response once again is, "Oh, well, can I have your receipt so I can process this?"

The employee is only doing his job and can't process your refund without this information, yet you get angrier and angrier. There is a disconnect here, and the problem will only get worse. The employee is doing what he has been trained to do, and you are doing what so many people in frustrating predicaments like this do: get angrier and angrier if somebody does not step in soon. And the second mistake can make things even worse. This second mistake is to say, "I'm sorry." It is a natural tendency to want to apologize to a customer when your company is at fault, and I would recommend its use to you if these words were of any use. Unfortunately they are not. Telling the customer you are sorry is the equivalent of waving a red cloth in front of a bull. It only makes things worse. "I'm sorry" has a hollow ring to it in business and usually only makes the customer angry. Usually it is not even the mistake of the person who is apologizing.

When I was a kid, my older brother Richard would come into my room and aimlessly fidget with things that did not belong to him. I would plead with him to "put that down" or "leave that alone," but the fiddling would continue. Eventually something would fall or break. These occurrences would always be followed with a monotone, "Sorry."

Symbolically, this is the same monotone "sorry" your customer hears. It is empty and useless. Your customer does not want you to be sorry. Your customer wants to be listened to and acknowledged, and so do you as you stand ready to bean the laundry clerk with your injured shirt.

The answer falls in the acknowledge step of the objection tactic. In this stage, you have been taught to restate the objection to make sure you understand it. Now let me make a little change in the way you need to acknowledge a customer concern.

When you hear a customer complaint about something you or your company caused, let your customer know you have heard him by saying something like, "I can understand your frustration" or "I can certainly appreciate how disappointing that must be." Then you can restate the objection and begin to address it.

If you ever have finally blown your top and demanded that a manager show himself to address your concern, the phrase above is really the only thing you hear. For example, if you demand that our laundry cleaner employee get the manager, this is what you typically hear:

Manager:  May I help you?

You:       Yes. Your employee here does not seem to know the first thing about customer satisfaction! I had my shirt cleaned here, put it on to attend a key meeting, and found your cleaners had cracked my button!

Manager:  I can certainly understand your frustration." [*acknowledge*] You bring your dirty shirt to us and wind up with a shirt that is unwearable. [*restate*]

You:       Exactly!

Manager:  What I will need from you is a receipt so I can process your refund as quickly as possible.

You:       All right then. That's more like it.

By following this process, you do not have a guarantee against irate customer reaction to your errors. What I can tell you from using this process and teaching it to numerous customer service people is that it will help to defuse the customer's emotion dramatically. The rest is up to you. Once the emotion is defused, do what it takes to turn this person once again into a satisfied customer.

## TRY IT FIRST AS A MISUNDERSTANDING

Now that you have had an opportunity to look over the two major categories of objections, I bet you would prefer that all of your objections be centered around misunderstandings rather than drawbacks. You also probably feel that most objections that you get in your particular line of selling are a result of drawbacks. If only all objections were misunderstandings, life would be a whole lot easier. Well, your wish may just have come true.

You must understand that what you might consider a drawback, I probably would categorize as a misunderstanding. This is not due to stubbornness. This is simply due to the nature of most drawbacks. Remember that a drawback is something the customer wants that you do not have. I would like to offer a quick dose of perspective. Think about those critical things that your competition has that you do not. Just how vital are they?

I have never seen Xerox build a machine without an on-off switch, for example. Most of the machines copy on both sides with multiple paper trays. The point here is this: Most companies are not foolish. They all have the fundamental features that require them to compete. After that, it becomes somewhat of a game—a bell here, a whistle there. I would hope you would not be making recommendations to customers if you are unable to satisfy their most important needs. What typically is represented in a drawback objection is something a little more obscure.

Consider two automobiles that face off against each other. One has an American manufacturer and the other, Japanese. Let's say that the customer has stated that one of his buying criteria is to buy American. If you were selling the Japanese car, I would guess that this would represent a clear-cut drawback objection. The customer wants something you do not have . . . or does he?

Seller:      It sounds as if buying an American car is an important buying criterion to you. Specifically, what appeals to you about buying American?

Customer:   I want to make sure that the money I am spending contributes fully to our American economy.

Now that the objection has been clarified, you could rename it:

Seller:   So you want to make sure that the car you purchase is not built overseas and is built in this country by Americans. Is that right?

Or you could go ahead and address it as a misunderstanding:

Seller:   Well, you know that many customers *feel* the same way you do. When they plan to purchase a car, they want to make sure that all the dollars they spend go toward our American economy. I *felt* the same way myself when I started working for this company. I wanted to make sure that the cars I bought and sold contributed to our economic gain, not our deficit. What we *found* was by moving the assembly line to the United States, we not only contributed to the American economy, we helped to create many more American jobs.

The worst that can happen by portraying everything as a misunderstanding is that your customer will not agree when you confirm that the objection has been answered. The real question is, Would that be so terrible? The worst-case scenario is that you would then have to handle the objection as a drawback.

Once you attempt to address an objection as a drawback, there is no going back. If stacking your benefits against the one criterion you cannot meet does not work, you will need to spin off into negotiations. If this suggestion of attempting to handle objections as misunderstandings works even half the time, you are way ahead of the game. This newfound success represents a significant amount of time you will not need to take a chance on working within the more difficult drawback scenario.

## ARE YOU THE LEAST EXPENSIVE?

One last suggestion may be helpful to you when battling price. This is an approach that may come in handy every now and then and should be saved for your image-conscious customers. The suggestion is to get your customers to relate to the way their company does business. Here is what it would sound like:

Customer:   I understand all that, but you are still too damn expensive!

Seller:   Mr. Kane, I am going to ask you a question, and I hope you can appreciate why I am asking you this question: Are you the least expensive company in town?

Customer:   Absolutely not! Our organization believes in taking care of our customers. These things take money. We believe in quality, customer service, dependability . . .

Seller:   Mr. Kane, my company is not the least expensive either, and we never will be. We also believe in the same things that you do, such as quality, customer service, dependability . . .

Sometimes customers will explain to you why they are not the least expensive company, and sometimes the customer will smile before answering and try to tell you why what they do is different from you. Either way, this approach certainly advances the conversation.

Let me give you a few words of caution before you take this little idea out for a spin. First, in no way is this suggestion meant to antagonize the customer. I strongly recommend you not use this approach unless you have had a few meetings with the customer or are nearing the end of the selling process.

I have had salespeople tell me they have used this process and met with resistance. After probing further, I have found that they have used this idea in their opening when challenged on price. Remember, if you are using the Customer Centered Selling process, you can't be challenged on price early because you are not talking about product.

And watch your tone when using this idea. You are treading on shaky ground here, and I strongly suggest you phrase the question to your customer *delicately*. This idea is not to be used as a weapon, but rather merely as another tactic to draw from.

Finally, remember that this idea is designed for image-conscious customers. It would be awkward asking a customer if he is the least expensive vendor in town and hearing the answer yes.

## "THAT'S WHY I'M HERE!"

Here is an oldie but goodie I picked up and have used from time to time. If you are at a loss for words, why not offer a simple statement: "That's why I'm here!" Here is what this would sound like in a variety of situations.

| | |
|---|---|
| Customer: | We don't have a need for any of your products. |
| Seller: | That's why I'm here. I am aware you are not currently a customer and . . . |
| Customer: | We currently use a different vendor. |
| Seller: | That's why I'm here. We believe that when you make a decision . . . |
| Customer: | We had a bad experience with your company. |
| Seller: | That's why I'm here. Our company has gone through various changes . . . |
| Customer: | We already are using some of your products. |
| Seller: | That's why I'm here. We appreciate your business and would like to . . . |

This method of defusing objections is just another of many ideas you might find helpful from time to time and should fit nicely into your growing arsenal of ideas. Please, don't thank me . . . that's why *I'm* here!

## BE CAREFUL WHAT YOU WISH FOR

Too often I see salespeople who become almost dejected at the hint of an objection from the customer. There are many reasons that people object. In this chapter I have touched on some of the more frequent reasons, but there are many, many more. Perhaps the most important point that needs to be made concerns your reaction to these objections. My hope is that you will welcome these objections with open arms.

Be careful what you wish for. It just might come true. Do you really want to spend time with a customer and get *no* objections? If my customer is harboring an objection, I very much want to hear it. I guess I have a choice: Either I can answer his objection, or my competition will hear it and answer the objection. Something tells me I would do a better job.

Xerox recently performed a study regarding the frequency of objections, and the results from this study had some startling implications. Sales calls without at least one objection had a 24 percent lower chance of resulting in a sale than sales calls with at least one objection. That's one in four, proof enough for me!

In the Customer Centered Selling process, there are trial closes strategically located throughout the model to confirm decision points with your customer. These trial closes have not been put in by accident. They are used to initiate an objection from your customer if an objection exists.

Many salespeople heavily focus their training around the need to study objection-handling tactics. If you do not commit to studying an approach with which to sell by, I would probably support this theory. To obsess on this tactic is a mistake. Your obsession should lie in your ability to communicate effectively with your customer and respect the decision process your customer follows. This will improve your selling and the way you are perceived as a salesperson.

Objections should never represent the big, bad, and troublesome obstacles so many salespeople attach to their mention. Objections are merely another natural step along the decision process that all customers go through. Their status as potential deal breakers is terribly exaggerated. To borrow a famous line we have all heard before, "The only thing we have to fear is fear itself."

# TWENTY

# STRATEGIC DECISION MAKING

*If you're not making mistakes, then you're not doing anything. I'm positive that a doer makes mistakes.*

*—John Wooden, UCLA College*

**N**ow that the Customer Centered Selling process is in place and the opening tactic and objection handling tactic are by its side, it is time to look at what comes next. In this chapter, I would like to show you the types of decisions that need to be made by salespeople on an ongoing basis while using this, or any true sales process.

The intent here is to provide you with the tools necessary to use the processes taught to you in a strategic manner. No two customers are alike and no two selling situations are alike either. Therefore, your ability to succeed with what you have learned will be heavily influenced by how you are able to adapt this process to unique customer situations.

302

The advantages of using a process to assist you in your selling, over a scripted approach, lies in your ability to react to various customer situations. A scripted approach is helpful as long as the customer cooperates and allows you to dictate each and every move. You and I both know that this is not realistic in the real selling world. As mentioned earlier, the real value of scripts is in the vocabulary they provide the seller in articulating well-worded responses to key issues. Ultimately, you are left with a couple of good ideas and phrases to draw upon.

It's no secret that I am opposed to the act of boiling down sales training to the occasional use of "a couple of good ideas." I believe salespeople need to have a *process* to use in a repeatable, predictable fashion. This is not to suggest that the process should not be flexible. This is where what I refer to as "strategic decision making" comes in.

▶ *The ultimate test of any sales process is its ability to expand and contract to adapt to any sales situation.*

Up to this point, you have let me walk you methodically through the steps of the Customer Centered Selling process. Now, let's mess things up a bit and remind ourselves that people make decisions—not processes. Allow me to take you through eight questions you can ask yourself to adapt strategic decision-making principles to your use of the process. Each question has the potential to heavily affect the strategies you will employ and provide you with a better idea of how to let this process expand and contract around your customers.

# 1. WHERE IS THE CUSTOMER?

The process I created, "Customer Centered Selling," is called that for a reason. To me, no strategic decisions can be made until you know where the customer is in *his decision cycle*. This is the first domino that must fall to make any other decisions, and therefore is almost more like a mantra than a step within a process.

Determining where your customer is in the *decision cycle* should not be that difficult. If you are pursuing the customer, and not the other way around, you are most likely dealing with a customer who is in the acknowledge stage or possibly the satisfied stage. This will require a great deal more time using the probes recommended in the research and analysis stages.

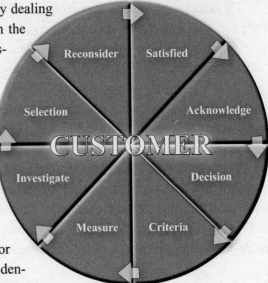

The key is to focus your strategy on your customers' location in the *decision cycle*. Listen for customer cues that would identify key decision points. If you are going to make an error, I would suggest you err on the side of the process. In other words, when in doubt, move backward and not forward in your choice of tactics within the *selling cycle*.

## 2. WHAT STEPS WITHIN THE SELLING CYCLE WOULD BE CRITICAL?

Going in to an appointment, there needs to be a game plan. Within that game plan are steps within the selling process you intend to use. These by no means are steps cast in stone, but they are necessary for you to complete your task.

Now that you know where your client is, what steps will you be following? What leads you to this opinion? This doesn't mean you have to defend this position with the client, but it does contribute to your game plan before you meet with the client. Depending on where your client is in their *decision cycle*, perhaps you will need to establish trust, or create urgency. Why not do your homework beforehand?

In the next chapter you'll see various job aids that may be helpful to you. However, here is an immediate example: some typical questions

| Research Stage | |
|---|---|
| Background Probes | *Tell me about your business? Tell me about your product mix? Over the past three years, how have you changed the way you do business?* |
| "Who, what, where, when, why . . ." | *What do you look for in a partner? What do you know about our particular company? What can I do to create more business with you?* |

| Analysis Stage | |
|---|---|
| Identifying Probes "Concerns, challenges difficulties . . ." Developing Probes "Effect, feel, relate, react, respond . . ." | *You mentioned that the relationship you have with your financial planner is not what you'd like. What sort of challenges has that created in the planning elements of your portfolio? What effect has that had on your business? What have you been doing to try to counter that loss? And? Tell me more? How much did that cost you? What did you do then?* |
| Impact Probes "Results, impact, consequences . . ." | *Overall, what are the consequences to you and your family?* |

plugged into a job aid that could be used to prepare some of the questions and steps you would use within the earlier stages of the *selling cycle.*

# 3. WHAT STEPS WITHIN THE SELLING CYCLE WOULD **NOT** BE NECESSARY?

I know you have heard these words a lot in this book, but it's time to say them one more time. Customer centered selling is a process, and nothing more. It is not a straitjacket and it is meant to be flexible. Based on client position, certain steps within the process will be more important than others.

Pause for just a moment and consider these words again, "What steps within the selling cycle would *not* be necessary?" These words are coming from the author straight to you. The author is telling you *not* to use all the steps he just taught you. That might make me a lousy author, but it makes for one heck of an honest sales process! I can assure you, I would not have created each and every step within this process if I didn't think they were important, but when we deal with the real world we find that different steps become more and less critical based on many factors, including where the client is in his *decision cycle*.

No, I not only think it's okay to dismiss certain steps within the process, I think it's imperative. I'm such a believer in connecting this process to the real world, a few years ago I changed every program my company delivers to reflect this change. You see, as a Xeroid, I was taught the only way to merge a selling process into the real world was to role play. Let's just say that type of thinking is half right. Learning a selling process is not something that comes from a lecture or solely from a book. There must be a way to connect the process to the client, and that traditionally comes from role playing.

Students traditionally hate role-plays, and I don't blame them. They feel stiff, they feel robotic, and they feel a numbness that comes from spitting back steps in a process. It's a necessary evil, and will never leave the sales training world; and like every other sales training organization, I dug in and held onto my opinion. The only way to learn a sales process is role playing.

Maybe I got worn down by the discomfort of my students, or maybe I started practicing what I preach. If this process is not a straitjacket, why do we keep teaching and monitoring the process like it is? After two decades of delivery I began to incorporate case studies, and I'm proud to report, I've found the light.

A case study allows participants to discuss strategies, and in a sense, the pre-call plan. There is no right or wrong answer, but rather an intelligent guess based on what we know to be true, and what we anticipate *may* be true. Rather than put participants under pressure to recite steps of a process, a case study allows participants to research clients, and prepare how they intend to use the selling process they have been taught. Bingo!

This not only applies to each client you visit, it applies to the products you sell as well. For instance, I work heavily in the financial industry.

There are exceptions to every rule, but for the most part, this is an industry that desperately needs to create urgency, but doesn't need a lot of the steps within the Requirement and Specification Stages. To accommodate this industry, I frequently will teach from a module that looks more like the one you see here. (Notice the expansion of the Solution Stage to accommodate the shortening of other stages.)

## 4. WHAT TRIAL CLOSES WOULD BE IMPORTANT?

One advantage to not just writing about Customer Centered Selling, but training customers on it as well, is seeing firsthand what is working and not working. I can't stress enough how important trial closes are, yet guess what parts of the selling process are typically forgotten at first? Yep, the trial closes. I happen to think they are so important, I'm going to dedicate one of our ten questions to back up this exact point.

As a reminder, customers make three crucial decisions within their decision cycle before they actually make the final commitment to change. These decisions are:

- Do I want to fix what's bothering me?
- What do I need in order to fix what's bothering me?
- Who am I going to allow to fix what's bothering me?

After you have determined where your customer is in the *decision cycle*, it is important to decide which trial closes would be appropriate, given the information you have learned about your customer. These trial closes take the guesswork out of determining where your customer is in the *decision cycle*. The customer's response to these trial closes will confirm your assumption as to what selling strategies to use.

Confirming your customer's location in the *decision cycle* not only allows you to confirm which trial closes will be necessary to use, it allows you to confirm which trial closes *not* to use! There is no need to ask a customer to answer an obvious question confirming a decision he has just made.

After a year or so of working with salespeople, I made an interesting observation regarding the flexibility of the Customer Centered Selling process. Customers do not mind moving around within the process, but they become frustrated when moved backward through decision points.

For example, when you are using the probing sequence in the analysis stage and feel you have created enough pain, you slide into the confirmation stage and begin to wrap things up. The first trial close, commit to change, asks the customer, "Would you like to look at some alternatives?" If the customer says "yes," you are on your way. If the customer says "no," it won't necessarily put you in a good mood, but after you clarify the objection and address it, the worst case scenario is that you go back one step and probe some more in the analysis stage.

Now, looking at the same example, consider what happens if you make a false assumption and prematurely move into the solution stage. Tracking the same worst case scenario, you are once again forced back into the probing sequence in the analysis stage. This produces a different result with the customer. The customer often becomes frustrated, making comments like, "Haven't we had this conversation already?" You just can't go from talking about your solution to probing a customer's problems and expect the customer to follow along without some frustration.

The first question in strategic decision making relates to where your customer is in the *Decision Cycle*. The best way to figure this out is to listen to your customer carefully and watch the use of your trial closes. These trial closes are your best clue for making the most important decision you will need to make if you want to properly use the Customer Centered Selling process.

# 5. WHAT ARE THE ANTICIPATED STRENGTHS AND WEAKNESSES OF YOUR POSITION?

When planning your selling time, your degree of preparation often depends on the specific solutions you represent. Your process will be affected by many variables, but a few generic assumptions can be made in your pre-call planning.

Typically, your amount of preparation will depend on the size of the sale you are planning, but there are a few questions that can be asked for all accounts. The first focuses on the anticipated strengths and weaknesses of your position with your customer. In other words, what solution do you have that would be particularly useful to this customer. Once you have determined your anticipated strengths, you can begin to prepare your background probes to see if there would be any potential for these strengths to be positioned down the line within the *selling cycle*.

You can even try to get a head start on your identifying probes within the analysis stage. If you have something that you believe the customer would find useful, prepare questions that would get your customer to discuss difficulties they would experience without this solution. Remember, you are not using any specific information to tip your hand.

For example, if you were selling stocks and felt one of your key strengths was your market research, some background probes you would want to prepare ahead of time would look into how your client currently goes about picking a stock. Identifying probes would zero in on difficulties in keeping up with trends and being able to make key financial decisions adequately.

It is difficult to plan much further because the rest of the probing sequence will depend on the answers you receive from your customer. Given the right answers to the questions you prepare in advance, the rest of the probing sequence will take care of itself.

Analyzing your potential weaknesses will give you a head start on issues to avoid. Your frank and honest acceptance of your weaknesses may also help to prepare you for potential objections that you may be faced with and strategies to deal with those objections.

## 6. WHAT OBJECTIONS DO YOU ANTICIPATE HEARING FROM YOUR CUSTOMER?

Sometimes it is hard to anticipate what objections you will hear and other times these objections are no surprise at all. Instead of hoping you will not have to deal with an anticipated objection, why not prepare for it?

Study the account you are selling and study the industry your account is in. What are the typical objections you hear within this industry? Is this an overly price-conscious account or industry to deal with? Questions like these will provide you with an indication of potential objections.

You have already learned how to handle objections, so I will not restate the process here. I would suggest that you write out some clarification questions along with some well-worded responses. This should give you confidence and provide you with articulate, nondefensive responses to your customer's objections.

## 7. HOW WILL YOU ADJUST YOUR OPENING TACTIC TO FIT YOUR CUSTOMER?

The opening tactic is another important element in your strategic decision making. This tactic is affected by many variables within your selling. Where is the customer in the *decision cycle*? Judging by what you know of your customer, which of the key elements within the opening tactic will be more crucial than others? How will you adjust your initial benefit statement to fit this particular customer?

These are just some of the issues that will affect the first forty-five seconds and may be the most important moments of your sales call. The key, once again, is *preparation*. Study your opening and based on what you know about the customer you are visiting, try to anticipate what adjustments will be necessary.

If this represents an important sale to you (and what opportunity to sell is not), tailor your opening and write that opening out in advance. Remember a recommendation I made to you in chapter 18, which teaches openings, to create and memorize at least three different openings.

If you have created a library of openings, you will be able to mix and match key phrases. That will allow you to put your best foot forward even if you are forced to make strategic decisions regarding the opening on the spot, in front of the customer. Either way, be prepared to use your opening strategically to win the first battle that you face in those all-important first forty-five seconds.

## 8. WHAT TYPE OF PERSONALITY TRAITS WILL YOUR CUSTOMER EXHIBIT?

When I first wrote *Customer Centered Selling,* I included the following statement:

"Much has been written about personality and its effect on selling. I feel that personality certainly plays a part in selling. I do not feel, however, that it plays as large a part as so many will have you believe."

Not too badly written, and a rather interesting comment. There's only one thing wrong with it. It was wrong, and so was I. When I went to my publisher and discussed the possibility of moving Customer Centered Selling to a new edition, I had a few thoughts in mind. One of those thoughts you saw when you picked up this book, because it's the first sentence I wrote in my preface "I haven't changed my mind." My second thought was, if I am going to get a chance to breathe new life into Customer Centered Selling, I sure would like to take another crack at the merger between persuasion and personality.

Yes, I like how I started this book, but hey, authors, and particularly authors with the last name of Jolles, can be a bit dramatic at times. Maybe it would have been a little more accurate to have written, "I haven't changed my mind . . . except as it pertains to personality."

Now, in fairness to the author, I had a problem with personalities because of the overemphasis so many place on this topic. Of the salespeople whom I have personally surveyed regarding their previous sales training, at least two thirds have studied only personality-type training. That would make any sales trainer and author on the subject a little bitter. That's because learning only about personality does not teach an individual how to sell. I guess my mistake was letting my bitterness cloud my judgment a bit. No, the merger of persuasion and personality is not something that is nice to know; it's something you need to know.

So let's take another crack at this with the intent of enhancing your ability to apply the customer centered selling process you are using. While we're at it, we'll merge personalities into the real world.

Since *Customer Centered Selling* hit the shelves in the late '90s I have had over a decade to research personality models. Many, like my own ten years ago, will break personalities down to four personality groups. After polling over 50,000 participants, many within my own seminars, I have trimmed this list to three personalities.

The list was reduced to three personalities for two reasons. First, statistically I was having trouble validating the fourth personality. After polling audiences I would frequently see three healthy groups of participants, and a small group representing less than 5 percent of my participants.

That leads me to reason number two. When we try to read personalities, and merge these personalities into how we approach selling, we have to make extremely quick decisions. We cannot rely on assessment tools, but rather our eyes, ears, and instinct.

I have so completely changed my mind about the critical nature of persuasion and personality, I now fear that the following few pages may not be enough. However, rather than a detailed study of personality, we're going to briefly identify these three personalities, and figure out how to sell them, as our eighth, and final strategic decision making question.

## THE "DOMINANT" PERSONALITY

A person with a "dominant" personality is usually straightforward in his approach to most things and often the person with the final "say so" in making decisions. This type of personality usually takes a no-nonsense approach to most things, including the way he makes decisions. Not known for a gift of gab, they want to get to the bottom line and get there in a hurry. Finally, those who display "dominant" personalities tend to be entrepreneurial and often dress conservatively.

Often it will take a few moments to determine which personality you are talking to. That's not the case with "dominant" personalities. One day in New York I met with a classic "dominant" personality who revealed himself in the first sentence out of his mouth. I started the conversation by asking him how his day was going. He answered by saying; "Why?"

Here are some adjectives that describe "dominant" personalities:

- Pushy
- Decisive
- Aggressive
- Determined
- Strong willed
- Action oriented

Here are some suggestions on how to apply what has been learned to the "Dominant" personality:

- Be prepared to get to your points quickly. "Dominant" personalities hate to waste time with idle chatter.
- Watch your use of the opening tactic. Spend any extra time you might have working out a strong initial benefit statement, establish an agreed-upon length of time, and stick to it.
- Back up your facts with solid proof. "Dominant" personalities do not like a lot of "ifs" and "maybes," so make sure your numbers are together and be prepared to "prove it!"
- Be prepared to not run the entire wheel. You are selling a personality that tends to be impulsive, so get ready to move and move quickly.

The bottom line with "dominant" personality types is to be prepared and move quickly. Although this personality type requires you to be on your toes, ironically, when compared to the other personalities, it is typically the easiest to sell.

## THE "ANALYTICAL" PERSONALITY

These customers are typically much more methodical in their approach to doing things than our friends the "dominants." Precise, rational, and detail-oriented, "analytical" personalities are often heavily focused on meeting goals and objectives in the most logical manner. They are inclined to have technical backgrounds and, like "dominant" personalities, tend to dress conservatively.

Regarding occupations for "analytical" personalities, don't be surprised to find these individuals in mathematical, academic, or technical-type careers. Here are some adjectives that help to describe this personality:

- Orderly
- Serious
- Persistent
- Controlled
- Procedural
- Industrious

Here are some suggestions on how to apply what has been learned to the "analytical" personality:

- Be prepared for questions. This not only includes your asking many questions of the "analytical" personality, but answering questions as well. You can help to clear this up within the "process" of your opening.
- Make sure to focus on the trial closes located within Customer Centered Selling. These closes tend to appeal to an "analytical" person's logical tendencies.
- Focus on facts and away from feelings. "Analytical" personalities are much more interested in just the facts and are not as impressed with emotional feelings.
- Once again, stick closely to the selling process. Orderliness and a systematic approach appeal a great deal to the organized tendencies of an "analytical." Pay special attention to the requirement and specification stages. These are areas within the selling process where "analytical" personalities typically require the most time.

If you spend the time to get your facts together and stick to these facts, the "Analytical" personality is not that hard to sell. Your pre-call planning, and your ability to be prepared to answer even the simplest questions with facts, not feelings, will help a great deal.

## THE "SOCIAL" PERSONALITY

This type of personality is usually agreeable, friendly, and often outgoing. I remember another salesperson telling me one time that he usually found most of the "social" personalities hanging around the water cooler, holding court and telling stories. As silly as that might sound, check out the next water cooler you come across and see who is hanging around. Frequently gravitating to positions that require public contact, "social" personalities can often be found dressed casually.

Here are some adjectives that can be used to describe "Social" personalities:

- Polite
- Amiable
- Trusting
- Respectful
- Supporting
- Personable

Here are some suggestions on how to apply what has been learned to the "social" personality:

- Try to be empathetic and support his feelings. This might require spending a little longer than you would like in the rapport-building portion of your sales call.
- Try to aim your background probes at the personal side of business. This will once again give your buyer more time to talk about positive things and become more comfortable with you.
- Prepare to take most of the questions used within the probing sequence of the analysis stage in a positive direction. I believe "social"

personalities react negatively to fear tactics or motivation through consequence and tend to shut down. Build your questions and therefore your case through value and you should be better off.

- Take care in preparing your seating arrangement. If you meet in a "social" personality's office, you probably will not have to worry because he will take care to make you comfortable. If, however, this customer is coming to your office, try to create a warm, friendly environment starting with the seating arrangement.

Do not be deceived by this personality type. "Social" personalities might be extremely friendly, but that doesn't mean they are easy to sell. Many salespeople become so taken by the apparent ease with which this personality operates, they lose sight of his basic sales skills. Their careers are often centered around meeting with salespeople so they have heard all the tricks. Make your approach as personal as possible and do not forget to offer your personal support along with your close.

# SOME FINAL THOUGHTS . . .

Strategic decision making requires planning, reaction, and instinct. Your first job is to become comfortable with the Customer Centered Selling process. Once that has been accomplished, the eight questions that are contained within this section will go a long way to helping you to apply the process you are learning.

Unfortunately, as with the various parts of the process, not everything is as cut and dried as I would often hope. Here are some other considerations for your strategic decision-making pleasure.

## CONSIDER TWO BONUS QUESTIONS

There are certainly more than eight questions we can use when preparing to meet with a client and developing a strategic plan. I limited my list to eight, and have found in the seminars I conduct that this is about all most salespeople can absorb. Let me show you two more that did not make the cut, but can be critical as well.

## WHAT ARE THE ANTICIPATED STRENGTHS
## AND WEAKNESSES OF YOUR COMPETITION?

During the years I taught sales internally for Xerox, one of my favorite places to take my trainees was the competitive labs. In these labs were dozens of competitive copiers, fax machines, and typewriters. Like the Xerox equipment, each of the competitors' machines had its strengths and weaknesses. It was an invaluable time for the trainees to study these machines and develop sales strategies to knock out this equipment within their sales territories.

I was always amazed at the trainees who just didn't seem to get it. They would take their time in the labs, lightly boasting of the Xerox prowess and laughing at what they felt were far inferior machines. I would often tell them, "These machines would not be here if lots of people were not buying them."

Whether it's in a lab, or on the job, the study of your competition is critical to your success. Do not take these rare opportunities lightly. Find out what your customers like about your competition. As with your own weaknesses, develop strategies that would allow you to avoid these strengths. I'd prefer to not create urgency around a need I cannot fulfill . . . but maybe that's just me! You could possibly even use the renaming technique from the objection handling chapter 19 to minimize the impact within these areas. Either way, I'd do my homework here, and work this information into the selling strategies you select.

The weaknesses you discover within your competition must be handled carefully. You never want to be perceived as taking cheap shots at your competition, but I'm guessing I haven't taught you anything new here. You can, however, develop background probes, asking your customer, for instance, how often he performs a certain task that coincidentally your competition does not satisfy. Have your impact probes lined up and hopefully you will be able to take these deficiencies through the probing sequence. Let the "customer paint the picture" and strategically you can begin to plant the seeds of doubt within your customer.

## WHAT SUPPORT WILL YOU ANTICIPATE NEEDING?

Another consideration that should be made during your strategic decision making concerns the need for support. Too often salespeople underestimate the support that is needed while attempting to sell key accounts. Unfortunately, once again you only get one chance to make a first impression.

Often, when I was selling training for Xerox, I would take support personnel from accounting with me on key account sales calls. This accomplished two things. First, it allowed me to price out large training efforts on the spot for the customer. My sales strategy is directed toward creating urgency. It would make no sense to create this urgency in my customer and be unable to close the deal because I was unable to confirm pricing.

There is one other benefit I have noticed to bringing support personnel out with me on sales calls. Customers seemed almost flattered! It sent a message to my customers that I was very serious about their business.

When you bring out support personnel, everybody wins. The customer observes proof of your thorough approach to selling. Difficult questions can be answered on the spot, thus making your job easier. A statement is made: "We want your business!"

## WATCH FOR CLUES

When it comes to making many strategic decisions, specifically relating to personalities, one of my best recommendations is to look for clues. Typically, these clues are all around you. All you need to do is open your eyes.

For instance, if you go to a customer's office, pay special attention to its appearance. How is the office decorated? Does it have the flamboyance of a "social" personality, or is it more conservative like that of a "dominant?" What is on the walls or on the desk? Does it possess the warmth of a "social" personality or the orderliness of an "analytical?"

A lot can be learned by your first impression as you meet your customers. The language they use, the clothes they wear, the materials they carry, or even the wallpaper on the wall. Watch and listen as you meet with your customers and you should get a head start in making an early, intelligent strategic decision.

## WATCH FOR EMAILS

Physical appearance, a client's car, or even the pictures on a wall are great personality indicators, but let's face it, sometimes all we have is an email. Not a problem—personality comes shining through in cyberspace as well.

For instance, if you get an email from a "dominant" personality, it won't be hard to figure out. In the email below, pay special attention to two of factors:

- Lack of warmth. These people aren't being rude, they just don't see the need to embellish what is clearly stated.
- Lack of punctuation. They took the same grammar classes you did, but they will often not feel it's necessary to waste their time with that demanding shift key.

```
-----Original Message-----
From: A. Tad Aggressive [mailto:Me@Now.com]
Sent: Wednesday, June 22, 2009 10:07 AM
To: Rob Jolles
Subject: Re: Your Training Session

tomorrow's training session will take place at
10am. come prepared with questions and feedback.
speaker participation is mandatory!
```

An email from a "social" personality will look dramatically different. In the email below, pay special attention to these indicators:

- A lot of warmth. Emails will often start with "Dear" and end with a corny, "Take care!"
- A lot of writing. Giving you the message isn't good enough for a

"social" personality. They often need to bring you into the email with something light, and leave you with something light.

---

-----Original Message-----
**From:** A. Tad Relaxed [mailto:Me@Whenever.com]
**Sent:** Wednesday, June 22, 2009 10:07 AM
**To:** Rob Jolles
**Subject:** Re: Your Training Session

Hey Buddy,

What's happening with you? We fired up the grill this weekend and ate like kings. I even made my famous cobbler. I think I outdid myself!

Anyway, wanted to fill you in a bit on the training session tomorrow. I think you have participated in these in the past, no? We'll be starting around 10:00 am. It would be great if you could bring along any questions you might have or feedback you'd like to share. I highly recommend you try to attend, as they're a great way to sharpen both your professional and life skills, and we all want balance, right?

Take care.

The Tadster
(Don't forget to tell Helen I said, "hi!")

You have a say—Make it a GREAT Day!

---

An email from an "analytical" personality will take on yet another format. In the email below, pay special attention to these indicators:

- A sense of procedure. Emails will often have numbered or bulleted items. That goes for specific meeting times, places, and any other fun-filled facts they can put in their message.
- A sense of humor . . . *not*! As with the "dominant" personality, you will not be overwhelmed by the warmth of their emails, however, the

emails will not be as abrupt either. These emails are often dry, and to the point.

```
-----Original Message-----
From: A. Tad Analytical [mailto:Me@Exact.com]
Sent: Wednesday, June 22, 2009 10:07 AM
To: Rob Jolles
Subject: Re: Your Training Session

Hello Robert,
   I'd like to provide you with information re-
garding tomorrow's training session. Details are
as follows:

   1. Time: 10:00 am to 12:00 pm
   2. Location: Sunlight Peak, 3rd Floor
   3. Drinks/snacks will be provided
   4. Questions and feedback will be solicited
   5. Participation is mandatory

A. Tad Analytical
```

## WATCH FOR PERSONALITY COMBINATIONS

I would consider myself a little bit "dominant" and a good bit "social." It is rare to find any individual who possesses one and only one personality style.

The fact that your customer is made up of multiple personalities should not change what you have learned thus far. Despite the lack of clear-cut personalities, most of us tend to favor one or another. This is not to say that your customer might not switch from an "analytical" personality to a more "social" personality as he becomes more comfortable with you. Simply be prepared to switch your approach or tactics if you see your customer switch.

## TRUST YOUR INSTINCTS

There are many suggestions I could offer you when it comes to strategic decision making, but probably the most important one of all is to trust your instincts. Do not let the process, personalities, or any of the other tactics taught within this book dull the most important decision-making tool you possess: your instincts.

Too often sales trainers like me forget to remind you of this most important tool. Your instincts have been shaped by years of trial and error relating to your personal style and approach. Never lose sight of your own "gut feeling" in making key decisions along the way. When all is said and done, your instincts will be your best strategic decision-making tool in your selling arsenal.

# TWENTY-ONE

# MAKING THE PROCESS STICK

Experience is not what happens to you, it is what you do with what happens to you.

—*Aldous Huxley*

**M**any people do not know that Xerox got out of the training business during the late '80s and early '90s. Xerox had entered into a noncompete contract with a customer it sold its sales training to, which ran for five years. Once the noncompete was up, Xerox reentered the customer sales training arena. One of my jobs in 1992 was to assist in the development and implementation of the Xerox external sales training effort. As I began to benchmark and study all the sales training available to the public, I noticed a peculiar problem emerging. Customers began asking me the same question over and over again: "What comes *after* the sales training?"

Think back to the last time you attended (or sent someone to attend) a sales training course. If the course was taught properly, you probably came back to your job excited and motivated to use your new skills. Then what happened? Typically, what I am noticing from marketing sales training is that companies are somewhat happy with whatever sales training is being conducted. Unfortunately, they are bewildered by how to implement what has been taught. They are unaware that they have entered into a race without a finish line.

I have now spent years teaching companies how to sell more effectively. I see the people in these companies excited and motivated to use what has been learned. I am paid for my deliveries but I am not compensated in any way if a salesperson *uses* the techniques I teach or not. The problem is, I have a conscience. I care a great deal whether a salesperson uses what I teach. I am elated when I hear of a success story that is attributed to the techniques I teach. I am fulfilled when I contribute to a salesperson's successful turnaround or improvement.

I was given a clear view of the severity of the problem of what comes after sales training when I conducted my first follow-up sales training course for a major bank in Chicago. This bank had embraced the process and concept of the sales training that I teach with tremendous enthusiasm. Every investment counselor and manager had attended the two-day sales training program that I taught on behalf of Xerox. I created an entire one-day follow-up program because I was inundated with questions about follow-up. The intention of the follow-up was to spend one hour reviewing the process that had previously been taught and most of our day covering strategic decision making using the process that had been taught.

This follow-up program was taught to a group that had been sales trained about eight months before. The review lasted two and a half hours. Everyone in the room was stunned by how much the trainees had forgotten. From that day forth, implementation and follow-up became my top priorities as a sales trainer. No matter how enjoyable and motivating my training course is, if the salespeople who attend do not remember to use what I have taught them, it and I have failed.

## AVOIDING THE
## "FLAVOR OF THE MONTH" SYNDROME

The label "flavor of the month" is not a term I view positively. As a matter of fact, I find it haunting. For those who do not know what this term means, allow me to explain: Sometimes companies sign up for training, but do not really take its implementation seriously. By the water cooler you will hear the whispers of employees who have little faith in what has been taught. They will be reassuring others by saying things like, "Don't let this thing worry you, it won't be around for long. It's just another flavor of the month. It will be gone before you know it." Sadly, they are often right.

Let me provide you with an even more glaring example. How does the term Total Quality Management (TQM) grab you? Often I see customers wince at its mention. A few companies have had successful quality programs, but unfortunately not many. Many companies were swept up in the euphoria of the mid-'80s to adhere to the concepts of quality. Employees were herded into huge rooms and preached to regarding the necessity to adapt to the principles of quality. They left, excited and pumped up. And then the worst thing that could possibly happen occurred: nothing. Companies did not realize that without a strategy to implement the program, the concept was useless.

For many the term TQM stands for the "totally quit movement," representing a lot of money and time wasted. I am not insensitive to the plight of the TQM movement because I was a certified quality trainer for Xerox. I taught internal and external customers problem-solving and quality improvements processes and principles. It did not matter whether they were internal or external customers. They were just as excited to join the movement. Three months later, it would be sticking internally and falling apart externally.

Through this lesson in quality, I offer a benchmark for what I feel is the most important solution. With so many companies falling by the wayside in their pursuit of quality, how is it that Xerox seemed to get it right? In 1983, David Kearns saw TQM as the only savior for a Xerox company that was getting its head handed to it daily by serious competition. To me, it was not the course itself that was revolutionary; it was the implementation.

## HOW TO IMPLEMENT WHAT HAS BEEN TAUGHT

The first strategy that Xerox adhered to was to take from the teachings of two great men, W. Edwards Deming and Joseph Juran, the gurus of quality. We'll start with Deming. One of his key teachings was centered on top management's making quality a corporate goal. When a company decides to embrace the process of selling and commits to training its workforce, top management must take an active, visible role. Most of the larger companies that I have worked with put all their senior management through the training to prepare to support the system being taught. I believe it also demonstrates the company's resolve to use the system it has committed to.

A clear demonstration of the top-down approach to training was illustrated by David Kearns himself. Not only were he and all of his high-level staff trained in the same principles as everyone else, he truly walked the walk. Kearns never left his home without a business-sized laminated card in his shirt pocket, illustrating the basic principles of quality. Every employee at Xerox received the same card on the completion of their training.

Juran also believed in hands-on leadership by senior management and that the pursuit of quality should be ongoing, not a one-shot deal. Too many times I see companies put their sales force through a course in sales training and literally finish with the belief that they won't have to worry about having to train their force for a few years. When you learn a new system to sell by, you need to use that system on a regular basis. You also need to be updated and evaluated, or it becomes easy to slip into unconscious incompetency. This is why I believe that upon the conclusion of initial training, a few things need to occur.

First, to help with the transition of what is being taught back to the field, I believe in an immediate action plan upon completion of training. This chapter contains such a plan, a tool designed to transfer what is learned in training to what will be done in the field. An action plan should force you to examine your strengths and weaknesses. The strengths need to be identified to make sure they are not forgotten or misinterpreted.

The weaknesses not only need to be recognized; they must be strategically solved. This can be done by identifying what action is necessary and what support is needed, dates of completion, and a priority of steps necessary to complete your task. Too often I have witnessed the completion of training with trainees happily exchanging hugs and handshakes, but not really committing to change. Without an immediate action plan, our tendency is to move toward the areas that are easy for us and away from the areas that are difficult. The only thing more important than creating an action plan is the commitment to implement what has been planned for. When I train management on the principles I teach their employees, I encourage them, as I do you, to review the action plan created at the conclusion of training. Do not put this book down without filling out the action plan. If you are having your salespeople read this book, review their action plans with them as well.

Juran believed that training should be done on a massive scale for everyone. Kearns believed this too and committed many dollars and years to train and retrain Xerox employees. I believe that when a sales training system has been agreed upon, that system should be taught to all employees, regardless of tenure. Everyone should be able to speak the same language.

If possible, the system should be extended to many in the office who do not sell directly to external customers. For years, I have conducted seminars on a flat fee basis as opposed to a per head fee. The biggest reason is that it allows companies to fill up a class with salespeople and usually three or four support people—administrative personnel or simply people who interface with the salespeople in some capacity. Once the training is complete, these people have developed skills to assist the salespeople they work with and they will have a new sense of empathy for the sales staff they support.

The ideas I have outlined so far represent solid theory for implementation. Now I will provide you with the final, and most dramatic, approach to implementation there is.

## AVOIDING THE TEMPTATIONS OF AUTOPILOT

The system of selling that I teach is not a program with a few good ideas. It is a *process*. The fact of the matter is that when you redefine your process to selling, it requires a commitment to change. This means leaving your area of comfort and venturing into uncomfortable territory. For many, the temptation is to revert back to old tactics and tendencies, especially when faced with a live customer. I often refer to this as "autopilot."

One of the many strengths to learning a systematic approach is that this approach can be measured and monitored. Without a process, what exactly is measured and monitored when sales managers accompany salespeople? Often the exact things. For instance, often management will monitor the salesperson's product knowledge. Why do we need to subject the customer to a test that can be taken without the customer present? Accompanying a salesperson out to the field and walking away with notes on product information is a waste of everyone's time.

Without an observable process, style is often misinterpreted as technique and incorrectly evaluated. This creates resentment on the part of the salesperson being asked to change something he has no control over. Remember, techniques can be universal but your style represents the unique qualities that are your own.

The biggest problem of all (and one that is a heavy contributor to the perception problem that the profession of selling experiences) relates to closing. When neither the manager nor the salesperson has a clue about where the customer is in the buying cycle or what repeatable steps would be necessary to influence change, the focus falls on one thing only: Did you close the sale or not? If you did not, the manager will attempt to do it for you. To evaluate a salesperson solely on whether he closed the sale falls somewhere between naiveté and ignorance. When there is no system to observe, what else is there *to* observe?

When I left Xerox, I made a vow that my first undertaking would be to create follow-up sales training to what had already been taught. In addition, I studied and benchmarked companies that were successfully implementing (no thanks to me) what had been taught. I was welcomed by customers with open arms. Many even commented, "What took you so long?"

It took some trial and error, but here is my four-step approach to implementing what I have taught you. My intent here is twofold. First, by following along and doing what is outlined for you, you will be able to implement better what has been taught. Second, by being equipped with a conscious process to learn what has been taught in this book, you will be able to offer support to others in your office as well.

## STEP 1. CREATE AN IMMEDIATE ACTION PLAN

Step 1 is to create an immediate action plan. It is never too soon to begin forcing yourself to use what has been taught, and an action plan does just that. You must begin asking questions that pave the way to translate what you have learned to the real world. Questions that incorporate long-term goals or dates can be customized in this plan. The key is to plan an approach that uses what has been learned. In the worksheet that follows, here are some sample questions I recommend you address:

1. The old habit(s) I want to change or eliminate:

_____

_____

2. The new habit(s) I want to develop:

_____

_____

3. Steps I will take to be sure I begin strongly:

_____

_____

4. Consistency and persistence are the only ways to develop new habits. To keep myself from deviating from my new habit(s), I will

_____

_____

5. The people I will ask to help me and what I will ask them to do:

_____

_____

## STEP 2. INCORPORATE JOB AIDS

A second key to reinforcing what has been learned is through the use of job aids, simple tools that allow you to move from your conscious memory to your unconscious memory to the process you've been taught.

There are certain misunderstandings that go along with the use of job aids. The real aim of a job aid is to act as a type of memory jogger. For years now I have given out sample selling wheels that are small enough to fit into a wallet or suit pocket. From time to time I hear from former participants in my seminars, who politely complain that they have difficulty trying to see something so small while they are with a customer. My fault. I did not explain its use properly.

The idea behind a smaller job aid, like a pocket-sized wheel, is *not* to look at it with a customer present. The idea is to look at it when you are not in front of a customer—keep it in your briefcase, hook it to the back of your car visor, put in your front desk drawer. Those are some sample locations for your smaller job aids. Right before a customer walks into your office or right before you walk into theirs, stop and take a quick look. You probably will not be able to get through the entire process in one call, so all you really need to look at are the steps you anticipate going through on that particular day. Here is a sample wheel that you can cut out or copy and keep with you.

Another effective job aid that many of my customers have used successfully is a customized note pad. The benefit is that you can use this aid with a customer present. The idea behind it is to use most of the pad simply to take notes. Scaled way back lightly on the left side can be the stages and steps of Customer Centered Selling. Following is an example of this type of aid. Extra sample sheets are located at the back of the book.

## STEP 3. DEDICATED FOLLOW-UP

After some early uncomfortable times, the process will work its way out of the robotic conscious competency stage and into the wonderful unconscious competency stage. Dedicated follow-up is essential to make sure your control of the process in fact stays there.

One way to follow up is simply to put on every meeting agenda a discussion relating to the Customer Centered Selling process. Some of the companies I work with break staff into small groups to analyze case studies involving customers and seek recommendations involving the customer and seller perspective.

Role plays are crucial when trying to make stick what you have learned. I am very much a believer in this old Chinese proverb:

> *What someone hears, they forget;*
> *What someone sees, they remember;*
> *What someone does, they learn.*

| **Research Stages** | |
|---|---|
| *Background Probes* | _____ |
| "Who, what, where, | _____ |
| when, why . . ." | |

| **Analysis Stages** | |
|---|---|
| *Identifying Probes* | _____ |
| "Concerns, challenges" | _____ |
| *Developing Probes* | _____ |
| "Effect, feel, relate" | _____ |
| *Impact Probes* | _____ |
| "Results, impact" | |

| **Confirmation Stage** | |
|---|---|
| *Any Other Concerns?* | _____ |
| *Commit to Change* | _____ |
| "Are you committed to | _____ |
| making a change?" | |

| **Requirement Stage** | |
|---|---|
| *List & Confirm Needs* | _____ |
| *Any Other Needs?* | _____ |
| *Prioritize Needs* | |

| **Specification Stage** | |
|---|---|
| *Transfer Need to Specs.* | _____ |
| *Commit to Specs.* | _____ |
| "Will you be basing | _____ |
| your decision on this | _____ |
| list of criteria?" | |

| **Solution Stage** | |
|---|---|
| *Commit to Seller* | _____ |
| "If I could . . . would | _____ |
| you . . . ?" | _____ |
| *"FABEC" Statements* | |

| **Close Stage** | |
|---|---|
| *Confirm Benefits* | _____ |
| *Ask for Commitment* | _____ |
| *Discuss Logistics* | _____ |
| *Reassure Customer* | |

When I am teaching the process, I will not conduct a training session without at least three role plays. To explain the importance of a role play, I like to think of the analogy of teaching someone to swim. You can spend as much time as you like on the side of a pool showing this person how to float, how to hold his breath, or even do a dolphin kick. Until he actually goes under the water, he can learn only so much. It amazes me how quiet a training session can be until after the first role play!

Regular discussions and role play are two things you or your company can do to reinforce what has been taught. This is not to say that future training is unnecessary. It is. One reason for follow-up training is to instill a sense of commitment on the company's part to the process taught. This will help to exorcise the "flavor of the month" demons. A funny thing happened when I first went out on my own and approached companies to see if they were interested in follow-up training. Their response was a mixture of agitation and frustration because it took so long for *me* to call on *them!*

If you are the person who will be responsible for keeping the process in place, here is one last word of advice on follow-up training. First, a couple of weeks before training send out a small packet of materials that refamiliarizes participants with the terms of the process. During the first couple of sessions I conducted, participants claimed to have known what I was asking them (because they used it all the time) but could not remember the terms. I sent out packets from that day forth. This will remove that potential excuse and allow you to get a clear look at what has been retained and what has not been retained.

## STEP 4. CREATING THE CULTURAL CHANGE

The last step, and perhaps the most important, solves the true mystery to making the process stick. In this step, I am once again addressing management. I want to provide the real secret that so many companies seek. I refer to this step as a cultural change because when it is implemented effectively, that is what you are creating. It is also the best way to keep the process in place.

Once again, allow me to benchmark the Xerox Leadership Through Quality process in illustrating how to effect a cultural change. When Xerox made its commitment to quality in 1983, it really made a commitment to saving the corporation. Many intelligent maneuvers were made, but in my mind, the smartest was what happened *after* the training for each employee. A type of action plan was created, numerous job aids were provided, and follow-up was arranged. That was all well and good, and it served its purpose in moving the training to the field. Then came a subtle move that kept it there: performance appraisal.

In most organizations, new employees are given a set of expectations, which are then converted into goals or objectives. These goals usually carry some sort of measurement and weight—for example:

---

- **BUSINESS RESULTS:** Achieve agreed-on sales production plan of $_____. (50%)

- **PRODUCT/ENVIRONMENT KNOWLEDGE:** Maintain product expertise to ensure up-to-date knowledge based on assignment. (20%)

- **CUSTOMER SATISFACTION:** Achieve agreed-on customer satisfaction rating of _____ percent. (20%)

- **LEADERSHIP THROUGH QUALITY:** Demonstrate initiative by identifying and actively participating in Leadership Through Quality projects on an ongoing basis. (10%)

---

By including quality in the performance appraisal, Xerox essentially developed a system to create the change it so desperately wanted. At the end of the year, employees and their managers went over the agreed-on performance goals. At this meeting, the employee's entire year (and possible raise or promotion) would come down to one number. The numbers roughly translated to the following definitions:

Level 1:  Consistently does not meet agreed-on expectations. This employee will most likely be terminated, and quickly. Whatever actions were taken in the past are not working. Equate this level with a failing mark in school.

Level 2:  Meets some agreed-on expectations. This is no prize either. This evaluation would land an employee into a corrective action or personal improvement plan. An employee who did not improve soon would be terminated. Equate this level with D work in school.

Level 3:    Meets and sometimes exceeds expectations. This is supposedly the norm. This is not going to get anyone fired. However, as I used to like to say, "Go ahead and put nails in the wall; you're not going anywhere!" Equate this level with C work in school.

Level 4:    Exceeds expectations in all areas. To advance within the company, this is the level that is required. It requires consistent overachievement in all agreed-on goals. Equate this level with A work in school.

Level 5:    Superior performance in all areas. This level is viewed as more of an award than a level of achievement. A rating that requires sign-off permission from way up in the corporate ladder, it is scarcely given. Many managers I have spoken with who use this system will never give a level 5 review, on principle. Their thinking is that there is always room for improvement. This level is a rare accomplishment.

With the Level 5 review considered somewhat unrealistic, look carefully at the wording of the Level 4 review: "Exceeds expectations in *all* areas." You can triple your assigned sales plan, have fantastic customer satisfaction ratings and tremendous demonstrated abilities in product expertise. Without demonstrated involvement in quality, you do not exceed expectations in all areas.

How do you measure involvement in quality? Let me assure you, it is not measured by someone's vocal support of the quality principles. We have all heard that talk. Unfortunately, that's all it is—talk. The Xerox Leadership Through Quality program involves two documented processes: the Problem Solving Process (PSP) and the Quality Improvement Process (QIP). The required amount of participation can vary, but typically it calls for participation in a minimum of two completed projects using either process. It must be documented so that the use of the process is not compromised.

When a quality project is analyzed, 85 percent of the evaluation of the project is credited to the process that was followed and documented; 15 percent of the project evaluations is credited to the actual monetary savings or value. This teaches the employees to focus on the process they follow as hard, if not harder, than they do on the actual results.

The pieces of the puzzle of cultural change are almost in place. The only thing left is a watch to make sure that management reinforces what has just been outlined. In a sales environment where numbers do the talking, it would be easy to overlook this requirement. That won't work either. Management must document the projects that employees are involved in, because the results are directly tied to its own advancement as well! In my career with Xerox, I had managers from time to time who were not enamored with the quality process. However, they cracked the whip and stayed on top of their employees to ensure their own potential success.

Now let's turn this example away from quality and toward maintaining the sales process. There must be a percentage within each employee's performance goals that measures the employee's adherence to the selling process. This will create accountability by both employee and manager. In order for the employee to advance, he must keep the process in place. The weight of this particular goal need not carry more than 5 to 10 percent of the evaluation. Without documented success in the process—the way the salesperson achieves these numbers—achieving level 4, "exceeds expectations in all areas," would not be obtainable.

The next step is to equip management with the tools necessary to monitor the use of the selling process. Monitoring the selling production has always been fairly simple. Sales figures are usually easily available and easy to track. The selling process can be just as easy.

One benefit of making management accountable for tracking the selling process is what happens before the sales call. Customer Centered Selling is fairly simple to use and master *if* you are using it on a regular basis. Customer Centered Selling (like other effective selling processes) is nearly impossible to implement on the spot when it is not being used regularly. When a salesperson knows he will be monitored on a regular basis for the technique he uses in selling, he is more likely to perfect the process to protect himself.

A second benefit of monitoring the selling process is the effect it will have on the quality of support given to observed salespeople. Too often sales managers accompany salespeople out on sales calls, take over the sales call if they don't like how it is going, and end up alienating the sales-person. If comments are made by managers, they are usually directed to sales style and are of little value to the salesperson. Behaviors are not changed, and the salesperson goes back to the way he was performing before the evaluation. When a manager is equipped with an evaluation sheet that monitors the sales process, the conversation afterward is directed to the process being observed. Style can be questioned because it often involves feelings. Process can't be questioned because it involves facts. Steps were observed or they were not. These evaluations can be tracked and monitored. On the following page is an example of an evaluation form that can be tailored for your use.

If you are intending to use the selling process yourself and do not have a mechanism in place to have a third party evaluate your sales call, word-smith the evaluation form, and use it when you have a moment to evaluate your own sales call—in the car, on the street, or over lunch, but use it as quickly as possible following a sales call.

If you are intending to manage others who are using the selling process, it might be comforting to note that customers rarely object to the use of this form. I strongly recommend they be told in advance that you are accompanying the salesperson to ensure the quality of the service the customer is receiving. Maybe I am just lucky, but I have conducted hundreds of evaluations asking customers for their permission and have never had a customer tell me no.

# *Customer Centered Observation Form*

**Seller Observed:** _____

**Date:** _____

## *Opening Tactic*

- ❑ Did the seller identify themselves and their company?
- ❑ Did the seller provide a rationale for being there?
- ❑ Did the seller address the process for this sales call?
- ❑ Did the seller establish a sense of time for this sales call?

## *Research Stage*

**Background Probes**

- ❑ Did the seller use open questions?
- ❑ Did the seller avoid problems?

| Open Questions | Closed Questions |
|---|---|
|  |  |

## *Analysis Stage*

**Probing Sequence**

- ❑ Did the seller use identifying probes? Notes: _____
- ❑ Did the seller use developing probes? Notes: _____
- ❑ Did the seller use impact probes? Notes: _____

| | Concern #1 | Concern #2 | Concern #3 |
|---|---|---|---|
| ❑ **Identifying Probes** | | | |
| ❑ **Developing Probes** | | | |
| ❑ **Impact Probes** | | | |

### Confirmation Stage

- ❏ Did the seller make sure there were no other difficulties?
- ❏ Did the seller use the first trial close, "Would you like to look at some alternatives?"

### Solution Stage

- ❏ Did the seller use the second trial close: "If I could . . . would you . . .?"
- ❏ Did the seller use features, advantages, and benefits in the product recommendation?
- ❏ Did the seller confirm each feature recommended?

### Close Stage

- ❏ Did the seller confirm benefits with the customer?
- ❏ Did the seller commit the customer to the highest realistic level of commitment?
- ❏ Did the seller discuss a logistical plan with the customer?
- ❏ Did the seller reassure the buyer?

### Objection Handling Tactic

- ❏ Did the seller clarify the objection?
- ❏ Did the seller address the objection as either a misunderstanding or a drawback?
- ❏ Did the seller confirm that the objection had been addressed?

### Overall Rating:

| Very Poor | | Average | | Outstanding |
|:---:|:---:|:---:|:---:|:---:|
| 1 | 2 | 3 | 4 | 5 |

Strength: _____

_____

Strength: _____

_____

Alternative: _____

_____

Alternative: _____

_____

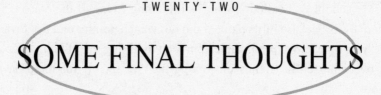

# SOME FINAL THOUGHTS

Wisdom consists of three things: success, failure, and an awareness of the lessons learned from each.

—*Robert L. Jolles*

Your journey through this book is about over. Your journey through Customer Centered Selling is just beginning. The question I must ask you now is, How will you proceed from here?

If you are now ready to implement a "couple of good ideas" that you picked up along the way, I have failed. I have failed to deliver one of the most important messages that needed to be said. I failed to prove to you that selling is not about a "couple of good ideas." *Professional selling requires a repeatable and predictable process.* This process must be measurable, and the process must be logical.

If you are now ready to implement the Customer Centered Selling process, but only on important occasions in critical situations, I have failed again. I have failed to impress upon you the need for continual practice to prepare for those critical situations. Watch LeBron Dame and see if he plays hard only in the "big" games. You do not develop a touch by waiting for important situations to practice your touch. You develop touch by practicing and practicing until what you do becomes muscle memory.

Recently I attended gold school for the first time. I had played the game for six years and took a lesson from time to time, but I wanted more. The occasional lessons were as helpful to me as the occasional seminars so many salespeople attend. I decided I wanted to improve seriously, so off to school I went.

My school was called "Swing Is the Thing." One of the reasons I selected it was because of its name. I did not want a pointer or a tip. I wanted to learn a repeatable, predictable approach to hitting a golf ball. After selling two other close friends on joining me, we set off for three days of school.

In those three days, we took clinics covering every shot imaginable. By the end of the first day my hands were hurting. By the end of third day my ego was hurting as well. I was frustrated and depressed by my perceived lack of improvement. Unfortunately, I had forgotten a lesson that I never fail to deliver when I am the instructor.

The lesson I had forgotten concerned my immediate expectations. You do not attend three days of golf school and leave knocking ten strokes off your game. As a matter of fact, when you leave golf school you are lucky if you have not *added* a few strokes to your game. If this sounds a little depressing, hang in there; it gets much better.

After three days of golf school, you leave with the tools to improve your game. Your swing is not muscle memory, but you have received something almost as good. You may have a somewhat mechanical swing, but the fundamentals are in place. These fundamental skills will continue to improve with practice. The more you practice, the better you play.

What's more, as you practice and play even more, you begin to become a true student of the process. The guesswork is removed. Muscle memory is not far behind. I left golf school mired in the same slump that kept me from improving from a 25 handicap for three years. Within three weeks after I returned from golf school, that handicap dropped ten strokes. It dropped because I worked hard to perfect the process I had been taught.

You are now the owner of a *sales process*. This process will feel clumsy and stiff as you begin to use it. As you may remember, this beginning is referred to as "conscious competency." If you use the process on a regular basis, unconscious competency will develop. As with a well-grooved golf swing, the sales process will become more effective and easier.

My question to you now is simply this: Do you want to approach your selling as you would an occasional hobby, or do you want more? I am asking you to risk leaving your area of comfort and take the steps necessary to implement what you have learned. This might mean taking a step or two backward, but the risk is well worth it.

You will succeed if you are willing to put up with some of the discomfort that go along with the implementation of any new process. I hate to stoop to the use of old clichés, but if what I was teaching you were easy, all salespeople would be using this process.

You will succeed if you are willing to put up with the pain and frustration that go along with mastering the techniques you have learned. There is always the temptation to want to go back to the safe and easy way of doing things.

Finally, you will succeed if you are willing to put up with the robotic feelings that are present while struggling through your conscious competency. There is only one way to achieve unconscious competency, and that is to pass through conscious competency first.

Like learning to play a violin, the struggle can be hard and the sound—well, let's just say the violin can put out a rather painful sound. With hard work and dedication, that painful sound becomes beautiful music. With hard work, your control of the process can take on similar beautiful sounds. Successful selling, like playing a violin, must be practiced daily.

I leave you with a story to illustrate a final point that needs to be made. One of my favorite writers, Mark Twain, had a habit of cursing a lot around the house. His wife found this habit annoying and steadily reminded him of her displeasure.

Once he cut himself while shaving and, out of anger and frustration, began to curse wildly. In the next room, his wife fumed at the words she heard. Determined to teach him a lesson, she wrote down each and every word that she heard coming from the bathroom.

As Mark Twain entered the bedroom, his wife greeted him with her list of words. Methodically she read each and every word back to him. When she had finished, Mark Twain, with a sly grin, scratched his chin and calmly remarked, "That's quite good, honey. You've got the words. You just don't know the tune."

Up to this point, you too have the words and will be wrestling with the tune. Two words can assist you with implementing what I have shown you: *energy* and *enthusiasm* Without these two words, Customer Centered Selling will be a pretty useless process.

I often call these two words, *energy* and *enthusiasm*, the great equalizers. Most customers are a lot more forgiving than we give them credit for. No customer is ever going to complain because your probing sequence was weak or your trial closes lacking. The customer will be totally unaware of the process you are attempting to perfect and will forgive your perceived clumsiness in using the process you are learning. Your energy and enthusiasm will compensate for any lack of expertise in mastering the process.

There is one thing your customer will not forgive: a lack of energy and enthusiasm. No matter how competent you are in using the Customer Centered Selling process or any of the tactics taught, without the great equalizers, what you have learned will be of no benefit to you.

Your challenge from here is to become not only more comfortable with the words, but to gain comfort with the tune as well. While you continue to develop your transitions and the key principles within the process, rely on your energy and enthusiasm to help you through.

Winning and losing can be contagious. Keep your head up and continue to seek perfection within your profession. You would not have bought this book if you were not interested in personal improvement. Now it's time to implement that change.

When you started this book, I asked a favor of you: to let me know what is working for you and what is not working. I want to hear from you. Please fill out the reply card in the back of this book, and write me at the address listed or visit me on the Web (www.jolles.com) and drop me an email (Book@jolles.com). When completing a project like this, there is no greater pleasure than hearing from you, my reader and my customer.

Learning a consultative approach to selling is not just another good idea. It represents an approach to selling that will make you more successful in your career. It will allow you to approach your customer in a professional manner, the way top salespeople expect. This is what I know to be true about the profession of selling: Being Customer Centered is not just a slogan; it is a way of life. Good luck, and good selling!

# THE STAGES OF THE DECISION CYCLE AND THE SELLING CYCLE

## The Decision Cycle

1. Satisfied Stage: The customer is totally content, perceiving no problems with his or her current situation.

2. Acknowledge Stage: The customer is aware that problems exist in his or her current situation, but feels no sense of urgency to do anything about these problems.

3. Decision Stage: The customer, feeling fed up, resolves to fix his or her existing problems.

4. Criteria Stage: The customer shifts the focus away from problems and attempts to determine what his or her buying criteria will be.

5. Measure Stage: The customer better defines his or her list of criteria.

6. Investigate Stage: The customer begins to compare various solutions to address his or her criteria.

7. Selection Stage: The customer chooses the solutions that best address his or her criteria.

8. Reconsider Stage: The customer reevaluates the decisions that were made.

## The Selling Cycle

1. Research Stage: The seller asks questions about the customer's current situation.
2. Analysis Stage: The seller asks more-in-depth questions allowing the customer to see the size and scope of his or her existing problems.
3. Confirmation Stage: The seller verifies that the customer is ready to fix the existing problems.
4. Requirement Stage: The seller helps the customer to list his or her needs.
5. Specification Stage: The seller assists the customer to define his or her particular needs.
6. Solution Stage: The seller recommends his or her products to meet the customer's needs.
7. Close Stage: The seller asks for commitment from the customer.
8. Maintenance Stage: The seller works with the customer to maintain a long-term relationship.

# CUSTOMER CENTERED SELLING WORKSHEETS

# Customer Centered Selling Sheet

## Research Stages

Background Probes _____

"Who, what, where, _____

when, why . . ."

## Analysis Stages

Identifying Probes _____

"Concerns, challenges" _____

Developing Probes _____

"Effect, feel, relate" _____

Impact Probes _____

"Results, impact"

## Confirmation Stage

Any Other Concerns? _____

Commit to Change _____

"Are you committed to _____

making a change?"

## Requirement Stage

List & Confirm Needs _____

Any Other Needs? _____

Prioritize Needs

## Specification Stage

Transfer Need to Specs. _____

Commit to Specs. _____

"Will you be basing _____

your decision on this _____

list of criteria?"

## Solution Stage

Commit to Seller _____

"If I could . . . would _____

you . . . ?" _____

"FABEC" Statements

## Close Stage

Confirm Benefits _____

Ask for Commitment _____

Discuss Logistics _____

Reassure Customer _____

# Customer Centered Selling Sheet

## Research Stages

| | |
|---|---|
| *Background Probes* | _____ |
| "Who, what, where, | _____ |
| when, why . . ." | |

## Analysis Stages

| | |
|---|---|
| *Identifying Probes* | _____ |
| "Concerns, challenges" | _____ |
| *Developing Probes* | _____ |
| "Effect, feel, relate" | _____ |
| *Impact Probes* | _____ |
| "Results, impact" | |

## Confirmation Stage

| | |
|---|---|
| *Any Other Concerns?* | _____ |
| *Commit to Change* | _____ |
| "Are you committed to | _____ |
| making a change?" | |

## Requirement Stage

| | |
|---|---|
| *List & Confirm Needs* | _____ |
| *Any Other Needs?* | _____ |
| *Prioritize Needs* | |

## Specification Stage

| | |
|---|---|
| *Transfer Need to Specs.* | _____ |
| *Commit to Specs.* | _____ |
| "Will you be basing | _____ |
| your decision on this | _____ |
| list of criteria?" | |

## Solution Stage

| | |
|---|---|
| *Commit to Seller* | _____ |
| "If I could . . . would | _____ |
| you . . . ?" | _____ |
| "FABEC" Statements | |

## Close Stage

| | |
|---|---|
| *Confirm Benefits* | _____ |
| *Ask for Commitment* | _____ |
| *Discuss Logistics* | _____ |
| *Reassure Customer* | _____ |

# Customer Centered Selling Sheet

## Research Stages

*Background Probes*
"Who, what, where,
when, why . . ."

_____
_____

## Analysis Stages

*Identifying Probes*
"Concerns, challenges"
*Developing Probes*
"Effect, feel, relate"
*Impact Probes*
"Results, impact"

_____
_____
_____
_____
_____

## Confirmation Stage

*Any Other Concerns?*
*Commit to Change*
"Are you committed to
making a change?"

_____
_____
_____

## Requirement Stage

*List & Confirm Needs*
*Any Other Needs?*
*Prioritize Needs*

_____
_____

## Specification Stage

*Transfer Need to Specs.*
*Commit to Specs.*
"Will you be basing
your decision on this
list of criteria?"

_____
_____
_____
_____

## Solution Stage

*Commit to Seller*
"If I could . . . would
you . . . ?"
*"FABEC" Statements*

_____
_____
_____

## Close Stage

*Confirm Benefits*
*Ask for Commitment*
*Discuss Logistics*
*Reassure Customer*

_____
_____
_____

# QUESTIONS & COMMENTS

Thank you so much for taking the time and effort to read this book. The greatest joy of writing a book is hearing from those who are reading it. Please feel free to send me any questions or comments you would like to make. I can assure you I take every correspondence seriously, and will respond personally to every one that I receive.

Sincerely,

Robert L. Jolles

Email:   Training@Jolles.com
Mail:    Jolles Associates, Inc.
         P.O. Box 930
         Great Falls, VA 22066

# Index

# About the Author

**Robert L. Jolles** is a master corporate trainer and one of the most sought after business speakers in the country. His programs and twenty-plus years of delivery have allowed him to amass a client list that reads like a Who's Who of Fortune 500 companies. He not only successfully sold for two of the most respected sales institutions in the nation, New York Life and Xerox; he was instrumental in creating, delivering, and managing Xerox Corporation's highly touted customer sales training programs. A published author of three best-selling books, and president of Jolles Associates, Inc., his programs teach you the lessons Xerox taught to its sales force and customers and are now taught in over twenty countries around the world. He lives in Great Falls, Virginia.

*"We need to demand more from outside presentations. Real presentations don't just entertain; they motivate, inspire, and, most important, inform."*

Over 75 Fortune 500 companies, including Toyota, Disney, NASA, Nortel, Honeywell, G.E., a dozen universities, and over 50 financial institutions have been through Customer Centered Selling programs.

### *Keynotes:*

Programs delivered provide instruction on basic, repeatable, predictable steps that participants can measure and implement in their own business practices. Participant materials include slides, speaker's notes, and job aids.

## THE CONFIRMATION STAGE

The Confirmation Stage represents an opportunity to check your work. This is accomplished by performing three steps. They are:

- Summarize concerns
- Any other concerns?
- Commit to change
- Commit to seller

### *Summarize Concerns*

After a lengthy conversation centering on clients' issues, the first step of the Confirmation Stage is to summarize concerns. This will allow the client and seller to make sure there are no misunderstandings and pave the way to move on to client needs.

### *Any Other Concerns*

Once you have finished the Probing Sequence, it is necessary to ask the customer if there are any other concerns he or she has not yet told you about. If you have done a thorough job in the *Analysis Stage* this might be a wonderful opportunity to find out other critical information.

### *Background Probes*

The first probe used is designed to uncover information about the customer's current situation. These probes should be open, avoid an indication of problems, and center around a perceived strength. Examples include:

*"How are you currently planning your vacations?"*
*"What type of vacations have you taken in the past?"*
*"What have these experiences been like for you?"*

### *Workshops:*

If you are seeking a true cultural change, we can accommodate. Half-day, one-day, and two-day programs are available incorporating small group activities, role-plays, case-studies, and Mental Agility® exercises. Presentation materials include tailored buyer briefs, participant guides, and books authored by the speaker.

If you're looking to not just "learn a new idea or two," but create a real cultural change within your organization, drop us a line!

**Visit: www.Jolles.com**
**Email: Training@Jolles.com**
**Call: 1-888-Jolles8 (565-5378)**
**Write: Jolles Associates, Inc. • P.O. Box 930 • Great Falls, Virginia 22066**